The Greenland Mummies

Edited by JENS PEDER HART HANSEN,
JØRGEN MELDGAARD, JØRGEN NORDQVIST

SMITHSONIAN INSTITUTION PRESS
WASHINGTON, D.C.

Taqamut iseqassuseq
isusissaanngitsoq
meeqqap pia
qanga maannalu
iternganut aperineq.
Suisi
Pilluarpisi
Sumut killippisi?

Front cover and frontispiece: Mummy I/1
a six month old baby. See also Fig. 80.

Page 13: Drawing of a wooden doll at a settlement in the Uummannaq fiord.

Page 37: The grave of a child with mourning parents. Drawing by the East Greenlander Karale, about 1920.

Page 53: A spirit in the form of a child. Drawing by the East Greenlander Karale, about 1920.

Page 64: The helping spirit Isitooq, 'The Melancholy'. It specialises in finding people who have broken a taboo. Drawing by Anaqqaaq the exorcist, the Iglulik people, 1922. Half the original size.

Page 102: An Iglulik woman. Drawing by Eqatlioq, 1922.

Page 116: An Iglulik woman. Drawing by Eqatlioq.

Page 150: Igtuk, 'The Boomer', who is different from all other beings. He is a creature of nature and is responsible for the boom-like noises heard in the mountains. Drawing by Anaqqaaq the exorcist, the Iglulik people, 1922. Half the original size.

Page 168: Women dressed in skins with long tails encourage a man before he undertakes a test of strength. Drawing by the Iglulik woman Pakak, 1922.

The original drawings are all in the Danish National Museum, Copenhagen.

© This English edition 1991 The Trustees of the British Museum

© Text, photographs and drawings 1985 The Greenland Museum

First published simultaneously by Christian Ejlers' Forlag, Copenhagen, and by The Greenland Museum, Nuuk, in Danish and in Greenlandic, 1985, *Qilakitsoq, De grønlandske mumier fra 1400–tallet*

This edition published by British Museum Press
46 Bloomsbury Street, London WC1B 3QQ

British Library Cataloguing-in-Publication Data

The Greenland mummies.
1. Greenland. Eskimos. Cultural processes, history
I. Hart Hensen, Jens Peder II. Meldgaard, Jorgen
III. Nordqvist, Jorgen
998.2004971

Library of Congress Catalog Number 90-63715

ISBN 1-56098-045-1

Jacket designed by John Hawkins
Photoset in Linotron Palatino by Rowland Phototypesetting Ltd,
Bury St Edmunds, Suffolk
Printed in Hong Kong

First published in
The United States 1991
by Smithsonian Institution Press

Contents

Note

Inuk means person or human being in English. *Inuit* (plural of *inuk*) is the general term for Eskimos in Greenland and Canada and is the term used throughout this book.

List of Contributors

A. Ammitzbøl PH D, Engineer, Department of Dermatology, Rigshospitalet, Copenhagen

Professor S. Ry Andersen MD, Institute of Eye Pathology, University of Copenhagen

H. P. Andersson, Detective Chief Superintendent, National Police Commission, Copenhagen

C. Andreasen, Director, Greenland Museum, Nuuk

M. Bencard, Director, Chronological Collection of the Danish Kings at Rosenborg Castle, Copenhagen

J. Bodenhoff DDS, Head of Section, Serum Institute, Copenhagen

Professor J. Bresciani, Institute of Zoology, Royal Veterinary and Agricultural University, Copenhagen

Dr M. Eiken, Chief Physician, Department of Radiology, Gentofte Hospital, Copenhagen

Professor B. Eriksen, University Institute of Forensic Serology, Copenhagen

Professor B. Fredskild PH D, Greenland Botanical Survey, Copenhagen

Professor N. Foged PH D, Odense

M. Ghisler PH D, Director, Geological Survey of Greenland, Copenhagen

R. Gilberg, Curator, Department of Ethnography, National Museum of Denmark, Copenhagen

Dr A. Gotfredsen, Department of Clinical Chemistry, Glostrup Hospital, Copenhagen

Professor P. Grandjean MD, Department of Environmental Medicine, University of Odense

H. C. Gulløv, Department of Ethnography, National Museum of Denmark

Professor H. E. Hansen PH D, University Institute of Forensic Genetics, Copenhagen

Professor J. C. Hansen MD, Institute of Environmental and Occupational Medicine, University of Aarhus

Professor J. P. Hart Hansen MD, Chief Pathologist, Gentofte Hospital, Copenhagen

Professor N. Haarløv PH D, Institute of Zoology, Royal Veterinary and Agricultural University, Copenhagen

J. Jakobsen DDS, Vice-Chancellor, Royal Dental College, Copenhagen

J. Johansson, Director, A/S Nunc, Roskilde

Dr J. Balslev Jørgensen, Chief Surgeon, Laboratory of Biological Anthropology, University of Copenhagen

H. Kapel, Curator, Department of Ethnography, National Museum of Denmark, Copenhagen

Dr T. Kobayasi, Chief Physician, Department of Dermatology, Rigshospitalet, Copenhagen

Dr N. Kromann, Department of Dermatology, Gentofte Hospital, Copenhagen

Professor B. Lorentzen, Royal Danish School of Pharmacy, Copenhagen

K. J. Lyberth, Institute of Eskimology, University of Copenhagen

Professor L. Lyneborg, Zoological Museum, Copenhagen

J. Meldgaard, Curator, Department of Ethnography, National Museum of Denmark, Copenhagen

Dr Fl. Mikkelsen, Næstved

J. Møhl, Conservator, Zoological Museum, Copenhagen

G. Møller, Conservator, National Museum of Denmark, Copenhagen

Dr R. Møller, Department of Dermatology, Rigshospitalet, Copenhagen

Dr J. Myhre, Department of Pathology, Gentofte Hospital, Copenhagen

Professor P. Nansen PH D, Institute for Hygiene and Microbiology, Royal Veterinary and Agricultural University, Copenhagen

J. Nordqvist, Director, Department of Conservation, National Museum of Denmark, Copenhagen

Professor P. O. Pedersen DDS, Royal Dental College, Copenhagen

Professor J. U. Prause MD, Institute of Eye Pathology, University of Copenhagen

E. Løytved Rosenløv, Chief Photographer, Department of Dermatology, Finsen Institute, Copenhagen

Professor A. M. Rørdam, Royal Danish School of Pharmacy, Copenhagen

Dr O. Sebbesen, Department of Clinical Microbiology, Gentofte Hospital, Copenhagen

Dr E. Svejgaard, Chief Physician, Department of Dermatology, Rigshospitalet, Copenhagen

H. Tauber PH D, Carbon-14 Laboratory, National Museum of Denmark, Copenhagen

D. D. Thompson PH D, University of Connecticut

Dr V. Frølund Thomsen, Chief Physician, Serum Institute, Copenhagen

Dr L. Vanggaard, Chief Surgeon, Royal Danish Defence Command, Vedbæk

Acknowledgements

D. Berenstein MS C, Risø National Laboratory, Roskilde

B. Berg, Conservator, National Museum of Denmark, Copenhagen

L. Bjerregaard, Conservator, Næstved

Professor A. Björk DDS, Royal Dental College, Copenhagen

Dr J. Boberg-Ans, Gentofte Hospital, Copenhagen

M. Bolet, Radiologist, Gentofte Hospital, Copenhagen

J. Borg, Technician, Glostrup Hospital, Copenhagen

Professor P. Bretlau MD, Gentofte Hospital, Copenhagen

G. Brockmeyer, Secretary, Gentofte Hospital, Copenhagen

Professor C. Bruun PH D, Royal Dental College, Copenhagen

T. Buhl, Hospital Porter, Gentofte Hospital, Copenhagen

Professor O. Carlsen DDS, Royal Dental College, Copenhagen

Dr C. Christiansen, Glostrup Hospital, Copenhagen

Dr W. Christiansen, Gentofte Hospital, Copenhagen

Professor T. W. Clarkson PH D, University of Rochester, New York

Dr K-E. Eldon, Frederiksberg Hospital, Copenhagen

B. Fortling, Radiology Technician, Gentofte Hospital, Copenhagen

L. Fredebo, Laboratory Technician, Royal Dental College, Copenhagen

Professor P. Geertinger MD, University Institute of Forensic Pathology, Copenhagen

Aa. B. Hansen, Laboratory Technician, University Institute of Forensic Genetics, Copenhagen

O. Hansen, Chief Hospital Porter, Gentofte Hospital, Copenhagen

Professor B. Harvald, Odense Hospital

F. Heilmann, Conservator, Greenland Museum, Nuuk

S. Aa. Henriksen, Danish Veterinary Serum Laboratory, Copenhagen

Dr G. S. de Hoog, Central Bureau for Fungal Cultures, Holland

B. Hueg, Engineer, Gentofte Hospital, Copenhagen

K. Haagendal, Laboratory Technician, University Institute of Forensic Genetics, Copenhagen

K. Jensen, Hospital Porter, Gentofte Hospital, Copenhagen

Professor S. Keiser-Nielsen DDS, Royal Dental College, Copenhagen

A. Klitlund, Secretary, Gentofte Hospital, Copenhagen

Professor J. Lewinsky, Botanical Museum, Copenhagen

Professor G. Lindemann, Royal Dental College, Copenhagen

Professor F. Melsen, Aarhus County Hospital

A. G. Muhs, Laboratory Technician, University of Rochester, New York

Dr R. de Myranda, Central Bureau for Fungal Cultures, Holland

K. Nørgaard, Chief Laboratory Technician, Frederiksberg Hospital, Copenhagen

Professor N. O. Prøjs, Zoological Museum, Copenhagen

Dr O. Collin Rasmussen, Royal Dental College, Copenhagen

Professor I. Sewerin DDS, Royal Dental College, Copenhagen

Professor J. Simonsen MD, University Institute of Forensic Medicine, Odense

A. Sommer-Larsen, Conservator, National Museum of Denmark, Copenhagen

Professor A. Stenderup MD, University Institute of Medical Microbiology, University of Aarhus

L. Svendstrup, Hospital Technician, Gentofte Hospital, Copenhagen

Professor B. Thomsen, University Institute of Geology, Copenhagen

Professor T. Y. Toribara PH D, University of Rochester, New York

Professor J. Westergaard PH D, Royal Dental College, Copenhagen

H. Vraa, Radiology Technician, Gentofte Hospital, Copenhagen

Dr G. A. de Vries, Central Bureau for Fungal Cultures, Holland

Foreword

It is with great pleasure that we accept the invitation to contribute some thoughts and comments on the publication of this popular book about the important find of mummies from Qilakitsoq.

The book is the product of much effort by scholars and laymen in Denmark and Greenland. Extensive investigations were undertaken by medical specialists, conservators and historians, investigations which had the character almost of detective work. The different sections of information were pieced together in an effort to present a complete picture. It is worth noting here that some of the results not only illuminate the past but can also be used in the study of modern man. In the course of the work there have been attempts to reach beyond the facts for a perception of the physical appearance of the people, their culture and way of life. This has created a better understanding of the prehistoric Inuit.

The work was carried out with a keen sense of scholarly curiosity, but also with due respect for the people, as if they were still alive today. It is this respect combined with the desire to discover how man has adapted to living conditions and opportunities through the ages which have been the major driving forces in the whole work.

It was again respect for the past and concern for the dignity of the dead which motivated Hans and Jokum Grønvold to report their find to the Greenland National Museum and to protect the site for several years until the museum staff could collect it. This circumstance particularly deserves a mention because such a vulnerable find could easily have been destroyed in the hands of ignorant or unscrupulous people.

We wish to thank Jens Rosing, the former director of the Greenland National Museum, who, on seeing the Grønvold brothers' photographs, immediately realised the importance of the find and thus initiated the process now brought to completion with the publication of the book.

We wish further to thank everybody who has contributed to the production and publication of the book which we hope will be a source of much interest and pleasure to its readers.

Stephen Heilmann
Minister of Culture, 1985

Aqigssiaq Møller
Director, Department
of Culture and Education, 1985

Map 1 Qilakitsoq is the name of the settlement where the
mummies were discovered. Its literal translation is 'the sky is low'
and it is pronounced *krilakittork*.

Introduction

The decision by the Greenland National Museum to send the Qilakitsoq mummies to Denmark for study and conservation provided an opportunity for collaboration between scholars of many disciplines. This book presents the results of their work.

While the find is of particular importance to Greenland, it is of great interest to the world beyond the Arctic. It was the wish of the Greenland National Museum, therefore, that the results of the investigations should be summarised in a book to be published not only in Greenlandic but also in Danish and one or more world languages.

Investigations by scholars from the medical, natural historical and historical professions had a common aim; they wanted to find out about the living conditions and environment of the Qilakitsoq people, what illnesses they suffered from and how they died. Many different scholarly groups have contributed larger or smaller pieces to the picture and while many questions have been answered, some remain unresolved. A number of more detailed articles have been published in 1989: 'The Mummies from Qilakitsoq – Eskimos in the 15th century' in *Meddelelser fra Grønland, Man & Society*, Vol. 12, 1989.

The list of contributors include all those responsible for various aspects of the investigations and thus for material presented in this book. All those whose assistance and continued interest has been of the greatest importance for the completion of the work are acknowledged separately. The editors have combined the reports into a single narrative for which they take full responsibility. It is their hope that the result is an easily readable book.

Among the contributors special thanks are due to Gerda Møller, the conservator who had the find in her charge for the three years it stayed at the National Museum in Copenhagen, to Rolf Gilberg, Curator of the Ethnographical Collections, for his editorial work, and to Hans Christian Gulløv for the preparation of the drawings.

This unique find of the oldest well-preserved bodies and skin clothing from Greenland is now in the Greenland National Museum. Three of the women, the six-month-old child and most of the garments are on permanent display. The child, above all, invites reflection. Aqigssiaq Møller, now Director of the Home Rule Administration, expressed his thoughts in the poem introducing this book.

Jens P. Hart Hansen

Jorgen Meldgaard

Jorgen Nordqvist

1
Inuit and Norsemen

H. C. Gulløv, Jørgen Meldgaard

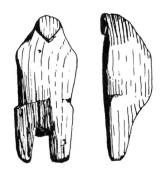

Fig. 1 Polar Inuit woman with children. Photographed at Thule, North Greenland, 1909.

Greenland around 1475

In about 1475 six women and two children were given a traditional Inuit burial at Qilakitsoq, a small settlement 450 kilometres north of the Arctic circle on the west coast of Greenland. They were well clad in warm clothing for the journey that Inuit believed took place after death – the journey to the Land of the Dead. Buried with them were the pertinent grave goods for this journey.

Nearly five hundred years later two Greenlandic brothers on a hunting expedition discovered their graves. The combination of low ground temperature and dry air had preserved their bodies and their clothes in such excellent condition that the Qilakitsoq mummies are the oldest and most important find of humans and clothing in the Arctic. Who were these people and how did they live and die in late medieval Greenland?

In about 1475 Inuit had settled in all the good hunting areas along most of the coast of Greenland. They had sailed around the north coast in their umiaks – large skin boats – laden with household goods, tents, dogs and sleds. The well-preserved remains of one such umiak were found on the coast of Peary Land. They also rounded the southern cape, passing the furthermost colony of Europeans (Norsemen), some of whom still lived along the fertile fjords of the East Settlement, near Juliane-haab. In addition, Inuit were evident north of the headland on the east coast, where ships sent out in 1472 or 1473 by the Danish king Christian I were attacked by men in 'small ships lacking keels, in great number'. Yet despite being spread out along the coast and thus divided into many groups, the Inuit constituted one people, speaking the same language and observing the same customs.

Greenland had been inhabited for thousands of years – the first Stone Age people, known as the Saqqaq culture, had hunted there three thousand years before the people of Qilakitsoq in 1475. Other tribes existed, known archaeologically as the Dorset culture and in legends as the Tunit, an enemy tribe, but they vanished in the ninth and tenth centuries. The forefathers of the mummies at Qilakitsoq had lived in Greenland for about five hundred years. Like the Saqqaq culture they had spread from Alaska and Canada to the gateway to north-western Greenland, known today as the Thule district; Thule culture is the archaeological term for these tribes. The Thule Inuit took advantage of the abundance of whales and seals and in the course of a few gener-ations the first families arrived at the Greenland side of Smith Sound. They built solid winter houses of stone and whalebone at the settlement Nuulliit on Smith Sound, and the carbon–14 dating method has shown that one of these houses was built in about 975 AD. In the twelfth century the Thule Inuit spread south over Melville Bay to West Greenland and, in about 1200 AD, there would have been settlements in the excellent hunting areas of the Uummannaq district and probably also at Qilakitsoq.

While the Thule Inuit were arriving in North Greenland, Norsemen were sailing up from the south. They came in summer, hunting for polar bears and large marine animals, especially the walrus with its precious ivory tusks. Eric the Red, an explorer from Iceland, had first come to Greenland in 982 AD, and four years later he had sailed from Iceland with twenty-five ships, fourteen of which arrived safely in Greenland. More ships followed the next year, and thus Norsemen colonised South Greenland.

They based their subsistence on cattle, sheep and goats. Their farms were concentrated in two fertile areas: the East Settlement mentioned earlier; and the West Settlement, in the fjords of the Nuuk area. According to written sources, there were 190 farms in the East Settlement and 90 in the West Settlement around the year 1300. An episcopal seat with a cathedral, sixteen parish churches and two monas-teries took care of the spiritual well-being of the three or four thousand inhabitants. The Norsemen were farmers and pioneers in a frontier land, but with their Scandinavian background they were ex-perienced hunters and fishermen and had a proud sailing tradition as traders and explorers on long-distance voyages. Their love of adventure had brought Scandinavians to Markland in Labrador and Vineland in Newfoundland in the early eleventh century, and the need for trade goods brought them on summer voyages northwards along the west coast of Greenland during the next three or four centuries.

Inuit and Norsemen made contact with one another as early as the twelfth century. A short and reliable history of Norway written in Latin just before 1200 briefly and clearly relates encounters during the Norse journeys northwards from their settle-ments. We learn that the Norsemen met small people, called Skraelings (the name Norsemen gave to Inuit): 'They have no iron whatsoever and use walrus teeth for spears and sharp stones for knives'. This information is no doubt based on a practical mercantile point of view that Greenland would be a

Left Fig. 2 Self-portraits, carved in walrus ivory. *Far left* An Inuk of the Thule culture. Thule district, probably 10th century. H. of face 4 cm. *Left* A Norseman. Found at Sandnæs farm, West Settlement, 12th–14th century. H. 5 cm.

Below left Fig. 3 The runic stone left by three Norsemen in a cairn is the northernmost reliable evidence of Norse voyages along the coast of West Greenland. Soft siliceous slate common to the island of Kingittorssuaq. Found in Kingittorssuaq, Upernavik district, 300 km north of Qilakitsoq, probably 13th century. L. 10 cm.

Below Fig. 4 Norsemen and Inuit in battle. The Inuit costume is that of 18th-century West Greenland. This is part of a map accompanying a document, sent by Hans Egede in 1737 to the Missionary College of Copenhagen, proposing a voyage of investigation to the east coast of Greenland where he thought the Norse East Settlement lay. He went out as a missionary to Greenland in 1721 in the hope of finding surviving remnants of the Norse people.

good market for trading iron for ivory. The text continues and describes the character of the meetings between the two peoples: 'When they are struck by weapons, their wounds are white, with no flow of blood while they are still alive, but when they die, the bleeding is almost endless . . .'.

In the thirteenth century relations probably included both peaceful trade and conflicts. The Inuit continued to spread further south and established permanent settlements along the Disko Bay while the Norsemen continued their summer trips to the same regions, occasionally venturing even further north. Late in the century, at least one ship reached the Thule district. On both the Canadian and Greenland shores of Smith Sound, finds have been made of Norse objects which can be dated to about 1270. However, these objects – chess pieces, iron ship nails, woven garments and fragments of chain mail

among other things – lay among Inuit ruins and do not seem to have been trade goods; nor is it likely that the Norsemen relinquished them willingly.

Another Norse journey went further north than the Uummannaq fjords and Qilakitsoq. The evidence is a small runic stone, probably dating from the thirteenth century, found by one of three collapsed cairns at the top of the island Kingittorssuaq in the Upernavik district. The runes translate as: 'Erling Sigvatsson and Bjarne Thordsson and Enride Odsson built these cairns on the Saturday before Rogation Day and . . .'. The last part of the inscription is illegible.

In the following centuries, however, the Norsemen had to abandon their travels to the north and their settlements gradually fell into decline. The reasons may be climatic deterioration, possibly creating problems in providing fodder for the cattle and in sailing conditions. Communication across the Atlantic to Iceland and Norway became irregular, and there were periods of many years during which no ships from Europe called. By about 1350 the West Settlement was deserted. The priest Ivar Bårdsøn visited the East Settlement at this time, and commented thus: '. . . The Skraelings now have the entire West Settlement'. By about 1500 the East Settlement was also deserted.

Contemporary European thoughts on Greenland were concerned largely with religion, expansion and new trade routes among other things. The papacy was worried about the neglected bishopric which lay 'at land's end'. Already in 1448 Pope Nicholas v

Far Left Fig. 5 Fresco depicting Hans Potthorst, leader of the expedition sent to Greenland by Christian i in 1472 or 1473. Church of St Mary, Elsinore, Denmark, *c.* 1480.

Left Fig. 6 Bishop's crozier, carved in walrus ivory. Found in grave beneath ruins of Gardar Cathedral, East Settlement, *c.* 1200. H. 14 cm.

Right Fig. 7 An Inuk as a bearded pygmy, fighting a European. Potthorst's expedition came under attack by Inuit at the cliff of Hvidsærk. Despite this direct confrontation, Inuit remained figures of myth in Europe. Map of Greenland in Olaus Magnus' *Carta Marina*, 1539.

had bidden the Icelandic bishops to send priests and a bishop to the inhabitants of Greenland. The last bishop on Greenland had died in 1378 and the following year a priest on Iceland noted in the Icelandic *Annals*: 'The Skraelings raided the Greenlanders [Norsemen], killing 18 men and taking two boys as slaves'. The pope had been informed that the heathens had attacked and destroyed most of the churches and taken many inhabitants prisoner. The authenticity of the papal brief, however, is doubted by some historians and there is disagreement as to what is meant by the phrase that the Greenlanders,

that is the Norsemen, were attacked 'from the heathens' neighbouring coasts'. The attackers may in fact have been pirates from Europe, though more probably they were Inuit, whose fifteenth-century settlements have been found by archaeologists along the 'neighbouring coasts'.

None of the many bishops who were later appointed felt any pressing call to travel to Greenland. In 1492 Pope Innocent VIII appointed the Benedictine Martin Knudsson as bishop of Gardar in Greenland. Knudsson was exempted from having to pay for his appointment as Rome recognised that this bishopric had for a long time had no income. It was probably more than a century since the Norsemen had paid a tithe, in the form of walrus ivory either hunted in the north or obtained in trade with the Inuit; and according to the papal brief in 1492, no ship had called at Greenland in the past eighty years.

In about 1475 the Danish king Christian I grew anxious about his subjects in Greenland. For nearly a century royal concern had been minimal and official voyages to the country had stopped; but in return the crown had not received its rightful duties and taxes. However, other countries were apparently calling illegally at Greenland and other ancient Norwegian tributary countries in the North Atlantic. In the early fifteenth century King Erik VII of Denmark, Norway and Sweden was forced repeatedly to request the English king Henry V to prohibit the illegal English traffic. Unfortunately, no written sources tell what was really happening in Greenland.

In 1472 (or 1473) King Christian I sent an expedition to Greenland, led by the German Didrik Pinning and the Dane Hans Potthorst. A Portuguese, Joao Vaz Corte-Reale, accompanied them. The initiative for the journey came from the king of Portugal, who was determined to 'seek out new islands and lands'. The Portuguese had long been searching for a sea-route to India and the Orient. The expedition arrived at the cliff of Hvidsærk on the east coast of Greenland, and was attacked here by 'pirates' sailing 'in small boats without keels, and in great number'. The expedition was subsequently driven westward by a storm and reached the coast of Labrador or Newfoundland before returning home. It was undoubtedly regarded as a failure, and the discovery of land west of Greenland was not new – centuries earlier the Norsemen had landed at Markland and Vineland in Labrador and Newfoundland respectively. However, Corte-Reale's report was probably instrumental in encouraging continued voyages of exploration, which culminated with Columbus in 1492. As for Greenland, Europeans had now been confirmed in their belief that the Skraelings controlled the Greenlandic coasts. In about 1475, however, there were still Norsemen in the East Settlement and they were buried in the Christian manner.

From the start of the fifteenth century historical sources of information about Greenland diminish considerably, leaving only rumour and conjecture. However, archaeological evidence from the cemetery at Herjolfsnæs (Ikigait) provides a few facts.

For five hundred years Herjolfsnæs had been an important farm. It lay far to the south, closest to the open sea, and its pastures were poor; but it was the place where ships from Europe first touched the Greenland coast. Since the *landnám*, or settlement, period, it had been the 'customary harbour for Northerners and merchants'. The cemetery has been excavated and the finds have become world famous. They show how profoundly different the Norsemen were to the Inuit of Qilakitsoq: although both groups had the same basic ideas about good and bad kingdoms of the dead with varying degrees of ease of entry, their beliefs about life were not at all similar. Despite what the papacy believed about the destruc-

Fig. 10 Two coffins at the Norse cemetery at Herjolfsnæs. The permanently frozen earth had preserved wooden coffins and clothing, although traces of the dead were few. Excavated (and here photographed) by Poul Nørlund in 1924.

Left Fig. 8 Inuit women from Igloolik in the Canadian Arctic. Drawn during W. E. Parry's expedition, 1821–3.

Below Left Fig. 9 Inuit costume from Baffin Island. Drawn by John White, 1577, and Norse costume from Herjolfsnæs (worn by a contemporary Dane), dating to 14th–15th century.

tion of the churches, the decline of the faith and the conversion of the Norsemen to the heathen beliefs of the Inuit, or Skraelings, the graves, even the last one at Herjolfsnæs, reflect a respect for the precepts of the Church. The deceased were properly equipped for the journey to heaven where, as faithful Catholics, the Norsemen believed they would continue their existence; they were placed in solid wooden coffins oriented in the correct direction; and all corpses were given a wooden cross, some with inscriptions such as 'Ave Maria' or 'Jesus Christ, help'.

At Herjolfsnæs the garments of the dead were well-preserved in the permanently frozen earth, and so for the first time the everyday clothing of the common medieval man was seen. In Europe the only garments preserved from the Middle Ages are ecclesiastical vestments, coronation costumes and other elaborate garments. The Norsemen of Her-

jolfsnæs wrapped their dead in the clothing they had worn while alive, and this included worn and patched garments. It is evident that the changing fashions of Europe were still followed.

An infant, a boy of about ten and many of the adults were buried with caps of a characteristic type, cylindrical in shape with a flat top and a rather high edge. This sort of hat was very popular in western Europe in the fifteenth century. One man was wearing a 'Burgundy cap', made of sheepswool and with a flat crown, but in addition having an elegant curve at the nape of the neck and a sharp, 25-cm-high incline above the forehead. This sort of hat was in style in the last half of the fifteenth century where it can be seen in paintings worn by worthy Dutch burghers and citizens of Louis XI's France. One woman was wearing a gown with narrow tucks at the waist and a pointed neck opening at the front which can be stylistically dated to the same period.

For the Norsemen to be so aware of the European fashions foreign ships must have called at the harbour of Herjolfsnæs. If the foreigners were peaceful merchants, however, it is difficult to imagine what trade goods of any value could be found in the destitute and badly-decimated East Settlement.

The burial clothing reveals an essential feature of the Norsemen's attitude to life: techniques, types and styles were European. No single design element indicated local adaptation to the unique living conditions and climate of Greenland, and no single feature had been influenced by the clothing of the Inuit. However, even though no remains of skin garments have been found, the Norsemen must surely have used skin clothing when travelling and hunting.

The Norsemen adapted themselves to conditions on Greenland only insofar as they could maintain the norms of their European form of agrarian society, and the Church required the greatest possible distance from their heathen neighbours. The fifteenth century consisted of one long crisis during which the settlement gradually perished. The graves at Herjolfsnæs leave the impression that the prime concern of the inhabitants was to cling to tradition and in all ways maintain their identity. Thus, the last ceremonies at the cemetery were most probably attended by men in tall impractical caps and women in narrow-waisted gowns with low necklines, providing little warmth; the children were miniature copies of the adults. The deceased were buried as Europeans.

By this time, Inuit and Norsemen had been in Greenland for five centuries, during which they lived for much of the time as neighbours. The Norsemen had traditions and prejudices which made it difficult for them to learn from the Inuit and perhaps survive in the country on their conditions. The Inuit simply had no need to learn anything from the Norsemen.

The burial to the north at Qilakitsoq was pervaded by ritual just as the burial at Herjolfsnæs, and common to both was a belief in life after death. But the Inuit had no worries about the future of their families and people in Greenland. In contrast to Herjolfsnæs, the last ceremonies at Qilakitsoq were probably attended by men and women dressed in double layers of skin clothing as insulation against the cold, the materials of their garments carefully chosen from various animals to obtain warmth and durability, the shape and cut of their garments to provide roominess and allow for movement. Theirs was the cloth-ing best suited for life in arctic Greenland. The Inuit survivors could hardly have felt – as the Norsemen probably did – that they were exiled to a dismal life in a country at land's end.

The Uummannaq district

THE ORIGIN OF THE INUIT

The settlements of the Inuit in Greenland in about 1475 lay scattered along the coasts. In the far south the Inuit surrounded the Norsemen in their remains of a European peasant community. To the west, in Canada and Alaska, the Inuit and other Eskimoan peoples covered about the same territory as they do today.

The origin of the Inuit is a most complicated and, as yet, unsolved problem. During the past two hundred years European scholars have offered various theories about the roots of the Inuit culture and the migrations of the Inuit. It has been suggested that the original Inuit were either, firstly, hunting people in northern Siberia, secondly, the earliest Stone-Age caribou-hunters from Europe who followed the edge of the retreating ice at the end of the glacial period, or thirdly, Indians in Canada moving northwards to the tundra and the shores of the Arctic Ocean. Between ten and fifteen thousand years ago, according to a new and well-founded theory, common ancestors of the Inuit, Aleutians and various Indian peoples spread from southern Siberia to the shore of the Pacific north of Japan and from there to Alaska. During this period the ice masses of the Ice Age were gradually melting. Asia and America were linked by a land bridge which was later covered by the Bering Strait and the Bering Sea. Along the south coast of this land area and continuing along the south coast of Alaska the abundance of marine fauna provided the basis for a hunting culture which may have been the forerunner of the Inuit culture.

However, the oldest settlement sites which archaeologists can term Inuit with some certainty appeared between four and five thousand years ago. These settlements have been found on the west coast of Alaska, close to the same excellent hunting grounds used by later generations of Inuit. Nothing is known of the language and race of this people, but their hunting implements of stone and bone are Inuit in character. These first Inuit spread surprisingly rapidly along the coasts of northern Canada to Greenland. 4300 years ago they had settlements in the Uummannaq fjord near Qilakitsoq.

However, the direct ancestors of the Qilakitsoq

Fig. 11 Inuit pulling a sledge onto the shore north of Thule during their journey from Canada to Greenland. The coast of Ellesmere Island can be seen in the background. Photographed by Christian Vibe, 1940.

people were a later tribe which originated in the cradle of Inuit culture on the coasts of Alaska. About one thousand years ago this people, the Inuit of the Thule culture, see above, spread to the east along the same coasts as the first Inuit. About eight hundred years ago they reached West Greenland and the Qilakitsoq region.

Natural resources
For thousands of years, Inuit have had settlements on the steep north shore of the Nuussuaq peninsula. The stretch from the outermost headland by the open sea in the west to the glacier at Qarajaq Ice Fjord is one hundred and fifty kilometres long and monotonous. This is the north side of the peninsula and its coasts appear to foreigners as barren and unhospitable. But to the experienced hunter the coast is inviting for settlement and the sea rich in game. Narwhal and white whales migrate past the winter camps and ringed seals are often seen. In the summer harp seals may be found close to the tent

camps, and narrow valleys open up to herds of caribou behind the ice-caps of the highland. Traces of ancient camps may be found along the coast wherever there is the least headland or cove together with a fairly flat and even foreland. The ruins of dwellings from both prehistorical and historical times have been registered at twenty-three sites. By Greenland standards this is dense settlement, comprising as it does a quarter of all known settlements in the Uummannaq district.

In the middle of this coastal stretch lies Qilakitsoq and the burial ground with the mummified women and children from about 1475. The first thorough historical and topographical descriptions of this region were made in 1789, shortly after the establishment of the colony of Uummannaq, and again in 1811. Some time later the site seems to have been abandoned as a permanent winter settlement. Both sources describe the district, and we learn that during this period hunting and living conditions were still as they had been in earlier centuries.

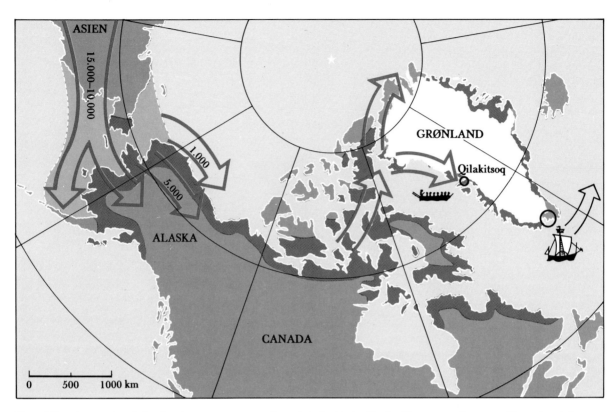

Map 2 Migration routes of about 10 to 15,000 years ago from Asia to Alaska (the Inuit's supposed ancestral home) and then to Greenland. The dark grey area shows the distribution of Inuit in the later 15th century. The last Norse inhabitants in the East Settlement disappeared at this time – some perhaps boarded ships from Europe.

In 1783 the Norwegian Peter Andreas von Cappelen was sent as a missionary to Uummannaq, and in 1789 he sent home a *Description of the Omanak Bay*, accompanied by a map sketch. He wrote:

Killekitok [Qilakitsoq] and Porusek [Poruseq]. Here are found the only fairly suitable landing places for boats along the entire mainland side. About a quarter of a mile from Killekitok there lies a sea bank where the Greenlanders sometimes catch many halibut with lines made of baleen. However this fishing cannot be relied upon, depending as it does upon how long the ice lasts in the springtime. For in open water there is usually such a strong current here that the ice disappears, which prevents fishing. These camps are only rarely inhabited. The Greenlanders also suffer want in the winter because the ice is usually blown away when the east wind blows. Therefore at this time of the year they cannot profit from the abundance of seal until there is ice again, and as long as

the ice is new and thin, they fear its being blown away. Many unthinking Greenlanders look forward in vain to open water in the icy period because they are sometimes fortunate enough to catch a few white fish [white whales] whose skin [mattak] they eat most greedily. However they are most often deceived in this hope and must admit how much better it would have been to live at the camps where the seal catch is certain. Therefore the Greenlanders ought not prefer these two camps due to the uncertainty of the white fish catch, unless they are compelled to go because of their great desire for mattak.

Cappelen referred to the settlements, including Qilakitsoq, as being rarely inhabited. The occurrence of white whales was noted as one of the main reasons for staying at the site. Cappelen's wish to see the Inuit population move was related to the desire to exploit as far as possible the netting of seals. Netting, catching seals in large nets beneath the sea ice, could take place only where the ice was fairly stable and durable, namely north of the Uummannaq Fjord. Just when Cappelen arrived in the district, this method of hunting became tremendously popular and remained the paramount source of income for the Royal Greenland Trade Company for over a century. It was introduced in its European form by the merchant J. H. Bruun, who launched the first trials in the district in 1763. This increased Cappelen's desire for the departure from Qilakitsoq of its Inuit inhabitants.

However, Qilakitsoq had never been a poor place for settlement, especially since sea mammals, fish and birds provided sufficient subsistence through-

Map 3 The region around Qilakitsoq and Uummannaq. 1:250,000 Scale.

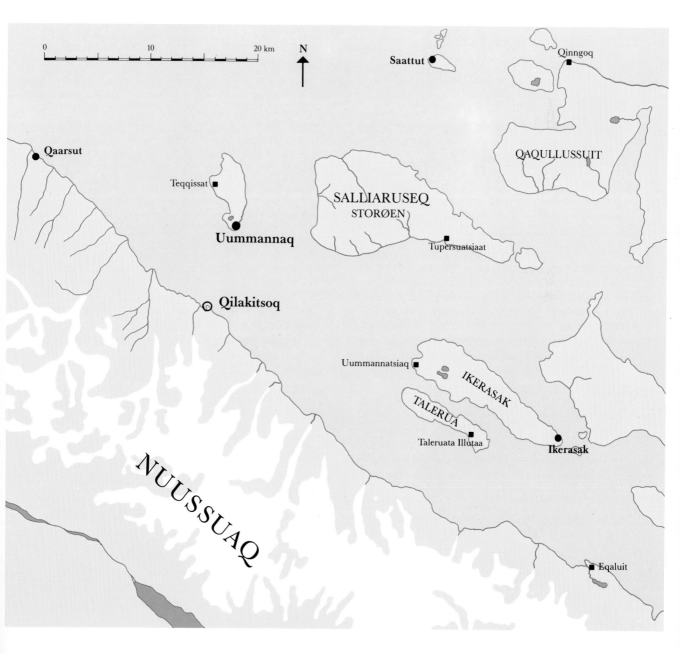

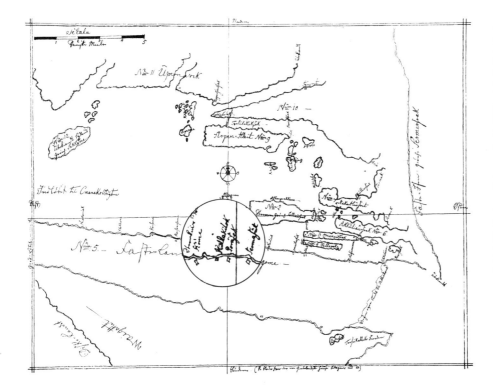

Fig. 12 Uummannaq Fjord, with Qilakitsoq (*Killekitoq*) circled. The colony of Uummannaq, founded in 1761, lies at the crossing point between the marked latitude and longitude lines. Drawn by the missionary Peter Andreas von Cappelen, 1789.

Right Fig. 13 Winter settlements of the Uummannaq district in the centuries before colonisation in 1761. The information on the living resources comes from the 18th and 19th centuries.

out the dark winter. But after a few years the inhabitants of Qilakitsoq undoubtedly moved to other hunting areas in the Uummannaq district. On the basis of information from the nineteenth century, the following picture of the hunting conditions here can be drawn.

The most important mammal was the ringed seal which was found throughout the year in the small fjords of the district, and was the mainstay of net-hunting. The harp seal appeared in the fjord in June, when the ice had melted. The hooded seal was found throughout the summer in the outlying areas, Nuussuaq and Ubekendt Eiland. The bearded seal was found everywhere, though most often to the west. The harbour seal was rare, but could be caught off Hare Island. The walrus is believed to have been common in the fjord although in historical times it has only been found off Nuussuaq point.

The most common whales were the white whale and the narwhal. The white whale migrated to the fjord in the autumn and could be caught almost everywhere. The narwhal came to the fjord slightly later and was also abundant. Larger whales were rare.

As for fish, Greenland halibut was particularly important in winter and could be found in the fjords;

Cappelen mentioned a 'bank in the sea at Killetok'. Sea trout was caught in the summer at such places as Eqaluit.

The polar bear arrived with the ice in the winter by the coasts of Svartenhuk, Ubekendt Eiland and Nuussuaq.

Among the land mammals the caribou was the most important. Caribou could be hunted every-where on the inner islands and peninsulas between Svartenhuk and Nuussuaq. In historical times there was caribou-hunting on Nuussuaq in the autumn and winter and up behind Svartenhuk through the Ukkusissat Fjord in the spring. Fox and hare were also hunted. Birds were hunted mostly in the sum-mer, and the most important ones were the eider, the king eider, the guillemot, the black guillemot and the kittiwake. Bird eggs were also collected.

The site of winter habitation was determined by the living resources. Around Qilakitsoq it was poss-ible to catch Greenland halibut and to combine the hunting of whale, seal and caribou. About three hundred years of local experience had provided the basis for the society in which the people of Qilakitsoq lived, and the mummies in the graves were perhaps the tenth generation after the *landnám*, or settlement, of the Thule culture in Uummannaq.

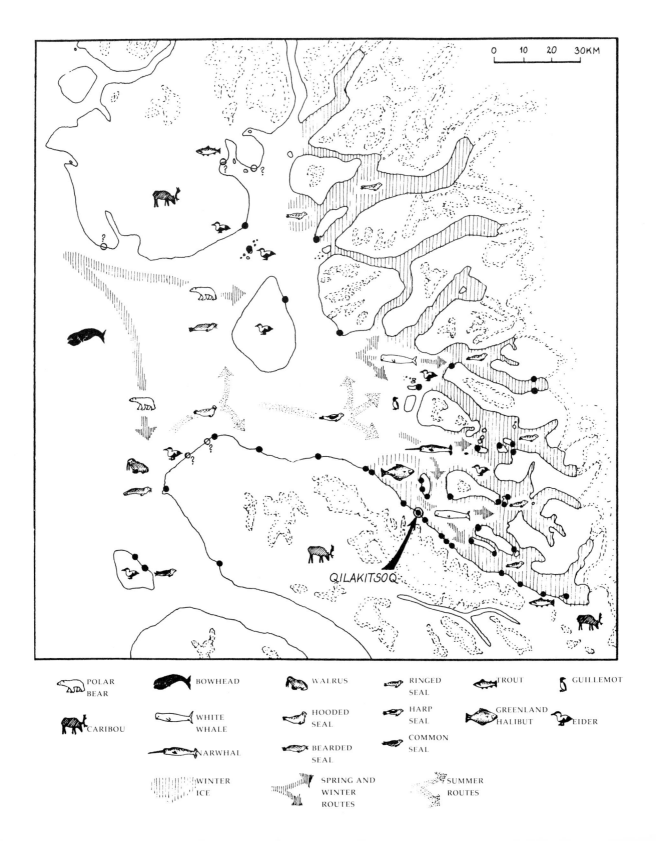

QILAKITSOQ

POLAR BEAR

CARIBOU

BOWHEAD

WHITE WHALE

NARWHAL

WALRUS

HOODED SEAL

BEARDED SEAL

RINGED SEAL

HARP SEAL

COMMON SEAL

TROUT

GREENLAND HALIBUT

GUILLEMOT

EIDER

WINTER ICE

SPRING AND WINTER ROUTES

SUMMER ROUTES

0　10　20　30KM

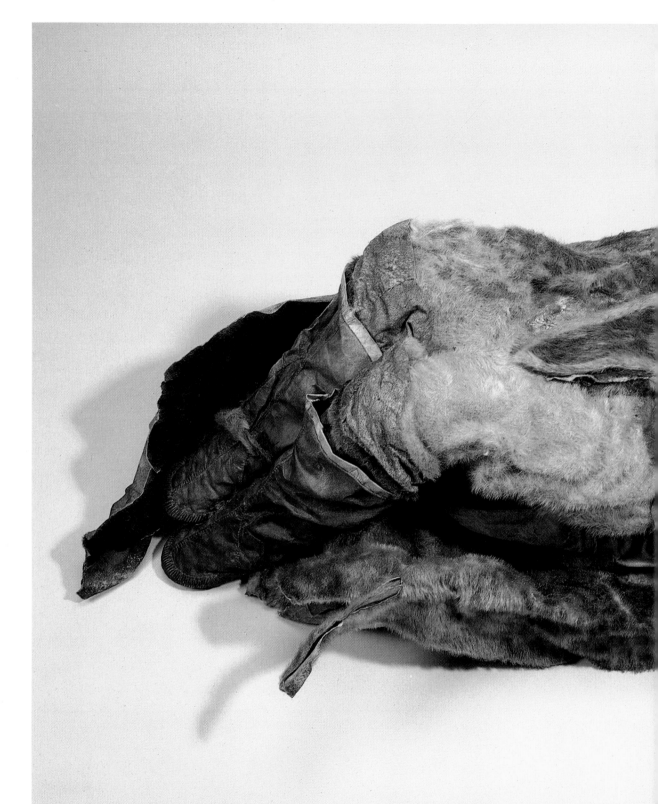

Fig. 14 Mummy I/4, a 30-year-old woman.

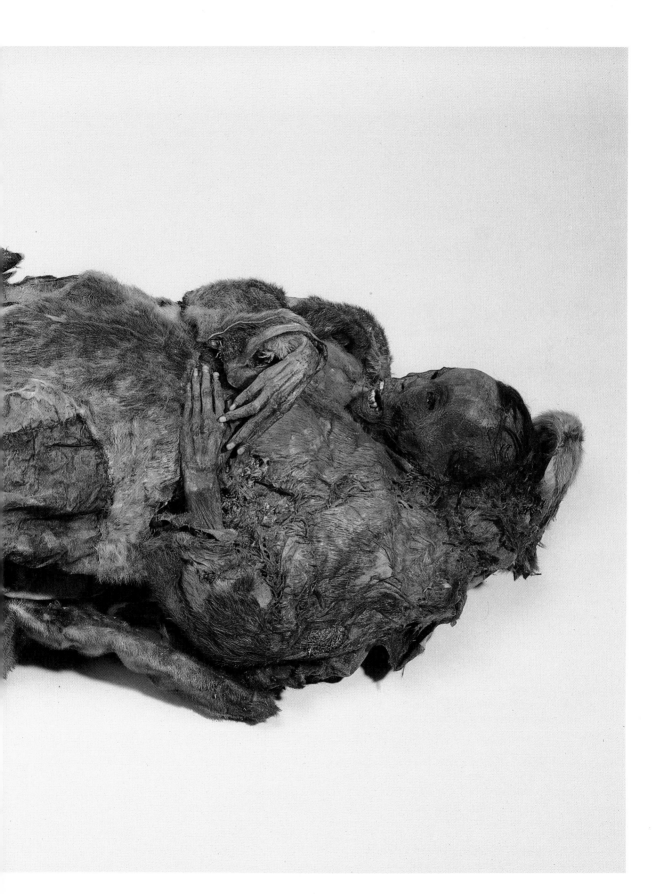

Fig. 15 The old winter settlement of Uummannatsiaq which is now abandoned. Some hunting huts built of stone and turf are still used by hunters for short stays. Qilakitsoq lies at the foot of the mountain wall on the other side of the fjord.

Right Fig. 16 Grave from 13th to 17th centuries at the Taleruata Illutaa settlement. Photographed July 1981.

PATTERNS OF SETTLEMENT

In 1811 the geologist Karl Ludwig Giesecke travelled in the district. On 18 June 1811 he noted, among other observations, that the layered sandstone massif 'in which these lignite deposits occur begin at Tuaparsoit, west of the mountain and the settlement Killekitok . . .'. Giesecke's detailed journal reports unfailingly whether or not settlements were abandoned (in ruins). Since then, numerous ancient settlements have been mapped in the Uummannaq district, and in the archives of the Greenland National Museum 102 localities with traces of settlement from prehistorical and historical times have been registered.

The winter camps in the pre-colonial days were concentrated especially in the south-east part of the district and along the north and west coasts of the Nuussuaq peninsula. This is partly owing to the character of the landscape, for the north part of the district consists of steep mountains, at the foot of which there are only very few possible settlement sites. The Svartenhuk peninsula is also fairly un-suited for winter habitation, and the boundary to the Upernavik district is ill famed as a long coastal stretch where it is difficult to find a landing place and where the ice is unsafe in winter. The route to the south to Disko Bay went either around the west point of the Nuussuaq peninsula or overland at Kuussuaq at the base of the peninsula.

The Uummannaq Fjord and its south-east branches are particularly rich in examples of settlements which were inhabited over several periods. In 1981 the Greenland National Museum visited and surveyed many of the settlements in this region. Three noteworthy camps are: Qinngoq at the southern outlet of Itilliarsuup kangerlua; Taleruata illutaa on the south-east coast of Talerua; and Teqqissat, north-west of the town of Uummannaq. Together, these three settlements constitute a cross-section of the cultural history of Greenland from a four-thousand-year-old Stone-Age find to contemporary hunting huts.

The location of graves at these settlements is the same as at Qilakitsoq – that is, removed from the centre of the site – and there are both single and common graves. This feature is ubiquitous along the

Fig. 17 Uummannaq Island as seen from the graves at Qilakitsoq.

west coast of Greenland, although burial grounds with no nearby settlement exist. There is one such example from the Nuuk Fjord region where a number of people were drowned and buried at the place where the corpses were washed ashore. This site was named Iliverpassuit, 'the burial places', and the accident was attributed to sorcery.

Round or oval ruins represent the house type of the Thule culture. When such ruins are found at a settlement site, one can be fairly certain that it was inhabited before Danish colonisation in 1721. The houses were not particularly large and were probably intended as single-family dwellings. Some were of a size, however, that must have sheltered an extended family consisting of several generations. At Qilakitsoq there are a small number of the old rounded type of ruin.

ARCHAEOLOGICAL FINDS

As early as 1903 objects were found in the graves at Qilakitsoq. N. W. Thron, the colony factor, had these finds sent to the National Museum in Copenhagen. They included household items – three wooden bowls or dishes and a wooden ladle. Fig. 22 shows an intact wooden bowl with a hollow bottom and vertical wooden sides fastened to the bottom with wooden pegs, along with the wooden ladle. The other two objects are an oval wooden box made of two halves lashed together with baleen, and half a wooden dish with traces of holes for wooden pegs made for repairing the piece. These objects, typical of the late Thule culture, must have been placed in graves with women, probably later than the mummy graves.

Many settlement sites in the Uummannaq district have yielded objects which shed light on the Eskimo hunting culture at the time when the six women and two children were buried at Qilakitsoq. Finds of sled-runners of whalebone and harness-traces bear witness to dog sleds and winter transportation along the edge of the ice and overland. Contact with Upernavik in the north and Disko Bay in the south could be maintained during the winter and spring by sled-runs over the base of the Svartenhuk and Nuussuaq peninsulas. Ice-chisels, snow-goggles, snow-knives, harpoons for hunting on the ice and ice-ladles confirm the impression of a technology geared to frozen conditions for half the year.

A rich diversity of implements used for hunting seals and birds from kayaks had been found in abundance in both graves and settlement middens in the district.

Hunting on land using bows and arrows has also been documented in archaeological finds. The bow was a stick wound with sinew along its back; barbed arrowheads have been found equipped with both knobs and screw-threads for fastening the point into the shaft. Knives with blade grooves and iron edges or stone blades were common until European knives were introduced. Axes were used for digging up turf and shaping driftwood. The most common form was the adze, which has the blade placed crosswise in contrast to the European axe.

Graves and middens have yielded objects related to activities in the winter house or the summer tent. In addition to those mentioned above, objects include soapstone lamps, wooden dishes and wooden vessels with staves (which seem to have

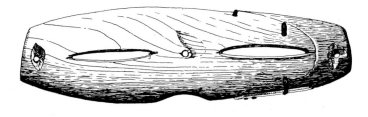

Fig. 18 Top Bone knife with cutting edge made of small pieces of iron that were presumably beaten into shape from small lumps of local iron. Bottom Snowgoggles carved out of wood and used to shield the eyes from sunlight reflecting off snow and ice. Two important items of hunting equipment, both found in graves around the Uummannaq Fjord, 15th to 17th centuries.

0   1   2   3 CM

been influenced by Norse cooperage techniques), ulus (women's knives), combs, bodkins, needle cases (both the 'winged' and the tubular types, see p. 126), thimble holders, wooden boxes, fire drills and drills, drum handles and small human figures of wood.

These archaeological finds have painted a fairly clear picture of the material culture of the Thule people and have shown how they adapted, with utmost ingenuity, to a harsh environment. We can see the true people of the Thule culture, the descendants, now mixed with Europeans, of today's Inuit.

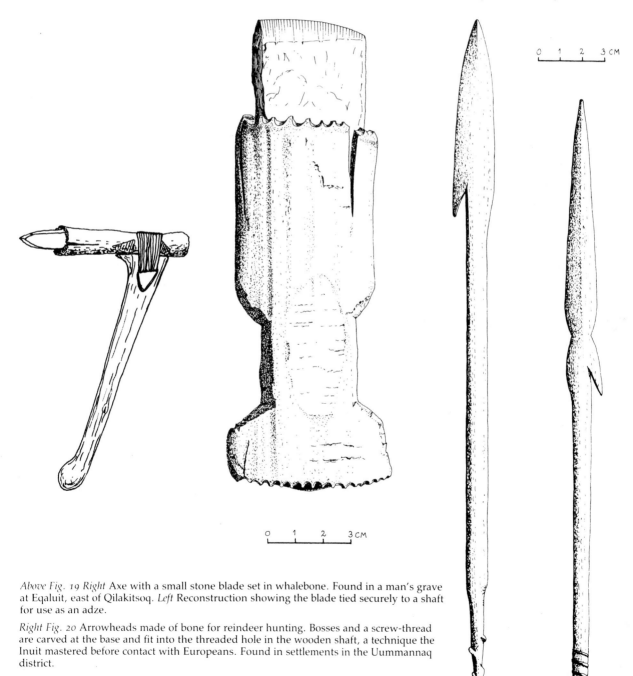

Above Fig. 19 Right Axe with a small stone blade set in whalebone. Found in a man's grave at Eqaluit, east of Qilakitsoq. *Left* Reconstruction showing the blade tied securely to a shaft for use as an adze.

Right Fig. 20 Arrowheads made of bone for reindeer hunting. Bosses and a screw-thread are carved at the base and fit into the threaded hole in the wooden shaft, a technique the Inuit mastered before contact with Europeans. Found in settlements in the Uummannaq district.

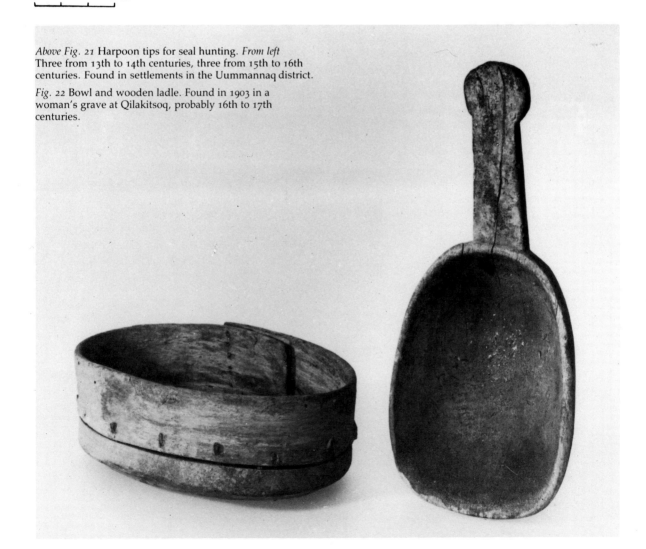

0   1   2   3 CM

Above Fig. 21 Harpoon tips for seal hunting. *From left*
Three from 13th to 14th centuries, three from 15th to 16th
centuries. Found in settlements in the Uummannaq district.

Fig. 22 Bowl and wooden ladle. Found in 1903 in a
woman's grave at Qilakitsoq, probably 16th to 17th
centuries.

2
The Find

Claus Andreasen, H. C. Gulløv

J. P. Hart Hansen, J. Lyberth, H. Tauber

Fig. 23 Jokum Grønvold, one of the two brothers who discovered the mummy graves while grouse-hunting, standing by grave I, the capstones of which are indicated by an arrow.

The discovery of the mummies

On 9 October 1972 during the ptarmigan-hunting season Hans Grønvold and his brother Jokum were getting ready to go hunting in a well-known ptarmigan area around the abandoned settlement of Qilakitsoq on the north side of the Nuussuaq peninsula. From this site they planned to follow familiar paths on the steep slopes. About two hundred metres west of the settlement Hans Grønvold suddenly caught sight of the two graves which were covered by flat stones in a crevice. He described his discovery in a letter to a friend:

Hello Juaakak,
I found the graves while out hunting ptarmigan. I fetched the others, including Juukorsi, and we investigated. We reported the find to the authorities right away but kept it a secret from everybody else. We knew that the climate, which is always dry, would preserve the things for many years. For a long time we've refused to help people who wanted to come and photograph the find. People started to look for the graves on their own and move the stones around. For a while we took care of the site, but we finally had to give up. The last time we fixed the stones was in 1975, and at that time everything was pretty much in place. We knew that one mustn't touch old graves, but we did it to preserve them. If the find had been damaged it's other people's fault, and you can tell the authorities from me that they're crazy. In Denmark they investigate the least little thing, regardless of costs. You know, if some seventeenth or eighteenth century corpses were found in Denmark, they would certainly be interested. What's the price of a ticket to Uummannaq compared to all the money people use for unimportant things?

As I said, I found the graves while hunting for ptarmigan along a route which I've always taken. I usually go past the foot of a cliff where the ground is flat and easy to walk on. That's when I noticed that the stone was irregular and the fallen stones were flat. Without thinking I picked up a large stone. And then I saw a corpse, covered by a skin, which seemed to be fresh. I started to poke around and realised that I had found a grave which had never been opened before. So I ran after Juukorsi and the others and we all explored further. There was a half-grown child lying on top, close to

what was probably its mother, and then we saw a doll which had fallen to the side, a doll which turned out to be a little child. We put them back in place, with the child to the very back, by the rock. Only the eyes and the mouth of the child were damaged; everything was dried up.

Then we found another grave alongside. At the very top there was a woman who seemed to have been young. She was wearing a very beautiful outfit and had a lot underneath her. Next to her there was a man who seemed to have been well-off. He was hefty, and also wore a beautiful outfit, with boots that seemed to be new. There was a lot of skin around the two others, high boots with laces, made of braided sinew. The man's neck was broken. I don't know if it had happened before or after he died. There was also another corpse visible.

Later we took pictures of the child and the woman as a remembrance. We were so disappointed that they showed so little interest in the find. I can't recall any longer whose boots were more beautiful, the man's or the woman's . . .
Yours truly,
Hans Grønvold

In 1972 the brothers' report was submitted to the municipal authorities who forwarded the information to the Greenland National Museum and the Greenland radio who, in turn, announced the news of the find. The information was filed in the archives of the museum, and was studied again by Hans Grønvold in 1977. Looking at the photographs which he and his brother had taken, it was suddenly realised that the find was truly exceptional. Both the excellent state of preservation and the cultural and historical information which the find could apparently yield made it incomparably more significant than all others known.

The board of the Greenland National Museum supported the idea of preserving the find for posterity. The first trip to Qilakitsoq was made at Easter in 1978, with the purpose of collecting material for dating and of gaining a better impression of the preservation condition. The two child mummies and some pieces of hide were sent to Denmark for further study. Preliminary examination of the graves showed that the material was preserved to varying degrees, but that in all cases there were rich opportunities to learn more about the people who had

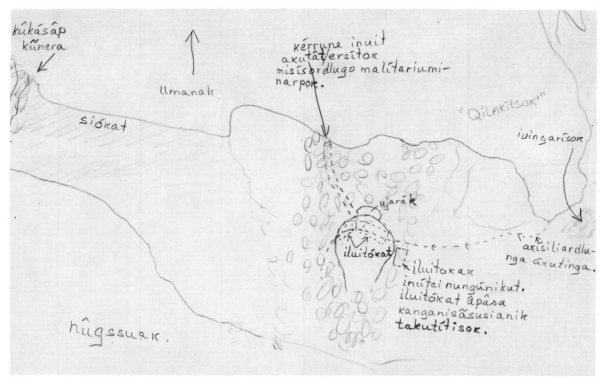

kûkásâp kûnera

ûmanak

Qilakitsoq

siôkat

ivingarisok

kérrune inuit akutát ersitok misisordlugo malitariumi narpok.

ujarâk

iluitôkat

iluitôkak inûtai nungûnikut, iluitôkat âpâsa kanganisâsusianik takutîtisok.

akisiliardlu nga akutinga.

nûgssuak.

Above Fig. 24 Qilakitsoq: the location of the old graves (*iluitokat*) on the path (the dotted line) from the house ruins of the settlement (*ivingarisok*, literally 'the place with fine grass'). Drawn and sent to the Greenland National Museum by Hans Grønvold.

Opposite Fig. 25 Aerial photograph of Qilakitsoq. The ruins are indicated by rings, the graves by an arrow and the path between them by a dotted line.

used the well-known finds of implements from fifteenth-century Inuit culture.

The first datings were made in August 1978 and placed the find in the later fifteenth century, within fifty years either side of 1475. The graves became the oldest known find of well-preserved humans and their clothing in Greenland and, indeed, the entire Arctic cultural community. Moreover, the find stemmed from the time before contact had been made with foreign whalers in the seventeenth century and before the Danish–Norwegian colonisation in the eighteenth century. The chronological difference between the Qilakitsoq mummies and the people whom the Norsemen encountered during their hunting expeditions in Nordsetur (the Disko Bay) in the thirteenth and fourteenth centuries is so slight that the mummies may be regarded as true representatives of the Skraelings, the Norse term for Eskimos. The excavations of the Norse graves at Herjolfsnæs and the Inuit graves at Qilakitsoq have revealed vital aspects of the two population groups which inhabited Greenland in the fifteenth century.

There was no doubt that the rest of the find had to be safeguarded before it was destroyed by inconsiderate visitors. Hans Grønvold mentioned that between 1972 and 1977 he and his brother had had

to maintain and fix the graves after visits from uninvited curiosity seekers. There are many instances elsewhere of souvenir hunters having removed pieces of clothing and skin, even parts of corpses. To prevent further theft, the authorities at the Greenland National Museum decided to transport the rest of the find to the Museum.

Thus in August 1978, representatives of the Greenland National Museum made another trip to Qilakitsoq. The remaining mummies were placed in solid wooden boxes which were sent to the Museum in Nuuk. After being exhibited for a short period, the entire material was sent to the Department of Conservation at the National Museum in Copenhagen. An ambitious programme of investigation began.

In 1982, the find was sent back to the Greenland National Museum. Here much of the material, including four of the mummies, is now in a permanent exhibition in specially designed rooms.

Qilakitsoq

The finding place of the mummies of Qilakitsoq lies on the steep north side of the Nuussuaq peninsula. A small cove has cut into the coast, creating a landing place on the sandy beach, behind which is a small

grassy area stopped by the abrupt rise of the mountain. A visitor to this place does indeed feel that, as signified by the word Qilakitsoq, 'the sky is low'. The mountains enclosing the area are nearly 250 m high and provide excellent shelter in the northwest-facing cove. The settlement site itself measures about 85 by 60 m and is encircled by a crescent-shaped area littered with boulders. The path on which the graves were discovered is clearly visible on the south side of the cove. It passes through the terrain strewn with boulders and runs along about 20–25 m above the coast. It leads to another settlement area about 6 km to the west by the outlet of the meltwater river Kuukassak and its sandy shores.

Traces of past settlements can still be found here. In total there are seven different structures at the site as well as about thirty-three graves or grave-like structures. The most distinctive ruin consists of the remains of a large house (Fig. 28, B) built of stone and turf, probably in the nineteenth century, so making it the most recent at the site. The house has extremely thick walls, an inner room measuring about 3.5 × 5 m, and exterior dimensions of about 10 × 15 m. The corridor, which is nearly 5 m long,

bends at the end. Inside the house, stone walls are visible and several small holes have been dug in the floor in recent times. Beside it there is a ruin that has been levelled off and is indistinct in shape (C). It measures about 7.5 × 8 m and is possibly one of the oldest at the settlement. By the shore lies another stone and turf house ruin (D) and a tent ring (E) which may be of a date comparable with B. House ruin D, like B, is that of a winter house, although it is somewhat smaller. The interior dimensions of D are about 3 × 3.5 m and the exterior dimensions about 6 × 11 m. Both ruins B and D are trapezoid. At the very back of the site lies a larger house (A), also constructed of stone and turf. This house was probably used in several periods, but the continuous back wall, measuring 15 m, indicates that the structure was originally built as a long-house (a communal dwelling), probably in the eighteenth century. The two dividing walls were probably built later, and the trapezoid shape of the westernmost room indicates that it was in use during the nineteenth century, like ruins B and D. At the east end of the building there is a storeroom, built up against a free-standing boulder.

Fig. 26 Qilakitsoq from the northwest. The ruins of the houses are on the grassy land.

Below Fig. 27 Opening grave I in 1978.

There are faint but unmistakable traces of a few more houses which, judging by their type, were contemporary with the mummies. These ruins are at the sides of the settlement, a fact which probably

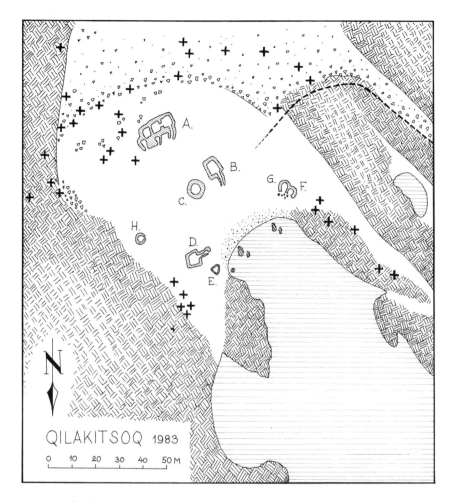

Fig. 28 Positions of the ruined houses and nearby graves of Qilakitsoq.

accounts for their survival: the later structures required so much space that they were moved to the large open area in the middle of the camp and so were not built on earlier foundations. One of these is a double house ruin (F and G). All that remains are the very low and badly delapidated back walls of turf and a façade which is only vaguely marked by small stones. The total extent of F and G is approximately 5 × 9 m, and the height is about 0.3 m. The other house ruin (H) lies far to the east of the area, under the bluff between large boulders. This ruin is round and appears as a depression, bordered by a low turf wall opening to the west and the water. The exterior dimensions are 3.7 × 4 m, and the height is about 0.2 m. At the back of this ruin are faint traces of a raised area, probably a sleeping platform. It is possible that the remains of earlier habitations, from the fifteenth century or perhaps even before that, lie beneath the other sites.

The graves

About two hundred metres from the settlement there is a ravine which cuts into the side of the mountain. In the course of its ascent, this ravine is increasingly filled with fallen stones. Where it runs into the mountain there is a protruding rock wall and the path by which the two mummy graves lie runs beneath this rock.

The graves lie close together and almost at right angles to one another. Grave I lies along the mountainside in a crevice between a fallen mountain wall and the solid bedrock and is nearly parallel to the beach. Grave II is partially under the mountainside. The capstones, or surface stones, are flat and have no lichens growing on them.

After the capstones had been removed even professional archaeologists were astonished to see how well-preserved the contents of the grave were. The entire find consisted of eight mummies, five in grave I and three in grave II, and they shall be referred to in this book by their scientific labels. In grave I a six-month-old baby (scientific label I/1) lay uppermost. Beneath him lay another boy (I/2) about four years old, together with three women (I/3, I/4 and I/5) aged about twenty-five, thirty and forty-five years old respectively. Grave II contained three

women, the uppermost (II/6) was about fifty years old, the middle one (II/7) between eighteen and twenty-two years old and the woman at the bottom (II/8) also about fifty years old.

When mummy I/1 was taken out of grave I and the clothing examined, it was judged that it was a baby boy. Beneath the baby and on top of the uppermost woman, lay a boy. He was lying on his

back with his arms by his sides and was resting his head on the woman's thighs. His legs were bent, both outwards, and in such a way that his feet almost touched. His feet were just below the woman's chin. He was fully dressed.

The uppermost woman in grave I, mummy I/3, was lying on her back on a sealskin with the fur side inward. Her shoulders were hunched as if she had a bundle on her chest beneath her arms (but this was not so), her hips were turned slightly to one side and her knees were flexed. (The reason for this is probably the position of the underlying mummy rather than shortage of space, since the grave at this point was of ample size.) Her face, hands and legs (clad in beautiful boots) were visible, as were her thighs, bare above her boots, her short trousers and her apparently long fingers, which stuck out of the sleeves of her bird-skin garment. Her hair had come loose from her head and had fallen to the back, making her seem bald.

Beneath mummy I/3 were some loose skins. When these were removed the body below, mummy I/4,

Left Fig. 29 Settlement ruins of Qilakitsoq from the southeast.

Below Fig. 30 Sole amulet. Two small pieces of leather with all the fur removed and shaped as kamik soles are tied to a piece of reindeer fur with sinew-thread. The amulet ensures that the wearer has warm kamiks on journeys. Grave I, Qilakitsoq, 15th century.

could be seen very distinctly. This woman also lay on her back with slightly bent hips and flexed knees which were turned a little to the right. She was immediately presumed to be pregnant because of her swollen stomach, upon which her hands rested. She differed from mummy I/3 in that, among other things, her trousers were long and were tucked into her boots. When she was removed from the grave a small amulet was found which had probably belonged to one of the children, mummies I/1 and I/2.

After the removal of the uppermost visible bodies, it was seen that grave I narrowed at one end. There was a large pile of skins at the bottom which the excavators attempted but failed to removed *en masse* because of the cramped space. During the removal process, the fifth mummy, I/5, was discovered, concealed by its wrapping of a large caribou skin. A closer examination of the bottom of the grave did not reveal any grave gifts, but showed that it consisted of flat stones overlain with grass and heather.

Grave II was less accessible than grave I because it was shorter and half of it lay under the mountainside. When the capstones were taken off a protective piece of skin was found lying on top of the uppermost body. When removed, mummy II/6 was revealed. This woman was at once seen to have been buried in a different position from those in grave I. She lay on her side in a sleeping position with her legs slightly bent beneath her. Her head was protected by an animal skin and her arms were wrapped around her, her hands almost reaching into the opposite armholes. She gave the impression of having died while trying to protect herself from the cold. When she was lifted out a beehive was found under her knee.

Loose grass and skin lay between her and the next woman, mummy II/7, who lay on her back with slightly turned hips and bent knees, so that she could be fitted into the narrow cleft. Her hands were folded at her hips. In contrast to the others, she had no wrapping around her.

The bottom corpse, mummy II/8, was at first difficult to discern below the covering of skin and grass. There were many loose pebbles and the grave seemed to be nearly full of hides and stones. However, after something of a struggle, she was at last lifted out. Her face was hidden, although her forehead and some hair could be made out beneath the edge of the parka hood.

When removed from the grave, the bodies at the bottom were clearly seen to be in a poor state of preservation. The grave floor was seen to resemble

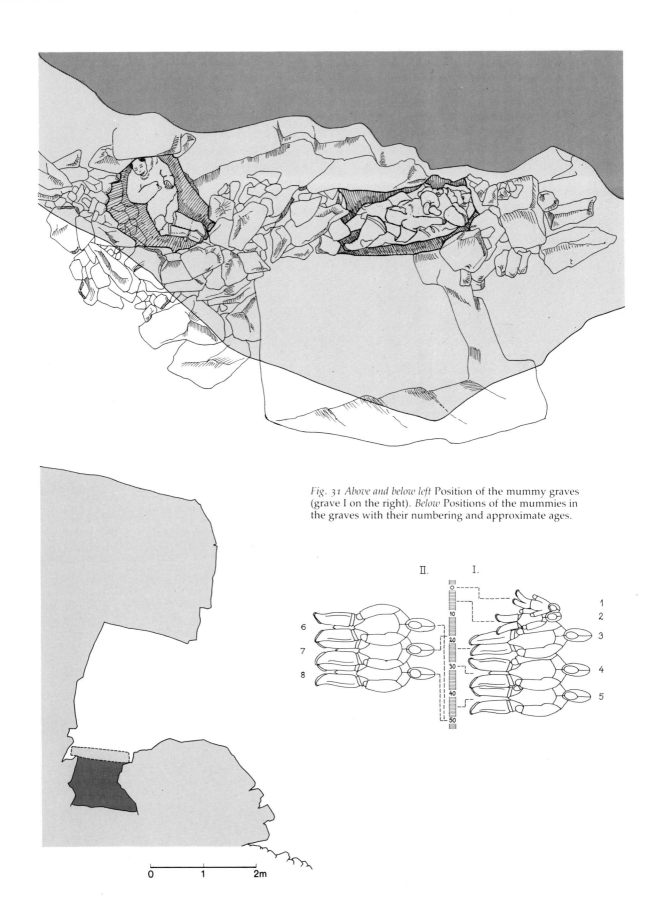

Fig. 31 Above and below left Position of the mummy graves (grave I on the right). *Below* Positions of the mummies in the graves with their numbering and approximate ages.

that of the other grave, with grass and heather on flat stones.

Close examination of both empty graves revealed that they were constructed of flat stones taken from the immediate vicinity. The base of grave I was roughly pear-shaped, while grave II was rectangular with no unusual features. However, in grave I it was clear that a large flat stone had been placed on its edge after the burial of the bottom woman, mummy I/5, and the pile of skins, on which part of the stone rested. This stone was probably set in place to increase the height of the grave and to ensure that it was not too wide when the capstones were set in place. On the whole, the graves seem to have been constructed rather haphazardly in contrast to the large, free-lying common graves in the area.

There are other graves in the area which testify to long-lasting habitation. Along the massif behind the settlement and along the west side of the cove there are about thirty-three graves and grave-like structures. However, not all of these structures can be human graves; several may have been pits for storing the meat of game animals, because almost half the graves at the settlement itself did not contain human bones. The remaining graves usually contained a skull, in some cases several skulls, but only rarely were other bones found. On the path from the settlement up to the mummy graves thirteen other graves were found, two of which contained fairly well-preserved remains such as hair, soft tissue and pieces of hide.

All the graves are built of stone. The ground plan is usually rectangular, with an interior length ranging from 1 to 1.5 m; the internal height does not exceed 1.2 m. This is a fairly large burial ground by Greenlandic standards, even when it is considered that the burials may have taken place over several centuries.

Fig. 32 Another grave near Qilakitsoq, built of stone and lying between large boulders at the foot of the rock face.

Dating the find

The find was dated to around 1475 by means of the carbon–14 method, which is based on a measurement of the content of radioactive carbon in the sample materials. All carbon compounds formed in living organisms can be dated by this method. Carbon atoms occur in different forms called isotopes, which appear in slightly varying amounts in different carbon compounds. In nature there are three types of carbon isotope, weighing respectively twelve, thirteen and fourteen times as much as a hydrogen atom. These isotopes are consequently termed carbon–12, carbon–13 and carbon–14. The first two are stable atoms whereas carbon–14 is radioactive. A determination of the ratio between the amounts of carbon–12 and carbon–13 in, for example, bones, skin and muscle tissue from animals and humans can yield important information concerning the diet of the samples. A determination of the carbon–14 content, however, can reveal the age of the samples.

Carbon–14 is formed in the upper atmosphere (see Fig. 33) and is oxidised into the gas carbon dioxide. As radioactive carbon dioxide, carbon–14 is mixed with the stable forms of carbon dioxide (carbon–12 and carbon–13). Therefore, when green plants photosynthesise and absorb carbon dioxide, they are also absorbing a certain quantity of radioactive carbon. As animals and humans ingest these plants, they also ingest radioactivity, albeit extremely low levels. When they die, the ingestion of plants and so of carbon–14 ceases. The number of carbon–14 atoms in the tissue slowly decreases by radioactive decay, at a known rate. The amount of carbon–14 which is left in a specimen is thus an indication of the time that has passed since the last ingestion of food took place and the age of the specimen can be calculated.

However, materials from the sea have a slightly different original carbon–14 content than materials from land, as is shown by the study of sealskin or caribou hide, and this must be taken into consideration. An exclusively seafood diet would result in about 5 per cent less carbon–14 in skin tissue than a diet of only plants and land animals. A difference of 5 per cent corresponds to a difference in date of four hundred years. Another important consideration is that the carbon–14 content of the atmosphere has varied in the past. This is known because measurements of carbon–14 taken from the annual rings of trees of a known age show differences from expected values. Dates which have been adjusted to allow for these variations are termed calibrated carbon–14 dates. Approximate calendar dates (after calibration, and adjusted for marine isotope differences) for the skin specimens of the mummy find are listed in the table on p. 49.

Each date has a margin of uncertainty of about fifty years either way. Therefore, conclusions cannot be drawn about a possible difference in time between the various deaths or between the burials. The small differences found may simply represent statistical variation of the measurements. Thus all the corpses may have been buried at the same time following, for example, an accident; alternatively the burials may have taken place at intervals of a few decades.

Seven specimens from the mummy find were examined by the carbon–14 method. These samples included caribou hide and sealskin as well as a sample of the skin tissue of the young boy, mummy I/2.

There is a problem in dating the skin tissue of the Qilakitsoq mummies because the composition of the Inuit diet is not known exactly – in particular, we do not know what proportion of seafood they ate in relation to plants and land animals. We can,

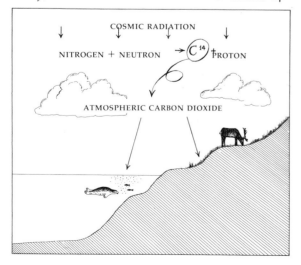

Fig. 33 The radioactive isotope carbon-14 is formed in the upper atmosphere by cosmic radiation and is oxidised to carbon dioxide gas, which mixes with carbon dioxide containing carbon-12 and carbon-13. The resultant mixture is distributed through the atmosphere, dissolves in the sea and, via the photosynthesis process, enters all plant and animal life. All living organisms therefore initially contain all three isotopes and can be dated by carbon-14. The most suitable materials in the mummy graves were the well-preserved furs, namely sealskin and reindeer hide.

Carbon–14 dating of the skins from the mummy graves.

Grave I		Grave II	
sealskin	1470	caribou skin	1510
sealskin	1465	caribou skin	1460
caribou skin	1480	sealskin	1470
average	1470	average	1480

however, presume that the age of the boy's skin tissue is the same as that of the six skin samples where the proportion of marine intake is known. Assuming that the boy died in about 1475, it is possible to calculate how many carbon–14 atoms would have decayed since then, and hence how many would have been in his skin tissue while he was alive, and so determine the composition of his diet (see pp. 157ff).

In complete contrast to this dating information a few elderly people in Uummannaq do not believe that the mummies date from the fifteenth century. Some claimed that the mummies had been victims of the great epidemic which ravaged the Uummannaq district in the early nineteenth century. In 1782 there was a serious epidemic of dysentery and in 1812 another epidemic disease that carried off 149 inhabitants. In a population that numbered 393 in 1805 this epidemic was catastrophic. The 1812 epidemic was at the time thought to have been caused by sorcery and the man believed responsible was killed that same year by a neighbour at his settlement.

Mummification

Mummification is the preservation, instead of decay, of the body tissue and is a process that can take place both naturally and artificially. Mummified tissue is brown, hard and dry and human skin resembles parchment.

In the case of the bodies at Qilakitsoq the mummification was natural. The explanation is a combination of low temperatures and dry air. The average annual temperature at Qilakitsoq is below freezing but the fluctuations may be great, ranging from −40°C in winter to +15°C in summer. However, the graves were protected from direct sunlight by the overhanging rock and each year there was probably no more than a few hours of direct sunlight on the capstones; the temperature in the graves can hardly

ever have reached much above +5°C. The overhanging rock also sheltered the graves from rain and snow, so that only minimal amounts of water came into contact with the grave contents.

The water which did get in was drained off through the bottom of the graves; in addition there must have been some sort of air passage between the stones of the graves which helped the mummification, or desiccation, process. Also, the humidity of the arctic air is very low. In fact, it can be said that a sort of freeze-drying process took place.

Bodily decay begins when the cessation of breathing and circulation stops the nourishment of the tissues. It gradually causes all soft tissue to disappear. An adult buried in well drained soil in Denmark, for example, normally becomes a skeleton in about ten years; for a child, it takes about five years. Parts of the body which are particularly resistant to decay are the bones, teeth, cartilage, hair, nails and crystalline lenses.

The process of bodily decay is very complicated. It consists of actual putrefaction involving decomposition of organic material because of bacterial activity, caused by the spread of bacteria in the dead organism. These bacteria stem mainly from the intestines, although they also come from the air passages, and spread through the circulatory system of the dead body; blood is an excellent nutritive medium for bacteria. Later, bacteria may also come from the earth and the environment. Decay is also caused by autolysis, the decomposition of tissue due to the activity of the enzymes of the dead body. Enzymes are bound to the cells during life but released after death.

There are different rates of decay. Temperature is a significant factor, as is apparent in the case of the Qilakitsoq mummies. A corpse decomposes rapidly when the temperature of the environment is high or when the deceased had a fever. Low temperatures hinder decay, which becomes extremely slight below +4°C. As the temperature drops and water freezes

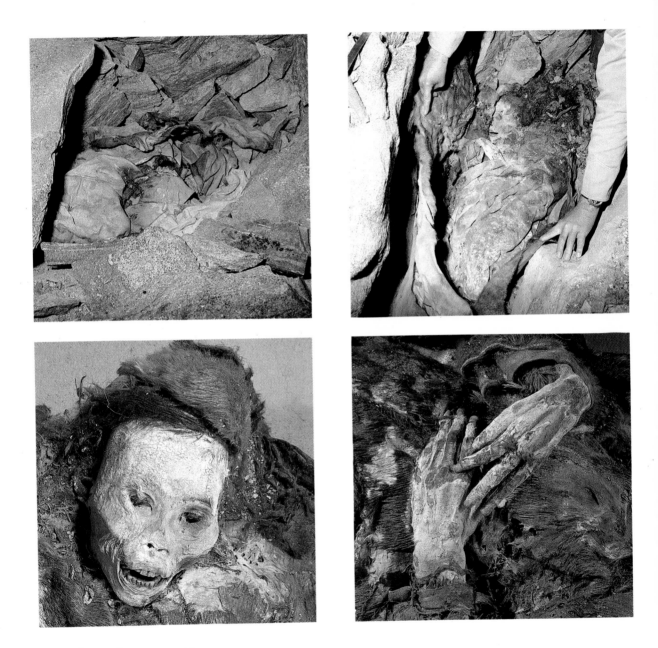

Fig. 34 Mummy I/4, a 30-year-old woman.

into crystals, water cannot be used in the processes of decay. Alternating periods of cold and thaw have a particularly desiccating effect because the water in the cells is released when the cell membranes are destroyed by the fluctuations of temperature, and subsequently evaporates.

Corpses which are covered decompose more rapidly because the body loses less heat. This also explains why overweight people begin to decompose relatively quickly, for the subcutaneous fat provides insulation against heat loss. If bacteria was already circulating in the blood before death, decay would be particularly quick. Newborn babies usually decay slowly – their body surface area is relatively large so they lose heat quickly, and at birth they contain no bacteria.

The presence of water is another significant factor. The growth of bacteria and, to a lesser degree, of fungi depends upon water. If water is scarce and desiccation is rapid, bacteria growth and thus putrefaction is hindered. In some cases decay is seen in the parts of a corpse's body which are covered, by bedding for instance, whereas the uncovered parts, forearms and hands which may be hanging over the edge of a bed, dry up and become mummified. There have also been finds of mummified infants who had been killed at birth and hidden away in dry attics, for example, where they were discovered years later. Therefore, differences in temperature, clothing, amount of body fat, and bacteria and water explain the various types and rates of decay among people who died at the same time.

Mummification, which occurs naturally when the process of decay is sufficiently hindered, is not characteristic of cold regions alone. In fact, it rather favours high termperatures, dry air and draughts. In warm and dry regions such as the Nubian desert it is not unusual to find a mummified corpse over a thousand years old. These desert people, preserved for an unlimited period of time, had died in the open and dried up rapidly because of the high temperature and low humidity of the air.

Artificial mummification has been practised throughout the world at different times – as early as 4000 BC the Egyptians were embalming their dead, with substances which halted the decaying processes and preserved the tissues. Artificial mummification is also known in Australia, China, South

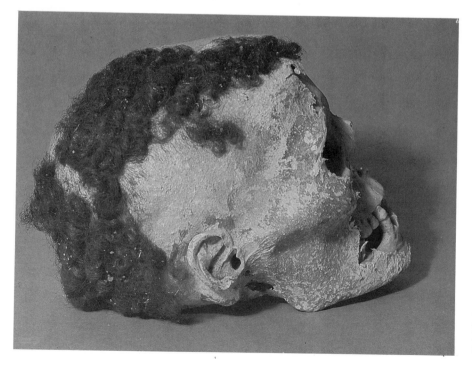

Fig. 35 Mummified head of a 25-year-old man discovered in the Nubian desert by the Scandinavian expedition to Sudanese Nubia in 1960–4. From around AD 350–500.

America and the United States. It was practised by the inhabitants along the west coast of Alaska and on the Aleutian Islands, where its purpose was to achieve immortality. The naturally mummified corpses had probably provided the model. Both naturally and artificially mummified bodies have yielded much information about ancient cultures and appearances.

Today embalming is done by injecting a formalin solution into the body. It is rarely practised in Europe, although it is widespread in the United States. The solution kills the bacteria and fungus and halts the activity of the enzymes.

In addition to mummification there are other ways by which the normal processes of decay in a corpse are wholly or partly stopped. In bogs, sphagnum peat can release acids which can conserve corpses if air is kept out. Skin is tanned to a leathery texture and calcium and other minerals disappear from the bones. Often the internal organs are completely pre-served, unlike those of mummified corpses. Some of the Danish bog corpses from the Iron Age were even found to contain abundant quantities of well-preserved stomach contents which, after close examination, yielded much information about their diet. The corpses found in peat bogs in Denmark and north-west Europe were probably mostly the victims of crimes, executed criminals, and perhaps human sacrifices.

Another way of delaying decay is the formation of adipocere, fatty tissue such as subcutaneous tissue changing into a white substance when in water or buried in humid soil. This is extremely resistant to decay and may preserve at least the outer contours of a corpse for a long time, sometimes up to several hundred years.

The bodies at Qilakitsoq are mummified. They were dessicated and thus preserved for an unlimited period of time, or as long as decomposing bacteria and fungus were kept away.

Fig. 36 The Tollund Man, one of several bodies discovered in peat bogs in Denmark. He was hanged (the rope is still round his neck) and then disposed of in a bog about 2000 years ago.

3
Death and Burial

Rolf Gilberg, Robert Petersen

Beliefs about death

The Greenland Inuit pre-Christian religion included the belief that everything was alive and contained an inner force, *inua*, as was so in man. People, called *inuit*, protected themselves against the powers of nature by using amulets and secret formulae. Many rules had to be obeyed in order to prevent disturbances in the world order. When these rules no longer sufficed, assistance was sought from an *angakkoq*, a shaman, who was the link between this world and the supernatural world.

Throughout the Inuit world existed the idea of *sila*, the ruler of the universe and especially of the air. Many regarded *sila* as the power with the greatest influence on souls. Man himself, *inuk* (singular of *inuit*), was thought to be composed partly of a body and partly of several kinds of invisible forces which, for the sake of convenience, can be called 'souls'. The most important of these were the name-soul, *ateq*, and the supernatural-soul, *tarneq*, which continued its existence after death.

Ateq remained in this world after death. The name of the deceased could not be used for up to a year after death, or before it was given to an infant, usually of the same sex. If the name was used, it would lose some of its power and would most probably attract the attention of the wandering name-soul, which would haunt the person who had defied the name ban.

The name had power in itself. Many of the good personal qualities of earlier bearers of the name were transferred with it to the next bearer. It was common for a person to have several names, and in pre-Christian days the Inuit used no surnames or family names, so there was no way of determining family relationships through names. However, it was not uncommon to be named after a close deceased relative, such as a grandparent, the power of whose name survived in the grandchild, who thus inherited the good qualities of his forefathers.

A person who bore the same name as one who had just died had to change and use another of his names. Also, if the name of the deceased was the

Opposite, above Fig. 37 Grave at the Illutalik settlement, Disko Bay.

Opposite, below Fig. 38 When opened, the grave at the Illutalik settlement displayed three skeletons. The one with the head on the right was the last to be buried hence its undisturbed position and bent legs. The bones of the other two are heaped together at the foot of the grave. L. of grave chamber 1.3 m.

term for an implement or some everyday item, this object had to be called something else. This custom led to the formation of many new words and so created considerable variation in the vocabularies of the various dialects.

Tarneq, the supernatural-soul, was the soul which gave a person his identity, consciousness, emotions and abilities to think and to procreate. It also seemed to be the driving force in a person's development from birth to death, through all phases of life. The body was the instrument of this soul.

There was no clear idea in Greenland as to where the *tarneq* came from. Inuit in East Greenland believed that the 'Man in the Moon' brought the soul to the body at birth. The Inuit of central Canada thought it arrived through reincarnation, although the reincarnate was not necessarily a person.

In answer to Knud Rasmussen's question in 1903 as to what the soul meant to a person, the Polar Inuk Majaq said: 'The soul is what makes you beautiful, what makes you a person. The soul alone is what gives you a will, enables you to act, to be bold. Your soul guides your whole life; and therefore the body collapses when the soul leaves it'. Only shamans could see this soul, which apparently looked like a person but was much smaller. It lived outside the body but followed it like a shadow, and body and soul were inseparable for as long as the person lived. After burial, the soul left the body and travelled to the Land of the Dead.

If the soul left the body for a short time while it was still alive, the body became sick; if it left for a long time, the body died. Only when a person was asleep could the soul leave the body briefly without harming it. A shaman, however, could voluntarily make his soul leave and return, often doing so to send it searching for an ill person's missing soul which it could bring back to make the person well again.

Inuit in Greenland did not view the borderline between life and death as absolute. They believed that a person was apportioned a certain number of days and that ultimately the length of his life was determined by fate. But fate could be changed by misfortune or sorcery. People who seemed to have died from an accident might be brought to life again through magical treatment, but only during the period before the soul departed for the Land of the Dead, that is, during the transition period between life and 'death'.

As the force of life, the soul was dangerous when not in its proper place, with the body. The transition from one phase of life to another was a time to be especially wary of such danger. During a birth, a number of taboos had to be specially observed: possessions in the house or tent had to be taken outside so that the soul would not collide with them, especially if the child was stillborn. This illustrates the belief that a stray soul could possess objects, which might thus become dangerous for the surroundings.

When the soul departed from the body at death it left behind all evil. The survivors thus had to exercise great care in burying the dead since all that was left was evil. Preferably, contact with a corpse was avoided. It was the dead body, rather than death, that Inuit feared. Touching a corpse and its danger-

Fig. 39 A human soul tucked under the arm of Toornaarsuk, a large and dangerous though helping spirit, whom the first missionaries equated with the devil. If Toornaarsuk intended to kill his victim, he placed the soul in his upper arm and squeezed him to death against his lower arm. Drawing by Karale from East Greenland for Knud Rasmussen, about 1920.

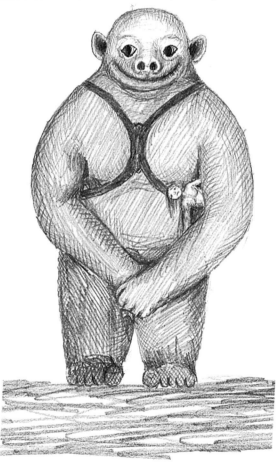

ous evil 'fluids' would bring about prohibitions which could last for up to a year.

When death occurred or was imminent, there were a number of rules regarding treatment both of the dead and the survivors. When on the verge of death, a person's possessions were carried out of his house or tent, and remained there for three or five days after the death. The survivors were then forbidden to do a number of everyday activities such as preparing or cutting their own food, and naming certain objects; they had to sit on their sleeping platform facing the wall. After three or five days the man of the house could be cleansed with a magic formula. He could then resume hunting, although he had to exercise certain precautions until he had made a catch. The woman of the house, however, had to follow many rules for up to a year before she could resume a normal life. For example, she could not go bare-headed and so had to wear a separate hood; she could not get into a woman's boat at the same place as others; nor could she mention game animals. If she saw a hunter with his catch, for example, she was prohibited from telling others, as would have been the normal custom.

If such rules were not followed correctly, the entire society might suffer, from poor hunting, for example. As no-one would voluntarily subject himself to the limitations in everyday life imposed upon those who had been in contact with a corpse, only the most closely related survivors would organise the burial. They had to arrange a traditional burial to prevent the soul from being homeless and so returning to haunt the settlement.

A person who died in a tent was brought out of it in the prescribed manner: the stones weighing down the back part of the tent were removed, and the corpse was carried out of the back opening. In winter in a house, the deceased was carried out either through a window or through an opening in the back wall of the house. This was done to prevent the soul from finding its way back into the dwelling through the entrance. A homeless soul was not at all beneficial and was feared for the harm it could do to the living.

In the case of murder, the fear that the soul would return to avenge itself was greater still, and there were a number of magic rituals to prevent this. One was for the murderer to eat a little of the victim's liver and heart, two organs closely related to the soul. Thus a vengeful soul would recognise itself in its murderer and abandon its mission. Another ritual was to dismember the victim, so that the various member-souls could not gather together as an avenger. Member-souls were part of the East Greenland Inuit creed: that a person consisted not only of a body, a name and a supernatural-soul (*tarneq*), but also of a great number of smaller souls dwelling in the joints of the body. A person who lost one of these souls would become sick in the corresponding part of the body. These member-souls resembled humans but were no larger than a thumb.

Fig. 40 Spirits in human guise illustrating the legend that these spirits are so evil that no flesh can grow on them. The Inuit thought that everyone had an evil spirit wandering in their wake and that whenever temptation arose, this spirit enthusiastically encouraged participation. Drawing by Karale from East Greenland for Knud Rasmussen, about 1920.

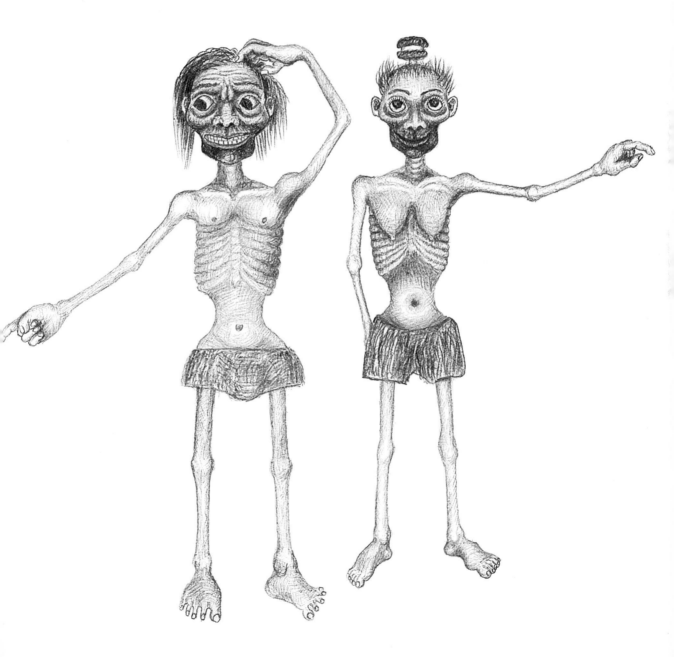

Burial and life after death

Before the mission period in the early eighteenth century the most common type of Inuit grave in Greenland was a burial chamber built of stone. Low stone walls were covered over with flat stones, after which the entire grave was heaped with large and small stones. These graves were usually airy, but as they provided little protection against humidity they could not prevent the normal decay of the buried corpse. Generally, only the largest bones were preserved, such as thigh bones and parts of the skull.

When people died of disease or hunger, their own house was sometimes made into their grave, with the walls torn down and piled on top of the corpse. Another burial custom, practised particularly in East Greenland, was to commit the body to sea. However, the procedure of simply leaving a corpse unprotected on the ground does not seem to have been followed in Greenland. In this form of burial, which has been observed among Inuit in Canada, the unprotected corpse is placed on the ground, with the head and foot ends marked by stones. It is, of course, difficult to find archaeological evidence of this practice.

Finally, there are cave burials such as those at Uunartoq in South Greenland and at the foot of Pisissarfik near Kapisillit (see p. 137), where mummified bodies have also been found. This custom exists at several other sites in West Greenland.

In preparation for burial, the corpse was fully dressed, often for the journey to the Land of the Dead, and was perhaps sewn into a hide and thus buried or committed to the sea. Nulouq, a successful hunter and the last adult West Greenland Inuit who died unbaptised, was dressed for his burial in 1858 in sealskin trousers, winter boots of furry sealskin, inner coat of bird-skin, outer fur of furry sealskin edged with dog-skin around the head and sleeves, and a separate hood made of the skin of a black dog's head.

Inuit believed that life never ended and that death was merely a transition to another form of existence in which the liberated soul of man could live on, provided that the proper precautions had been taken at his death. Life in the Land of the Dead was very similar to life on earth except that there was no unsuccessful hunting or illness.

Legends tell nothing about the route which the soul travelled. We know that some souls, most likely those buried at sea, went under the sea where they probably hunted sea mammals. Others, probably those buried on land, went up to the sky, where they lived by hunting land animals; both of these places were good to live in, though the land under the sea was thought to be marginally better. In the Land of the Dead one would be united with one's forefathers, providing they had chosen the same place. Shamans who came visiting while still alive could carry greetings from the living to the souls of the dead and could even take delicacies with them as gifts. An account of a visit to the Land of the Dead was given by the famous shaman from East Greenland, Avgo, and related by Knud Rasmussen.

The soul could not enter the Land of the Dead as long as it contained 'the earthly fluids'. It was cleansed of these fluids by being placed under a large, tightly stretched skin. Infants who had not done many things wrong in life lost the fluids quickly, whereas the souls of old people might take up to a year to have them removed. This was one of the reasons that survivors had to obey the taboos during this period, because until the fluids were removed, the soul was homeless. Its departure could also be facilitated by loosening the bands (primarily the spiritual and intellectual forces which held the soul and person together) which held the soul close to the body until the funeral was over.

At the funeral the survivors took care of the needs of the dead in the next life by giving them grave gifts. Men received hunting implements; women various household items such as a soapstone blubber-lamp, a sewing needle and an ulu. It was customary for a great hunter to be buried with his kayak, his sled and dogs, for he would need these in the after-life. A woman was often buried with a dog, even if she had none previously, for it was unpleasant to travel alone. Also, a dog's skull could apparently be placed in the grave of a child so that the dog could lead the child to the Land of the Dead.

In a society in which material goods were few, the temptation to steal grave goods may have arisen, but it was forbidden. However, it was acceptable to trade with the dead. For example, if someone took a hunting tool because his existing one was poor or he did not have one at all, he could pay for it by giving the dead a model of the implement. Payment could also consist of a small piece of meat. The soul of the dead person was able to make the model real or to enlarge the piece of meat. Therefore, finds of grave goods today depend upon what the deceased had owned and whether anybody had traded with him in his grave.

Food was also placed in the grave as victuals for the journey. The dead was to bring his own meat and water to the next life in the Land of the Dead in the sky, where there was not such an abundance of food as in the Land of the Dead under the sea. One could also give the dead sacrificial gifts as good luck tokens for hunting. In certain Inuit areas outside Greenland grave gifts were destroyed ('killed') so that the dead could use them more easily in the Land of the Dead than if they were intact, ('alive'.) In most places, however, including Greenland, the dead brought usable gifts with them. These gifts were often placed close to the grave, but not in it.

The Polar Inuit placed their dead with heads facing east, but elsewhere in Greenland the corpse was

Fig. 41 Inuit in East Greenland believed that when people died, they spent a year working their way from death towards eternal life – a year spent crawling from one side to the other of an outstretched tent or hide and thus ridding the body of all its 'earthly fluids'. The tears of those left behind attached the dead to the earth, making their journey much harder and more exhausting; thus survivors were obliged to control their weeping. The stillborn had the easiest passage since nobody cried for them and so they were able to crawl straight through and run unhindered towards eternal life. Drawing by Karale from East Greenland for Knud Rasmussen, about 1920.

commonly placed with its head to the west, perhaps because the Land of the Dead was believed to lie in that direction. In an area ranging from Alaska through Canada to Labrador, the corpses often lay stretched out in the grave. In southern Alaska and in Greenland, however, they were usually buried in a bent position. (Occasionally in Greenland, outstretched corpses from pre-Christian times are mentioned.) It is possible that the often-cramped conditions in the grave served to keep a corpse in a bent position. Also, it is sometimes said that the flexed position was symbolic of leaving life as it was entered, in the foetal position, for a new life was about to begin.

It was common to bury an elderly person at a site where he or she had, when alive, enjoyed the view. It is difficult to say whether this custom was simply out of the survivors' concern for the dead or whether it was believed that the soul would take pleasure in the beautiful view during the journey to the Land of the Dead.

It is said that screams could be heard from certain graves, perhaps before a change in the weather. A story from the eighteenth to twentieth century concerns a great young hunter from Nanortalik named Jarraajaaq. His sweetheart was forced by a Chistian Moravian priest to marry another man. That same day Jarraajaaq shot himself; his grave was

said to scream from time to time. Although it is understandable that no-one thought that Jarraajaaq's soul could enter the Christian heaven, the pagan belief that graves could be haunted still existed.

In certain cases, such as madness which was thought to be caused by magic, the sick person would have difficulty dying. This also held true of a *qivittoq*, a mountain wanderer, who had eaten bewitched food or inhaled the breath of a ghost. When a Greenland Inuk became unhappy with life with others he became a mountain wanderer. He left human society and became a hermit in the mountains. A mountain wanderer could spread fear and terror in an area because he was thought to possess supernatural powers, to be a sort of ghost. Some mountain wanderers had to travel far to the north to die outside the familiar world. Others were thought to endure the throes of death as many as five times before actually dying properly the sixth time. Other special cases were murderers who, as ritual protection for themselves, had eaten part of their victim's heart and liver and thus contained some of their victim's soul. Such murderers did not die easily. Tusilartoq, for example, was said to have

Fig. 42 Three watercolour depictions of Greenland legends dating back to the prehistoric (or precolonial) period. Painted by Greenland artist and seal hunter Aron of Kangeq. The main collection of 161 watercolours, painted between 1858 and 1868, is housed in the Greenland National Museum. *Above* Parents mourning by the grave of their son. 1863. Actual size. *Opposite, top* Burial according to ancient East Greenland tradition. East Greenland Inuit, to the astonishment of West Greenland Inuit, cast the dead Ivannissaq into the sea with the words: 'Should we bury him up here on the earth, his soul would suffer perpetual cold and misery. Therefore we will send him down where there is neither cold nor lack of food'. 1867. Actual size. *Opposite, bottom* Aariassuaq rises from his grave and frightens his enemies to death, illustrating the legend about a man who was envied and feared by his neighbours who mock him at his grave. 1867. Actual size.

Fig. 43 A ghost, or *tupilak*, in the form of a dog with a child's head. The *tupilak* here has enticed two men in a kayak to kill him with their harpoons. Drawing by Karale, about 1920.

Fig. 44 The creation of a *tupilak*. They are made to harm one's enemies and comprise various dead objects including bones from graves (often a child's skull) which were packed in a hide and brought to life by sorcery. This example shows seal bones as well as a human skull with seal jawbones. Drawing by Gert Lyberth from Sukkertoppen, about 1915.

Fig. 45 Tupilak carved out of wood showing human and animal characteristics. The faces on the shoulders probably reflect the old notion that the spirits had human guises. East Greenland, about 1930. L. 15 cm.

killed many people and eaten their hearts and livers, and he apparently walked the earth several times and first rested in peace only when buried in consecrated ground.

Haunting was regarded with horror. Canadian Inuit believe that a dead person whose survivors had not obeyed the prescribed taboos would return as a *tupilak*, in this case a ghost. Ghosts were spirits with no identity and thus with no will of their own. The Greenland Inuit *tupilaks* belonged to this group. They were forced to seek out the victim named for them by their creator, and if the victim turned out to have greater magical power, they had to return and attack the creator.

With such beliefs in mind, it is understandable that burial customs and death cults were intended to ensure that a dead person could enter his next life with his individuality intact.

4
The People

T. Ammitzbøll, S. Ry Andersen, H. P. Andersson

J. Bodenhoff, M. Eiken, B. Eriksen, N. Foged, M. Ghisler

A. Gotfredsen, H. E. Hansen, J. P. Hart Hansen, J. Jakobsen

J. Balslev Jørgensen, T. Kobayasi, N. Kromann, K. J. Lyberth

L. Lyneborg, F. Mikkelsen, J. Møhl, R. Møller, J. Myhre

P. O. Pedersen, J. U. Prause, O. Sebbesen, E. Svejgaard

D. D. Thompson, V. Frølund Thomsen, L. Vanggaard

Adaptation, acclimatisation and physical anthropology

The people of Qilakitsoq lived in a highly developed culture which was remarkably well suited to the arctic climate. What made it possible for them to exist in such a climate which is both cold and, for much of the year, dark, and which for centuries has often been regarded as impossible to survive in? It would be logical to presume that Inuit have a special natural ability to endure the cold, but this is not so.

Man's adjustment to such conditions as cold can be described in terms of adaptation and acclimatisation. Adaptation refers to hereditary changes occurring in a species. These changes are caused by the selection of certain genetic traits which make a species best fit for survival. Such changes have played a major role throughout the evolution of species: the concept is often expressed by the term 'survival of the fittest'.

Acclimatisation refers to changes occurring in an individual. Thus this term covers both physiological and psychological reactions to external influences which, for example, make the individual better able to survive and tolerate extreme cold or heat. Most people find that they soon become accustomed to cold or heat after arrival in arctic or tropical climates. Acclimatisation of the individual is closely related to cultural adaptation of a given society. Precautions and improvements in housing and clothing, for instance, help enable a society to survive.

The common belief that Inuit are especially well suited to arctic life because of their compact builds and abundant layers of fat beneath the skin is utterly groundless. No human type shows signs of being genetically adapted to cold. Everyone is identical in his reaction to the temperature of his environment. There is no essential difference between the temperature regulation of an Inuit and that of an African, despite the fact that one lives near the North Pole in a cold climate whereas the other lives in tropical sunshine and warmth.

Life most probably began in the tropics. Here the warm-blooded animals evolved, maintaining the original micro-climate close to the body. Beneath his clothing, a Polar Inuit has the same micro-climate – warm, moist and tropical – as for example a Lapp, who lives in similar conditions. Europeans and Africans, for example, are no different. This micro-climate determines the heat regulation which allows man to maintain 37–38°C as the normal body temperature.

It may at first seem strange that the body climate of all people is the same until one considers that, with regard to size, food consumption and metabolism, people are very similar regardless of ethnic background. The body temperature of 37°C is just above that of the hottest environment. If the body temperature were lower, man would not be able to regulate it; if it were higher, more food would have to be consumed, thus perhaps endangering the survival of the species.

Beneath their fur, the polar bear, caribou and musk ox also have the same micro-climate. Although it may be pointed out that many arctic animals have adapted to the cold by developing fur, man has always been, as far back as we can trace, the same naked animal, able to spread over the entire earth thanks only to his highly developed brain. Man's existence outside a narrow belt around the Equator is owing to his intelligence and his ability to live in societies which are structured to ensure the survival of the individual. Such adaptation is evolution over millions of years. Cultural development, initiating traditions that will be inherited, is far more recent, but its effectiveness has permitted the spread of man to the most remote regions.

So-called primitive peoples, however, have often been described as being particularly adapted to the cold. Darwin describes how in Tierra del Fuego he saw people barefoot and clad solely in loin-cloths in the falling snow. From Australia there are descriptions of Bushmen sleeping naked on the earth in winter, warmed only by a small fire. Investigations in Norway have also discerned a difference in the way Lapps and Oslo townspeople tolerate the cold. However, upon closer examination, all these reports show nothing but acclimatisation by the individual: Norwegians, who at first withstood cold more poorly than Lapps, could become accustomed to it if they had to. It is thus shown that the ability to sleep despite a slightly falling skin temperature manifests a physiological acclimatisation which can be trained. New arrivals to the arctic winter cold find the first weeks very difficult, but they become accustomed to it. Similarly, it takes a few weeks to become adjusted to a tropical climate, and a Greenland Inuk who has resided for some time in the south will have problems if he returns to the Greenland winter.

It is true that fishermen and Inuit, for example, who live and work in the cold often have somewhat warmer hands than people from more temperate regions. This higher hand temperature allows for increased manual dexterity in low temperatures, where nerve conduction, and consequently the ability to control one's hands and fingers, is decreased. At the same time there is greater protection against frostbite. But again this is the result of acclimatisation by the individual, not adaptation via an inherited trait.

The true difference between adaptation and acclimatisation lies in the way in which arctic man in his culture has been able to establish a society which completely protects him from his climate. It is typical that injury caused by the cold occurs almost solely to new arrivals to the arctic region, not to permanent inhabitants. This is another example of acclimatisation.

Inuit society has never existed on a minimum level, and it is incorrect to view it and its culture as a constant struggle for survival. Struggle may be encountered by the individual, but it is an isolated event. A society cannot exist in a constant battle for existence; instead it constitutes a collective protection ensuring existence. Hence Inuit society has survived by being able to live in and with the cold, and not by struggling against it.

Physical anthropology is the study of human races and is concerned with such factors as the physical characteristics of various ethnic groups. The great importance of the Qilakitsoq find lies in the well-preserved bodies and clothing. As the dress of the best preserved mummies has not been touched, and as the soft tissue of most of the other mummies has been preserved on the bones, no proper physical anthropological study of the skeletal structure has been made, for want of preserving the intactness of the find. However, since anthropologists today prefer to work with population groups instead of individuals, the superficial anthropological investigation of this small group of people is not felt to be a great loss.

Typologically, the mummies resemble the common Inuit in West Greenland prior to colonisation. There are no special features, and specifically no family resemblances, that can be distinguished.

Age determination has been made on the basis of physical anthropological studies together with dental and X-ray examinations. At the time of death mummy I/1 was about six months old, mummy I/2 about four years old, mummy I/3 was between twenty and twenty-five years old, I/4 about thirty, I/5 between forty and fifty, II/6 about fifty, II/7 between eighteen and twenty-two and II/8 about fifty. Thus they represent all age groups. It is worth noting

that one third of the dead were approximately fifty years old when they died, indicating that the survival potential in their environment was not particularly low.

All six adults seem to be women, in spite of physical anthropological evaluation of mummy I/3 which is indeterminable, meaning that the mummy could be male. However, the tattoos on the forehead, the lack of trace of a moustache, despite well-preserved hair and eyebrows, and the clothing imply feminality. The sex of mummy II/6 is also uncertain but is likewise thought to be female.

The average height of the adults is about 150 cm – respectively from I/3 to II/8 their heights are 165, 145, 158, 153, 148 and 150 cm, although mummy I/3 is noticeably taller. Studies of women from the Thule culture from about the fifteenth century reveal an average height of 151 cm, and recent studies of later skeletal material from the seventeenth century (shortly before colonisation) shows an average height of about 153 cm. Thus Greenlandic women remained at a constant stature from the Thule culture to the colonial period. Studies today of elderly women in the Thule district and in Aappilattoq and Nuussuaq in the Upernavik district also show an average height of about 150 cm. More specifically, in 1963 the average height of all women in the Thule district over twenty years old was 152 cm.

Detailed examination

X-RAY STUDY

The X-raying of both natural and embalmed mummies has become increasingly frequent over the past twenty years because the process does not damage the object of examination; in fact if necessary, the object need not be touched at all. X-rays provide a wealth of information about age and sex, old or new bone fractures, skeletal diseases such as tuberculosis or leprosy, or more common inflammatory changes. Bone tumours or other physical diseases, such as rickets, which may influence the development of the skeleton may be detected; and in some cases, it is also possible to identify disease in the internal organs, primarily the presence of stones in the gall bladder, kidneys or urinary bladder, but also tuberculosis of the lungs or kidneys and other diseases which can cause calcium deposits in the organs. Obviously such investigations may in some cases help determine the cause of death. X-ray examination can also detect the presence of amulets or ornaments made of materials which absorb the

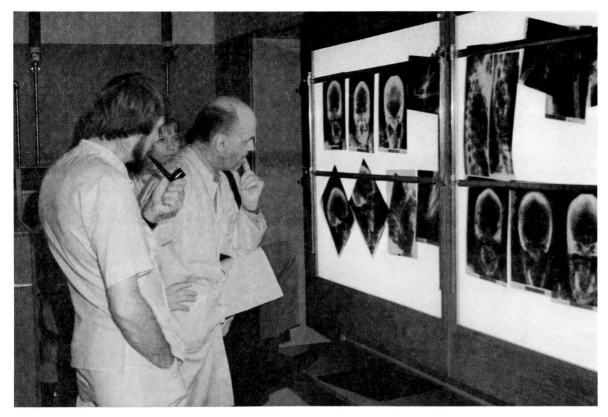

Fig. 46 *Above and below* The X-raying of the mummies. Whenever possible, the X-rays were taken with 150 cm between the X-ray tube and the film in order to reduce distortion.

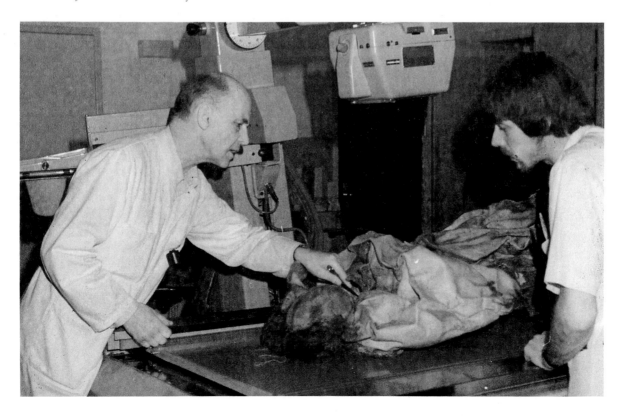

X-rays. In this case such objects would not otherwise be accessible without removing the mummy's clothing or wrapping and might thus remain undetected.

Upon arrival in Denmark, the eight Greenlandic mummies were in varying states of preservation, but on the whole they were in good condition. All of them were clad in skin clothes; several were also wrapped in large skins which, like the clothes, were as stiff as cardboard. Almost all the mummies had extremely flexed hip and knee joints, and the heads of some were bent sharply forward or to the side, which to some degree hampered the X-raying or resulted in an inconveniently long distance between the object photographed and the X-ray film. However, the mummies were fairly durable and could be turned in various positions without being damaged.

As mentioned, X-ray examination is helpful in the determination of age and sex. Radiological age determination is most precise in the case of infants and children up to the age of seventeen or eighteen years. The characteristic development of the bones means that evaluation of the growth lines and the degree of ossification can pinpoint age to within two or three months for infants and about one year for seventeen- or eighteen-year-olds. In adults, radiological age determination is far less reliable because it is based on the occurrence of incipient bone alterations caused either by ageing or by pathological changes such as degenerative osteoarthrosis.

Other methods of age determination include the degree of closure or the ossification of the sutures between the bones of the skull, and the appearance and size of the bone projections corresponding to certain muscle insertions. More advanced methods have also been developed. Our basis of comparison, however, with regard to people who lived about five hundred years ago is, of course, extremely meagre.

In determining the sex of each mummy, radiological evaluation, based mainly on the appearance of the pelvis, is somewhat uncertain. The X-rays of mummy I/1 showed a normal child about six months old, judging by the development of the teeth and bones. The X-rays, however, could not reveal the sex, but the clothing indicated that it was a boy. At the back of the head there was a small crack which must have occurred after death, as it was also visible in the overlying skin. In the posterior skull groove there was a little triangular bone which inspired fanciful conjectures of its being an arrowhead. Close examination, however, proved this triangle to be part of the occipital bone. This large flat bone, which extends far forward at the bottom of the skull, con-

sists in the foetus and in infancy of several bones connected by cartilage or connective tissue. The small triangular bone was the foremost part of the occipital bone which was twisted almost 180° to the back, probably from being pulled during the shrinkage of the brain. No other skeletal changes were seen, and no shadows made by amulets were discovered.

The older child, mummy I/2, was, to judge by the development of its teeth and bones, between four and four and a half years old. Its sex could not be determined from the X-rays, but when its clothes were removed, this mummy was clearly seen to be a boy. All the bones, both those of the skull and of the rest of the skeleton, were remarkably deficient in calcium. The shape of the pelvis was abnormal, with the hip crests turned outwards, a deformation similar to the characteristic pelvis alterations seen in children suffering from Down's syndrome. However, these pelvic changes can also be seen, with variations, in connection with other skeletal diseases. Other pathological changes, in the left hip joint, resembled those seen in Calvé-Perthes disease. This ailment, which most frequently affects boys between the age of five and ten, appears as a partial destruction of the head of the femur, and the cause is uncertain. Virtually identical changes can also be caused by infection in the hip joint. The other bones were normal, apart from the low calcium contents, and there were no signs of rickets. It is worth noting that all the cartilage corresponding to the articulations between the bones appeared more shrunken in the case of this child than in the adults.

Radiological examination of mummy I/3 inferred that it was probably a woman between twenty and

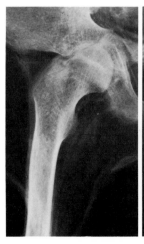
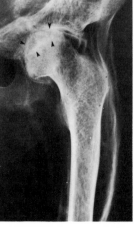

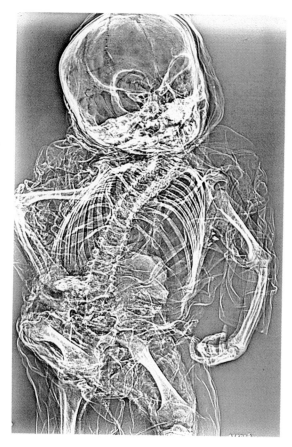

Opposite Fig. 47 The hips of mummy I/2. An increased and irregular calcium content can be clearly seen in the upper part of the left femoral head (see arrows). This may be a sign of Calvé-Perthes disease.

Above Fig. 48 Mummy I/1. A photograph, *left*, and an X-ray picture, *right*, taken with a special technique called xerography, which gives a laterally reversed picture. The clothing can also be discerned.

Below Fig. 49 Close-up of the right renal area of mummy I/3. The arrows indicate two shadow-casting structures. Closer examination proved the one on the left of the picture to be a piece of bone from a seal or polar bear and the other to be of the chemical composition of a kidney stone.

thirty years old. Apart from slight degenerative changes in the lumbar spinal column the skeleton was normal. Two upper teeth were missing but were found in the skin clothing to the right of her head, where they had probably fallen after death.

Directly to the right of the two uppermost lumbar vertebrae there were two distinct calcium shadows (lithiasis), one of them oval and the other irregularly curved and with a structure similar to bone tissue, and both measuring a few centimetres in size. Judging by their position, they might well be the traces of kidney stones. With a minor operation through the skin clothes and the back of the mummy, they were both removed and subsequent analysis showed that only the oval object had a chemical composition similar to a kidney stone. It had lain either in the

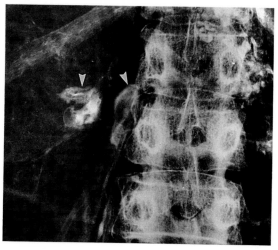

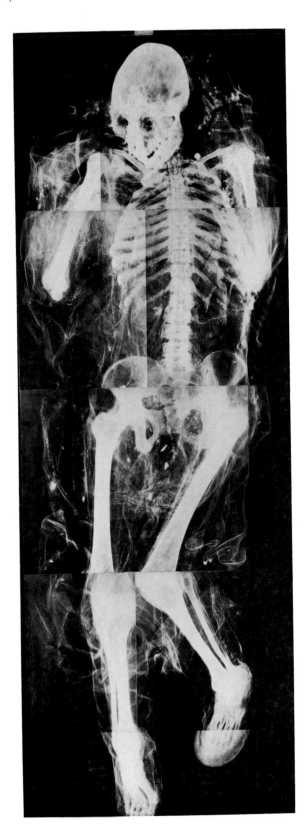

renal pelvis or at the upper end of the ureter, probably causing pain and interfering markedly with the functioning of the right kidney. The other object was proved by chemical and microscopic analysis to be bone tissue, and was probably a small fragment of the skull of a seal or polar bear. The bone fragment was most likely swallowed with food and left in the gastrointestinal canal. Examination of the surrounding mummified soft tissue did not help determine the position more precisely.

Mummy I/4, a woman over thirty years old, was above all remarkable for her distended abdomen, which was at first thought to be caused by pregnancy. If this theory were correct, the size of the woman's stomach would have placed her in her fifth month at least. A normal foetus of this age would have enough calcium in its bones to allow for radiological detection, but thorough X-ray examination failed to reveal any foetal evidence and the theory that she was pregnant had to be discarded.

As in the case of mummy I/3, very slight spinal changes caused by age were found, although otherwise the bones of the skeleton were normal. However, instead of the normal five lumbar vertebrae, six

Left Fig. 50 X-ray picture reconstruction of mummy I/3. Because of the large format of the frames, there is some distortion. Clothing and skin wrappings can be seen clearly, as can small stones.

Below Fig. 51 Close-up (taken from the side) of the abdomen of mummy I/4, who was initially thought to be pregnant. The spine is visible at the bottom, as is the pelvic ridge to the left. Folds of clothing can be seen over the somewhat distended abdomen. No foetal parts are visible here or in any other pictures.

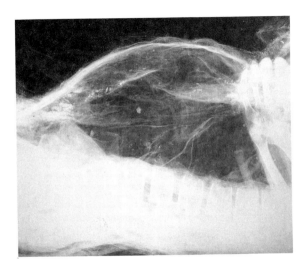

were found. Such a sixth lumbar vertebra sometimes occurs in otherwise normal individuals and has no practical importance. It was not found in the other mummies. This mummy also lacked two teeth, namely the upper wisdom teeth found lying on the large skin wrapped round the mummy.

Radiological examination of mummy I/5 seemed to indicate a man who was about fifty years old, but the garments and bodily remains proved to be female. The calcium content of the skeleton was markedly low, as is frequent in elderly people. Reduced calcium content makes the bones more brittle and the collapse of one or more vertebrae in the spine may be the result. A distinct collapse of this sort could be seen in the fourth and fifth thoracic vertebrae, while a slighter collapse of the ninth thoracic vertabra was also apparent. The eleventh and twelfth thoracic vertebrae showed another type of change, in that the eleventh vertebral body was

Fig. 52 Detail of thoracic vertebrae 8 to 12 and lumbar vertebra 1 of mummy I/5. Thoracic vertebra 9 (second from the top) is lower than the rest because of compression: the calcium content of the bones is low, so rendering them crooked, and liable to minor fractures which result in compression. Compression fractures occur after a fall and are supposed to be common in people who ride sledges – the uneven ride can cause severe shocks to the spine. A congenital, presumably insignificant, misdevelopment of vertebrae 11 and 12 has caused them to slant, as can be seen.

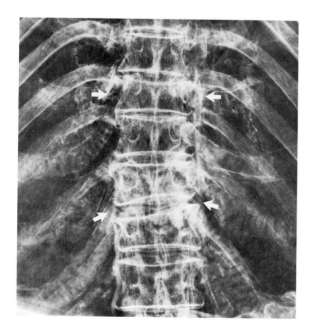

lower on the left side than on the right, whereas the body of the twelfth vertebra was lower on the right side than on the left. These changes thus counterbalanced one another. They can hardly be because of a collapse of the vertebrae but are more likely to be a congenital, probably insignificant malformation. In the lumbar spine a decrease of the height of an intervertebral disc was found with a marked bony spur formation on the adjacent vertebrae. There was also slight degenerative osteoarthrosis in the rest of the spinal column, in both shoulders, some of the fingers and the tarsal joints, while all other articulations were normal.

Mummy I/5 had considerable calcification of the rib cartilages, an instance found mainly among older people, although the age at which these calcifications occur varies greatly. However, the existence of arteriosclerosis of the medium-sized arterial branches in the pelvis indicated a relatively advanced age. At least two of the four teeth missing from the mouth must have been lost before death since the root holes were completely or partly closed. A single stray tooth and a root fragment were found in the skin clothing. Foremost and in the middle of the palate bone a tooth rudiment was found, a rare phenomenon but one which has been reported earlier in two ancient Greenlandic skulls.

Moving on to grave II, mummy II/6 was a woman, probably more than fifty years old. The calcium content of the bones was apparently not reduced. In the lumbar spine there was a wedge-shaped compression of the second vertebra and a decrease in the height of the cartilaginous disk between the first and second lumbar vertebrae. These changes were probably caused by an earlier fracture. There was also a decrease in the height of the fourth lumbar intervertebral disc with osseous condensation and spur formation of the adjacent fourth and fifth lumbar vertebrae. In the cervical spine slight degenerative arthritis was seen, while the rest of the spine was normal. There were no changes in the joints of the arms or legs, but the fingers were so bent that more detailed examination was not possible. There were calcifications of the rib cartilages and the medium-sized arteries in the pelvis.

The teeth of this mummy were in worse condition than those of the others. One upper front tooth was broken and five lower teeth were missing, all of which must have been lost before death, for the root openings were closed. Several of the remaining teeth showed traces of periodontitis.

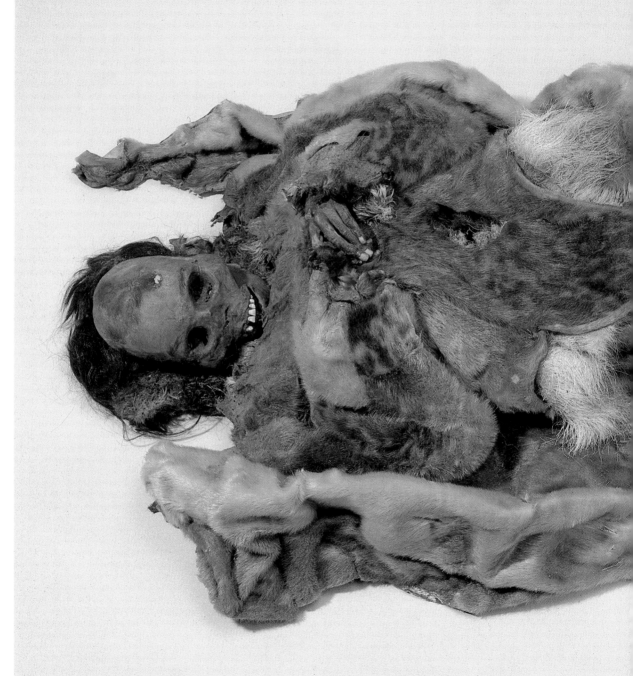

Fig. 53 Mummy I/3, a 25-year-old woman.

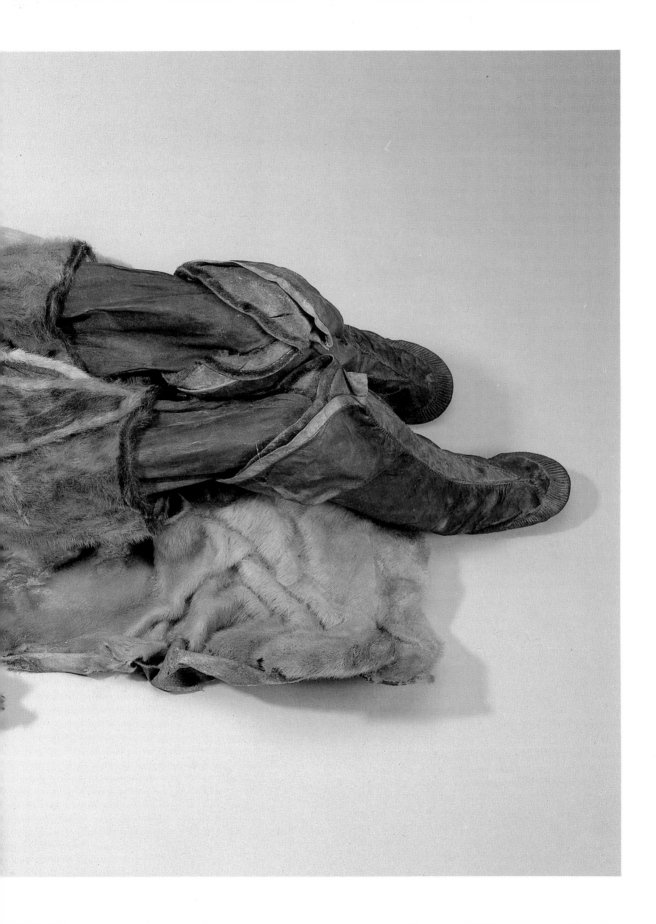

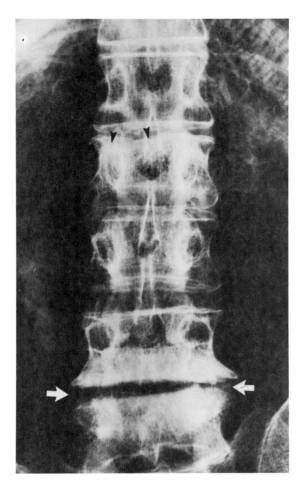

Fig. 54 The lumbar spine of mummy II/6. There is some compression of lumbar vertebra 2 (black arrows) as a result of an old fracture, and the collapse of the cartilage disc (a 'slipped disc') between lumbar vertebrae 4 and 5 is visible (white arrows).

Mummy II/7 was a young woman, eighteen to twenty-two years old, and was in a poor state of preservation. Her head and four uppermost cervical vertebrae were almost separated from the rest of the body and were held in place simply by dried-out shreds of skin and the hood of the skin garment. These changes no doubt occurred after death. The eleventh thoracic vertebra was slightly wedge-shaped, probably the result of a developmental anomaly rather than a spinal fracture. The skeleton was normal in all other respects. Seventeen teeth were missing from the mouth. They had probably all fallen out after death for the corresponding root holes were still open and some of the missing teeth were found in the skin clothes.

Several of the remaining teeth were loose.

The radiological examination of mummy II/8 revealed a woman of about fifty. Her condition of preservation was very poor; for example, her head was held in place only by the skin hood, out of which it could be lifted. The six uppermost cervical vertebrae were attached to the head, but the seventh lay by itself. All the soft tissue had disappeared from the lower jaw, which was also loose. Four of the upper teeth were missing, apparently having fallen out post-mortem. In contrast, some time before death the woman seems to have lost her lower front teeth, as a partial closing and ossification of the root opening of these teeth had occurred. The back of her skin clothing had disintegrated and the skin and soft tissue of the body had disappeared down to the level of the pelvic brim, thus exposing the spine and posterior part of the ribs. The left arm was also detached from the rest of the body.

The radiographs taken of the head frontally and in profile showed some changes in the bones at the base of the skull. The poor state of preservation of this mummy proved advantageous to X-ray examination – since the head was detached from the body, it could be examined more thoroughly than would otherwise have been possible. The examination revealed an extensive destruction of bone, including the part of the base of the skull which forms the roof of the nasopharynx together with the internal parts of both temporal bones, which contain the inner ear. Further there was destruction of the posterior parts of the left eye socket. Considering the mummy's poor state of preservation, one could deduce that the observed disintegration of the skull bones might have occurred post-mortem. But this theory can be rejected definitely, for all the other bones, including the exposed and rather thin ribs, were completely intact. The change in fact resembled the effects caused by a malignant tumour spreading in a bone which had probably affected both the woman's hearing and the sight of her left eye.

Most of the soft tissue of the left shoulder region had disappeared. Only the innermost two thirds of the left clavicle were in proper position; the outermost third was missing. However, some time after the recovery of the mummies a small bone fragment was found at the bottom of grave II. This fragment was at first believed to come from a seal but it was later identified as a human bone fragment. The two bone fragments proved to be compatible, constituting a fractured clavicle. Along the edges of both fracture surfaces, a thickening of the bone was

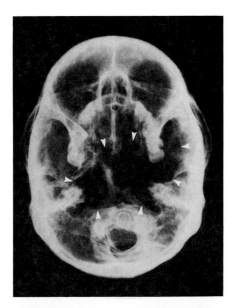

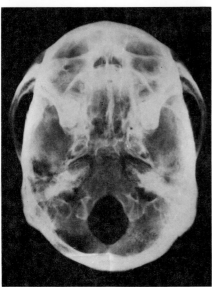

noted, and the surfaces themselves were partly sclerosed. These changes reveal that the fracture of the clavicle had probably happened at least a year before death, resulting in a fibrous union or false joint. There were no cancerous changes here as in the skull. The faulty union was probably the result of repeated movement of the arm during the normal healing process. As the woman would have had many daily tasks to carry out, she would have had little chance of resting her shoulder. This must have caused her considerable pain until her death and probably also reduced the strength of her arm.

The calcium content of her bones was normal. Several transverse lines were seen in the lower parts of the femurs, indicating periods of temporary growth arrest in childhood, caused perhaps by illness or malnutrition. Such lines were also visible in three other mummies. Considerable calcification of the rib cartilages was also found.

In three of the mummies (I/2, I/5 and II/7) the middle and inner ears were examined in special X-ray projections and showed normal conditions. In the X-ray of the skull, the frontal sinus was missing in all cases, but the other nasal sinuses were normally developed. The reason for the lack of formation of the frontal sinus, as is common among Inuit, is not clear. Some scientists have suggested that this lack is because of the Inuit gradual adaptation to the cold, but there is disagreement about this theory.

Left Fig. 55 Top Skull of mummy II/8 viewed from below. The large, irregular and dark area, roughly outlined by arrows, is because of deterioration of the bone, undoubtedly caused by a malignant tumour. *Left* Skull of a contemporary inhabitant of Greenland for comparison. Borrowed from Copenhagen University Laboratory of Physical Anthropology.

Below Fig. 56 Left collarbone of mummy II/8, showing the fracture that never healed. A false joint developed, probably because the woman carried on using her arm and so gave the fractured bone no opportunity to heal.

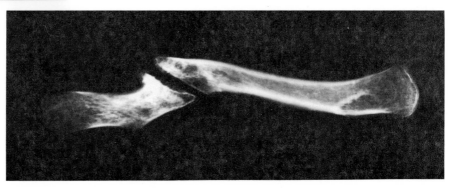

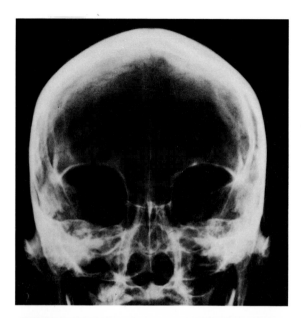

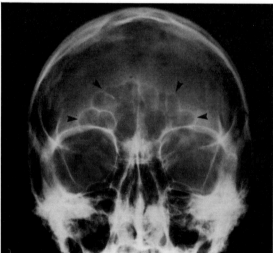

Fig. 57 None of the mummies had developed frontal sinuses although their other nasal sinuses were normal. Comparison of the X-ray of mummy I/4's skull, *top*, with that of a contemporary Dane, *above*, shows the difference. The frontal sinuses are marked by arrows.

Fungi

When the mummies arrived in Copenhagen, whitish-grey fungus coatings were found on the exposed body surfaces and scattered on the clothing and skins. When the clothing had been removed and the body cavities opened, similar fungus growths were found. It was necessary to identify the various types to ensure that none of the fungi were pathogenic for humans and thus liable to harm investigators and conservators, and also to determine the proper means of combating these fungi. The numerous fungus species discovered must all be assumed to have appeared post-mortem. A few of the fungi can cause an allergy, and in rare cases can be directly pathogenic, especially for debilitated individuals, but in the present case there was no risk for the staff working on the mummies.

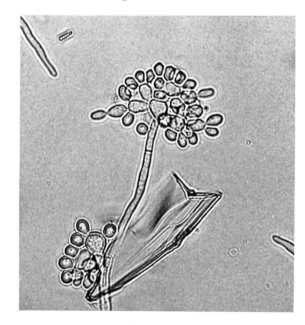

Fig. 58 The rare fungus *Sporothrix fungorum*. The mummies and skins were to a marked degree infested with fungus spores, cells and chains. *Sporothrix fungorum* was previously found in only three places in Europe and South Africa, and not Greenland. Only after thorough investigation will it be known whether or not this fungus exists in Greenland today. Another rare fungus was found, *Malbranchea Arcuata*, which was isolated earlier in America and Yugoslavia in earth samples, dog and bird excreta, rodent hairs and jackdaw feathers. None of the fungi found are pathogenic.

Skin

The four less well-preserved mummies (I/2, I/5, II/7 and II/8) were all in such a state that their clothing was removed and conserved separately. This permitted more careful study of the bodies. The process of mummification had made the skin of each body dry and shrunken, dark brown and very hard. To a varying extent there was a white, often cracked layer of mould up to one millimetre thick. On each mummy the skin of the abdomen (and in some cases the fronts of the thighs) was very dark, probably because of decay processes in the abdominal cavity after death.

Biochemical examination of skin samples showed that the collagen content in the dermis was about 5 to 10 per cent lower than in the fresh skin samples that were tested. Normally the skin of the cheeks contains far less collagen than body skin, and this difference was also observed in the mummies. The amount of ground substance was also decreased by about 45 per cent. Biochemical examinations as well as studies made with light microscopes and electron microscopes showed that the skin in the best preserved areas had changed very little after death.

The desiccating effects of the mummification process had caused the skin to shrink, thus enlarging the eye openings, nostrils and mouth, and sometimes creating cracks. The eye openings and mouth are asymmetrical in some cases. Mummy II/7 had one superficial skin lesion by the inner corner of the right eye and another one high in the abdominal wall. Her right eyeball was particularly well-preserved, with no lesions, and X-ray examination of the bone tissue beneath the lesion showed normal conditions without fractures. The lesion in the abdominal wall affected the skin only, for muscle tissue was found beneath it. There was nothing to indicate that these lesions occurred while the woman was alive. Mummy II/7 was the only woman to have a relatively large abdominal wall; it hung down toward the thighs, covering the external sexual organs. Her breasts were also relatively large. She had two small warts on the fingers of her right hand, and on the sole of her right foot there was a thick cornified area in the skin.

The only mummy whose eye sockets and mouth were not enlarged due to the tautening of the skin was mummy I/4. The lips of this woman were thus well-preserved. Perhaps she, like the infant I/1, had a thicker layer of fat in the subcutis of the face, as is often seen among Inuit. This layer of fat, together with the cheekbones, makes the face seem broad.

In the palms of the hands which were accessible for examination there were no traces of wear or pressure in the form of calloused skin. The natural lines of the skin were preserved to some extent, and in a few cases prints could be made of the fingers, palms and foot soles. The skin was often loosened or destroyed. All prints showed patterns and lines very similar to those found in present-day prints.

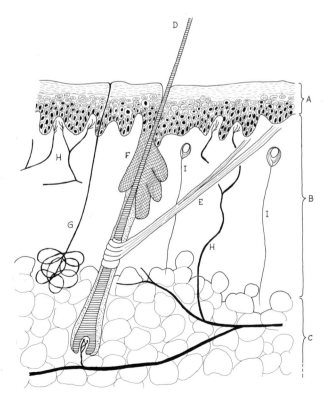

Fig. 59 Human and animal skin consists of three layers: the outermost layer called the epidermis (A) forms the thin, tight and wear-resistant surface of the body and has hair cover (D); the dermis (B), is a thick, tough layer which becomes leather after tanning and which contains the hair follicles (D), the sebum (F) and sweatglands (G); the subcutis (C) is the insulating layer of fat. The dermis consists primarily of collagen and ground substance. Collagen provides about 70 per cent of the skin's solid matter and consists of large protein molecules which accumulate to form threadlike fibres. These fibres toughen the skin. Between them lies the ground substance, large molecules of glucosamino-glycans. The ground substance is water-binding, acts as a spacer and lies like a jelly between the fibres, enhancing the smoothness of the skin.

Fig. 60 Head of mummy I/4 prior to cleaning. The wrinkles in the facial skin are made distinct by ultraviolet photography which renders the contours of the skin more visible. The nasal cartilage has deteriorated and only the impervious bony parts of the nose and mummified soft tissue remain.

Below Fig. 61 Underside of mummy II 7's right foot clearly showing the linear pattern of the skin. Remains of the straw insoles of the kamik are visible.

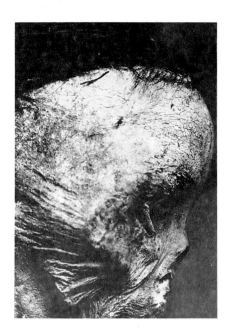

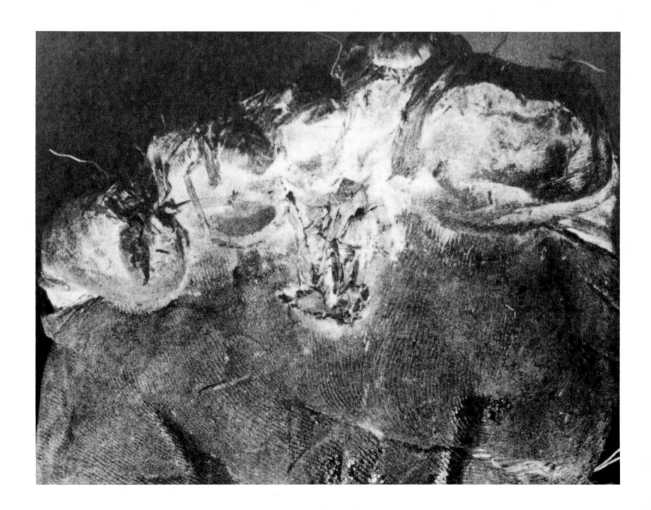

Fig. 62 Electromicrograph of collagen in the skin of the upper arm of mummy II/8. The fibres are characteristic of the light and dark striation. The fibres are so well-preserved that they are identical to those found in fresh skins. Enlarged 20,000 times.

In several places there were maggot holes in the skin, made post-mortem. Some of these holes were extremely enlarged as a result of the mummification of the skin. There was a scattering of empty reddish-brown cocoons both on the mummies and their clothing. There were also some mosquitoes and flies, desiccated and in fact mummified just like the humans and therefore well-preserved. Some of the insects were found inside the body cavities themselves.

The insects belong to four different two-winged families (*Diptera*); namely winter gnats (*Trichoceridae*), *Borboridae*, swamp flies (*Heleomyzidae*) and blowflies (*Calliphoridae*). The blowfly puparia originate from the deterioration of the corpses during the first summer after they had died, for this fly is in fact one of the means by which carrion is broken down in nature. A *Borboridae* puparium may also possibly stem from the first year after death, for the larvae of these flies live where there is liquefied rotten material. In contrast, the winter gnats and swamp flies are not proper carrion fauna. These insects may therefore have arrived at any time after death.

Hair

All the mummies had perfectly preserved, normal eyebrows. However, the eyelashes were missing in some cases because of their precarious position in the thin eyelids.

It was possible to examine the hair on the heads of all the mummies, apart from mummy II/6, whose hair was completely hidden by the parka hood. In several cases, the hair was loosened from the scalp. The children's hair was very thin and wispy. On none of the mummies could traces of a coiffure or a topknot be identified; nor were any headbands found. The topknot was very popular among the women and was a common reason for the loss of hair in Greenland. Constant pulling on the hair destroys the hair follicles at the temples, resulting in baldness. Mummy I/4 lacked hair on the crown of her head, but the hair follicles were preserved, indicating that her hair must have fallen out after death and not because of a topknot.

Loss of hair was also seen in the other mummies. Some had lost their hair while alive, others after death. Another possible cause of hair loss during life is *favus*, a fungus disease which affects the scalp in particular and which causes cicatricial baldness. This disease was once widespread in northwest Greenland, and as late as 1958 there were a number of new cases, especially among families living in turf houses, such as those probably inhabited by the Qilakitsoq people. The hair of mummy I/5 was extremely thin on the crown but thicker towards the temples and at the nape of the neck. There is little doubt that this thinning of hair is of the type prevalent among men, although it is also sometimes seen among women. The spreading to the crown is the same, although it is rare for women to be completely bald.

Nails

The shrinkage of the skin because of mummification causes the nail wall to recede (in some cases to the extent that the nail is loosened) and consequently the fingernails seem very long.

Accessible nails were scrutinised for signs of change attributable to manual work. Numerous transverse cuts were found in the left thumbnails of mummies II/7 and II/8. These marks were probably made when the nail was used as a support for cutting thread with an ulu (a woman's knife). Other traces of activity were small chips in the free edge of some of the fingernails, unevenly worn nails of the index and middle fingers of both hands, particularly the

Fig. 63 Right hand of mummy II/7, showing a wart 3 mm in diameter on the middle finger.

Below Fig. 64 Mummy II/7's thumbnail with transverse cut marks created by a knife.

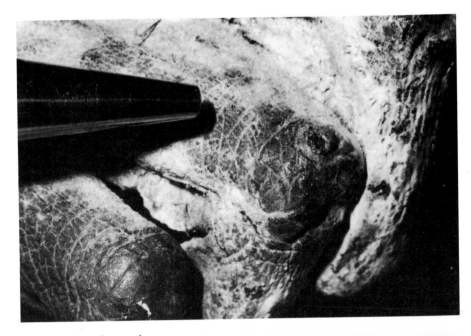

side towards the thumb, and the wearing-down of the relatively soft layer on the outer part of the nail, so exposing the thick and hard nail plate. This latter change may have been caused by working with water: notably warm water and chemical contents such as alkaline solutions. Hides were washed in old urine, which is alkaline. Some nails had slightly pronounced transverse grooves in the upper side of the nail plate. These furrows, which are probably caused by eczema or infection in the nail wall, are frequently seen today among those who work with their hands submerged in water.

The toenails of all were thickened; some were almost like claws. This is probably because of lack of care and insufficient clipping. The surface of the nails was smooth where they had rubbed against the kamik (a boot and stocking combined), and the outer edges of the big toenails were worn into shape by the sole of the kamik.

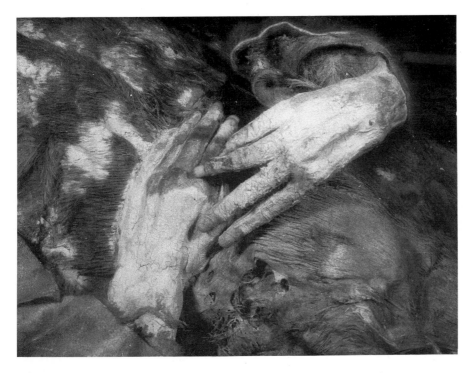

Fig. 65 Infra-red photograph of mummy I/4 prior to cleaning. The hands look fine and slender, and the nails well kept. However, the dessication and shrinkage of the soft tissue made the fingers thinner and the nails longer and more prominent than in reality.

Teeth

Dental conditions of ancient and modern Green-landers were studied by visiting dental researchers and practising dental officers between 1913 and the Second World War. In 1936 P. O. Pedersen and associates examined 526 skulls in Copenhagen mu-seums and in 1935 and 1939 surveyed 1634 and 702 South-west Greenlanders, respectively. In 1937 P. O. Pedersen examined 915 East Greenlanders at Ammassalik and Ittoqqortoormiit/Scoresbysund. The East Greenlanders lived traditionally and their lifestyle and diet were barely influenced by

Age of each mummy and number of teeth found in the graves.

| Mummy | Age | Number of teeth | | | |
		lost before death	lost after death	congenitally missing	super–numerary
I/1	6 mths	0	0	0	0
I/2	3½–4½yrs	0	1*	0	0
I/3	c. 25 yrs	0	1	0	0
I/4	c. 30 yrs	0	0	0	0
I/5	c. 45 yrs	1	0	0	1**
II/6	c. 50 yrs	5	0	2	0
II/7	18–21 yrs	0	11	0	0
II/8	c. 50 yrs	3	5	1	0

* deciduous teeth
** unerupted vestigial upper incisor

Europeans before the Second World War. This thorough background knowledge was a major reason why the examination of teeth and jaws proved to be an important step in the investigation of the Qilakitsoq mummies.

The mummy material, however, deserved particular attention because as a result of the mummification process, very few teeth were lost post-mortem. In most cases even a tooth with only a single short root remained in its proper position in the jaw or could be found beneath the dried skin. In contrast, numerous front teeth, canines and small molars are missing from the museum collections of ancient Greenlandic skulls because these teeth were lost during removal of the bodies from the graves, in transit, or later.

Dental conditions could be studied extensively in only four out of the eight mummies. The mouths of the other mummies were either closed or covered by clothing too precious to remove. Thus examination had to be limited to an evaluation of immediately visible front teeth and finds revealed by X-rays.

To estimate the age of the mummies, dental conditions, X-rays of the skeletal system and its microscopic structure, as well as anthropological findings, have been studied. In every case the dentition played an important role. However, dental age estimation is optimal with the three youngest individuals, namely the two children and mummy II/7, whose lower wisdom teeth were not completely formed.

Once all the teeth which had fallen out post-mortem had been found in the graves, tooth loss could be determined. The radiological examination had shown that many of mummy I/2's milk teeth lay beneath his clothing, which had partly disintegrated, and had fallen out post-mortem.

The three oldest women, mummies I/5, I/6 and II/8, had lost some teeth in their lifetime, and eight of the nine missing were front teeth. In addition, some teeth had fallen out after death. Three wisdom teeth had not developed and mummy II/5 had an extra front tooth which had not erupted. Supernumerary front teeth and, in particular, the absence of wisdom teeth are common among Greenland Inuit.

The heavy wear on the teeth meant that only a few of the typical features which characterise the teeth of people of mongoloid descent could be identified. However, the younger adults, especially mummy II/7, showed a pronounced shovel-shape of the upper front teeth, a feature typical among Inuit. There are various dental differences between Greenland Inuit and Europeans, namely that the first molar in the lower jaw of Inuit often has three roots instead of two, as in Europeans; and that Inuit teeth have short and strong roots, whereas those of the Europeans are longer and thinner.

Irregular shape, structure and calcification of the hard tissues of the permanent teeth can be caused by serious illness, malnutrition or periodic famine occurring in early childhood while the teeth are being formed and calcified but long before they erupt. After eruption of the tooth, the visible result is an irregular enamel surface, a phenomenon seen in mummy II/7. This young woman has irregularities in the enamel of the part of the crowns of the front teeth closest to the gums. In humans this part calcifies between the ages of two and four, that is, from the period during which breast feeding usually terminated among Greenland Inuit. The same condition was found in the Danish mesolithic people (from about seven thousand years ago) who were excavated at Vedbæk on Sjælland in the 1970s.

The most striking phenomenon in the teeth of the mummies is the extreme attrition of their crowns. When the attrition reaches below the largest circumference of the crowns the completely worn-down teeth look like pegs at gum level, at some distance from the neighbouring teeth. For centuries this phenomenon has drawn attention. In 1915 an article by Peter Freuchen on the health of Polar Inuit was published in the Danish medical journal *Ugeskrift for Læger*. On the basis of his special interest and experiences from his unfinished medical studies he had 'taken over the medical duties in the district as the person presumably best-suited' for the job. Regarding teeth, he wrote that 'due to many years

Fig. 66 Mummy II/7's shovel-shaped front teeth and moderately worn molars.

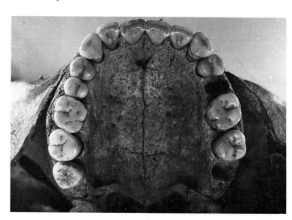

Fig. 67 Hard tartar on upper canine of mummy II/7. The upper limitation of tartar corresponds to the gum margin in life. The tooth to the right of the canine has had the tartar removed in order to reveal the uneven surface of the enamel.

of hard use, both in preparing skins and hunting implements as well as for chewing the often tough and gravelly food, the teeth were gradually worn all the way down to the gingiva [the gums] so that they can no longer chew their food but must swallow it whole instead, after which they have digestive problems, stomach pains, and die.' All phases of dental attrition are represented in the women of Qilakitsoq.

Not only were their teeth worn down by tough food, but also by the use of teeth as a tool. Inuit women especially prepared hides with their teeth, to make kamiks, for example; although men also wore their teeth down in a similar fashion, the wear was greater among women. The women would hold the skins, usually sealskin, with their front teeth as they scraped off the blubber. The skin was then 'rubbed' over the lower front teeth, with the mouth partly closed. Gradually the front teeth became rounded. The women also softened skin before sewing it by chewing its edge with their front teeth.

The considerable effort involved in making sinew-threads for sewing also wore down the teeth, causing transverse furrows in the chewing surface of the front teeth. First, thick bunches of tendinous material were split into thinner bunches with an ulu. Next, these bunches were alternately rolled against the cheek and drawn across the clenched front teeth, in which they incised one or more furrows. The purpose of this latter manoeuvre was to moisten and

soften the sinew. Sinew furrows were noted as early as 1937 in some women in East Greenland. They occurred only among those over forty years old. The Qilakitsoq women are the first West Greenland Inuit in whom these furrows have been found.

When a woman lost her front teeth, usually as a result of having used them as a tool for years, the sinew-thread had to be made with the canines and/ or the small molars. One example is mummy II/8, who had lost her front teeth long before her death. Instead, she had used her right lower canine tooth. Mummy I/5 displays furrows in two front teeth, one in the upper jaw, one in the lower. However, one is most clearly seen in her right lower canine.

Cracks in the enamel of the teeth are also frequently caused by strain. The front teeth of several of the women show cracks running all the way down the crowns. These cracks are particularly numerous in mummy I/3. The milk teeth of mummy I/2 are chipped in a number of places in the enamel, and the teeth of the adults have innumerable chip losses, both large and small, in the enamel edges of the masticating surfaces, caused by chewing hard foods such as bone fragments and by using the teeth as a tool. (Identical changes are found in the mesolithic hunters of Vedbæk in Denmark.) In mummy II/6 the whole crown is broken off from an upper front tooth, and X-rays showed that in mummy I/5 there was a broken root end on a worn but otherwise intact lower premolar. Examination of the surface of fracture

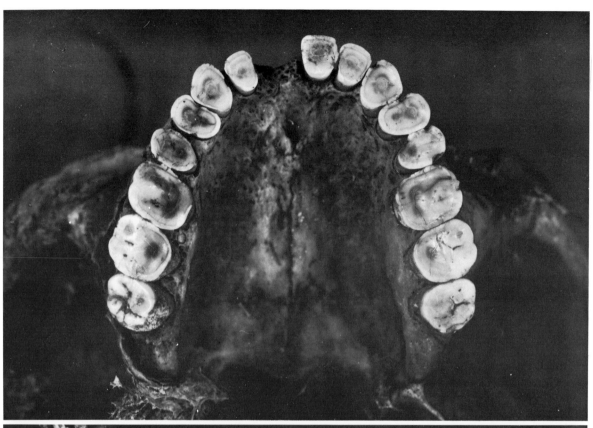

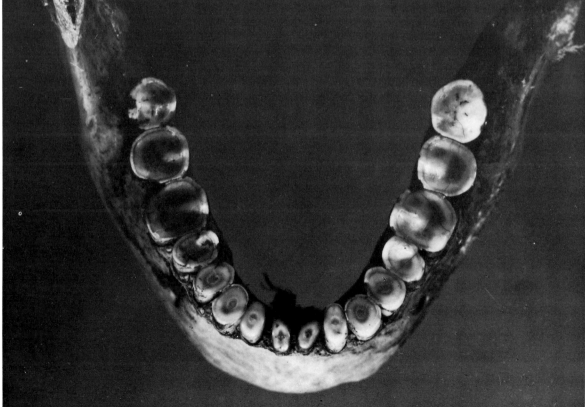

Above Fig. 69 Woman scraping blubber off sealskin. She is holding the skin taut with her teeth and scraping at it with the ulo in her right hand. Ammassalik, 1937.

Opposite Fig. 68 Mummy I/5's teeth in the upper jaw, *top*, and lower jaw, *bottom*, show advanced wear of both the chewing and contact surfaces. The front teeth of the lower jaw have rounded edges and chipping of the enamel of most teeth.

Below left Fig. 70 Woman chewing a piece of sealskin to soften it. The skin is to be used for kamik soles. Found in the Thule district in 1932.

Below right Fig. 71 Sinew-thread grooves in the right canine of mummy II/5 and chipping of the enamel of the molars. The front edges of the anterior teeth are rounded off. Enlarged 4 times.

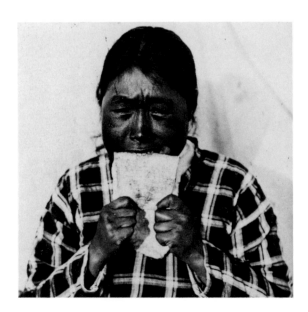

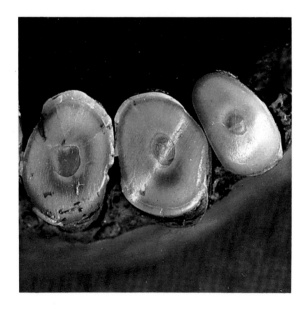

showed that the break had occurred some time before death.

Among the many consequences of the pronounced use and misuse of the incisors is, finally, the shortening of their roots as a result of reabsorption. The roots of the central incisors were notably shortened in the oldest Qilakitsoq women. Similar observations were made in elderly people in East Greenland in 1937. Today orthodontic findings have shown that roots can be reabsorbed by using exaggerated force. If too much force is used, the roots may disintegrate, a condition which may be unnoticed until much later.

There were no signs of tooth decay, i.e. carious lesions, in any of the mummies. Similarly there are almost no cavities in the large Copenhagen collections of Inuit skulls from pre-colonial Greenland, Canada and Alaska. During the twentieth century, cavities have become widespread among the Inuit populace, and virtually all modern Greenlanders have decayed teeth. There are many places in Greenland where people over forty years old are toothless. Despite intensive efforts by public health authorities to prevent and treat tooth decay (caries), it is extremely widespread, owing to the change from the traditional hunters' diet to a diet of imported food with a high sugar content.

A certain content of the element fluorine in food and drinking water protects teeth from cavities. However, too large a consumption of fluorine is harmful to tooth development. Drinking water is low in fluorine almost everywhere in Greenland except for the Narssaq district in the south. Today the occurrence of dental decay is far lower in Narssaq than elsewhere in Greenland. The surface enamel of both milk teeth and permanent teeth of the mummies has been examined for fluorine, and seems to exhibit the same concentration and distribution found among modern inhabitants of Greenland in the area.

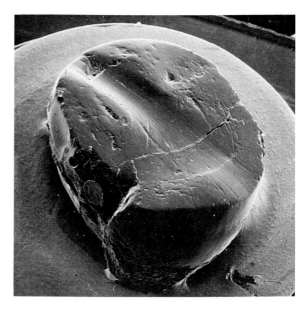

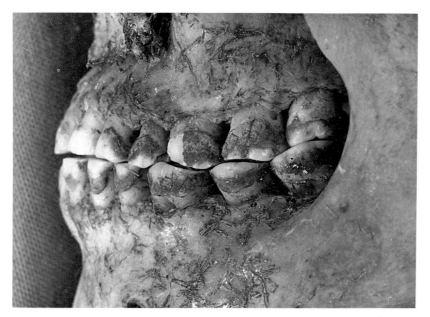

Above Fig. 72 Scanning electron-microscopic picture of mummy II/5's canine with sinew-thread grooves. Enlarged 10 times.

Left Fig. 73 Mummy I/5's bite is normal. Large deposits of tartar can be seen.

Above Fig. 74 Black arrows indicate chipping of the enamel of mummy II/8's teeth. The outgrowth *torus mandibularis* can be seen (white arrows).

Below Fig. 75 Mummy I/5's lower jaw showing the broken root tip of the premolar.

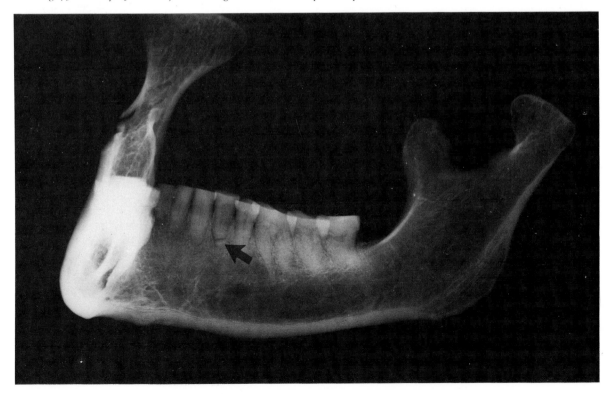

Fig. 76 Scanning electron-microscopic picture of the inner layers of tartar with many calcified micro-organisms. Enlarged 4000 times.

Below Fig. 77 Destruction of the bony socket around the upper first molar of mummy I/5, perhaps caused by a bone splinter.

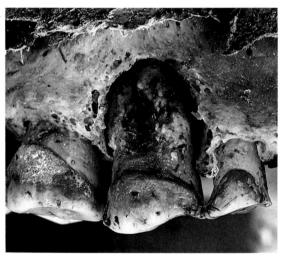

There was tartar on the crowns of all the adults' teeth, but none had tartar on the roots. The demarcation of the tartar coatings at the free margin of the jaw is sharp, indicating the level of the gum margin when the subject was alive. As tartar is infrequently seen in museum specimens of Greenlandic skulls, it was surprising to find such widespread and abundant tartar among the Qilakitsoq women, but it is probable that skulls in museums lost their tartar in the graves or later, as the 1937 study revealed quite widespread tartar. The nature of tartar deposits in East Greenland as well as among the mummies differs slightly from the tartar deposits among Europeans. The reason for this difference is not known.

It is probable that all the older and possibly also the younger adults had chronic inflammation of the gums (gingivitis) corresponding to the tartar rim. However, the loss of jaw bone along and between the teeth seen in connection with chronic inflammation of the gums, is slight. Deeper destruction of the bone tissue is seen only in limited areas. This is the case in mummy I/5 who shows a total loss of bone opposite the cheek side of the right first large molar. Similar changes are seen at the remaining central incisor in the same upper jaw. In both cases there must have been deep gum pockets, possibly with pus formation and tenderness. Most probably these changes were caused by bone splinters.

Two of the women had bony outgrowths on the inner side of the lower jaw opposite the molars, a so-called *torus mandibularis*. That of mummy II/8 was moderately developed, whereas that of mummy I/3 was strongly developed. A similar bone projection (*torus palatinus*) is seen in the middle of the palate in mummy I/5. Such bone projections are notably frequent among Inuit and other peoples living in the arctic regions, and are probably caused by the special conditions of life in the Arctic. They may have arisen in connection with strongly developed masticatory musculature.

All the adult mummies studied exhibit completely regular tooth position. Their front teeth have edge-to-edge bites and the molars show a normal occlusion. One exception is mummy II/7. She differs from the others in having a crooked bite with a jaw shift to the left and back. She had distinct changes in the right condyle of the lower jaw and the articular disk was thickened. These changes are probably due to an earlier injury such as a fall or blow. The shape of the condyle shows that a certain rebuilding of the temporo-mandibular joint occurred. This might have been the consequence of some slight damage to the joint which occurred between the ages of six and ten. At this stage, pains in the joint can alter the normal movement to such an extent that abnormal bite conditions develop. This would cause later changes such as those evident in the right joint. In addition, the X-rays of this woman showed several dense spots in the jaw bones which could not be explained.

In general the dental examinations may be said to have confirmed the significance of dental conditions in estimating age. They also show that the teeth of Inuit women were overworked and damaged and in the end might be lost because of lifelong use as a tool. It has been shown that under certain circumstances tartar can occur without serious damage to the supporting apparatus of the teeth, and that Inuit of the past did not have tooth decay.

TISSUE TYPES

Among the many questions which arose after the find of the mummies was whether the people found were related to one another. Clarification of family relationships has been attempted by means of tissue type determination. The tissue types in the HLA-system are found on the cell surfaces in all organs of the body.

Research in organ transplantation has shown that a patient and a donor must have compatible HLA types if, for example, a kidney transplantation is to succeed. HLA stands for Human Leukocyte system A, because the HLA traits were first discovered as a blood group system belonging to the white blood cells, the leukocytes. The genes of the HLA system are located on chromosome 6. As each individual carries one combination of genes on each of the two chromosomes 6 – one of which is inherited from either parent – the HLA trait-combinations found in a family can be followed for generations. There are at least seven series of genes on chromosome 6 determining those transplantation factors, but here only two of them have been studied, namely HLA–A and HLA–B.

In the HLA–A series, at least seventeen factors are known today: HLA–A1, A2, A3 and so on. In the HLA–B series at least thirty-two are known: HLA–B5, B7, B8 and so on. The frequency of the factors differs widely among various population groups. For example, HLA–A9 is found in about 18 per cent of contemporary Danes and 85 to 90 per cent of contemporary Inuit. In contrast, HLA–B8 is found among 24 per cent of contemporary Danes but only among 3 to 5 per cent of contemporary Inuit populations.

The fact that a tissue type determination could even be considered is because of the well-preserved and dried condition of the corpses. It therefore seemed possible that the tissue type structures could be preserved in the subcutis and in the large muscles. In fact, in the United States tissue type determinations have been made earlier on mummified tissue from burials between five hundred and two thousand years old in Colombia, South America. Although these corpses had been preserved under far less favourable conditions, it was still possible to determine at least one HLA factor in twenty-two out of the thirty-three specimens examined, although the method used differed significantly from the one used here. There was thus good reason to anticipate a positive result with tissue from the Greenland mummies.

An HLA type determination is usually carried out on live white blood cells isolated from freshly drawn blood which has been prevented from coagulating. There are no tissue type traits on the red blood cells. From an ordinary blood sample about fifty million cells will normally be obtained; these are finally suspended in a few drops of saltwater. These white blood cells are now mixed in small quantities with many different blood sera containing known tissue type antibodies. For example, if a person has the tissue type HLA–A9, A10, B8 and B17, the white blood cells from this person will bind and be killed by the antibodies directed against the tissue type factors A9, A10, B8 and B17, but *not* by antibodies directed against, for example, A2 or B40 or any of the other known HLA–A or HLA–B factors. The cell death is measured with the help of a blue dye (trypan blue) which only stains dead white blood cells. In the example mentioned, microscopic examination will show a blue colouration of the white blood cells in the drops in which the serum contained antibodies against A9, A10, B8 and B17, and only in these sera. The sera which killed the white blood cells thus indicates the tissue type.

This method could not of course be used to type the mummies. Even though there are still HLA structures on the cell surfaces, the cells are already dead, so all of them would be stained blue. Nor could an ordinary blood sample be taken. On the other hand, the method described could be used as a check system in an indirect type determination.

In such a determination, macerated tissue from the thigh musculature was brought in contact with many different tissue type antisera. With the help of live white blood cells from donors with known tissue types it was then investigated whether the sera in question had retained their tissue type antibodies or whether these had been bound to corresponding tissue type structures in the mummy tissue.

One example is a serum with an antibody against HLA–A10. This means that white blood cells from persons possessing the HLA–A10 type trait are killed by this serum. A sample of this serum was mixed with finely-ground tissue from mummy I/2. After an hour's contact with the tissue, the serum was sucked out again and mixed with white blood cells from a donor with the tissue type trait HLA–A10. These cells were no longer killed in this serum, and the antibody against HLA–A10 had to be assumed to have been bound to the mummy tissue, so that mummy II/2 consequently had to possess the tissue type trait HLA–A10. Another specimen of the same serum was now mixed with tissue from, for example, mummy II/8. After contact this serum specimen could still kill white blood cells from persons with type HLA–A10. Thus tissue from mummy II/8 could not bind an antibody directed against HLA–A10, and mummy II/8 could consequently not have had this HLA factor.

The above description illustrates in simplified form the principle used in determining the tissue types of the people of Qilakitsoq. In practice about fifty different tissue type antisera and blood samples from seventy-five to eighty voluntary donors with known tissue types were employed for each mummy.

Naturally, five-hundred-year-old tissue cannot bind tissue type antibodies as effectively as fresh tissue. It was necessary to work out a method to calculate how much antibody had been removed from the serum in each case. The result is seen in the table on p. 94. The findings here are compared with information on the age of the subjects at the time of death and their position in the graves. No tissue type determination has been made for the smallest child, mummy I/1.

The results indicate that there were two families, one in each grave. A logical interpretation of the findings is that grave I contained a grandmother (mummy I/5) with two daughters (mummies I/3 and I/4) together with one or two grandchildren (mummies I/1 and I/2). If this is true, mummy I/5 passed on the tissue type traits HLA–A10 and HLA–B40 to mummy I/3, and as in 99 per cent of all cases the HLA–A and HLA–B traits are inherited as a whole, she probably also gave HLA–A10 and HLA–B40 to mummy I/4. Mummy I/2 may be the son of either mummy I/3 or I/4. Considering that he lay by mummy I/3 and is completely identical to her in tissue type, mummy I/3 may be the most likely mother.

In grave II lay two middle-aged women (mummies II/6 and II/8) who may well be sisters, together with a very young girl (mummy II/7). This young girl probably received the tissue type traits HLA–A28,B5 from both of her parents, and as both mummies II/6 and II/8 possess these two traits, one cannot determine which of the two could be her mother.

Theoretically mummy II/6 may also be the mother of mummies I/3 and I/4, to whom she would in this case have passed on HLA–A10,B40. However, this seems less likely, judging by the position in the graves. It is possible that the three oldest women (mummies I/5, II/6 and II/8) could be sisters, namely the children of parents who, in this case, would have possessed the tissue types HLA–A1, B17/HLA–A28, B5, and HLA–A10, B40/HLA–A28, B40, but of course this cannot be proved. However, it is certain that mummy II/8 is not the mother of any of the younger people in grave I, and mummy II/7 cannot be the daughter of any of the women in grave I, nor can mummy II/7 be the mother of mummy I/2. While the above stated maternity exclusions are certain, it is not possible to calculate any odds for the correctness of the postulated ties of kinships.

In connection with the tissue type determinations an attempt was also made to answer the questions as to whether the HLA factors found are typical for Inuit, or whether some admixture of other genes, such as those of the Norsemen, could be detected. This question, however, cannot be answered on the basis of the available material. The frequencies of the various tissue type traits in the Danish population have been quite definitely established, and can hardly be expected to have changed over only five hundred years, thus the frequencies which are

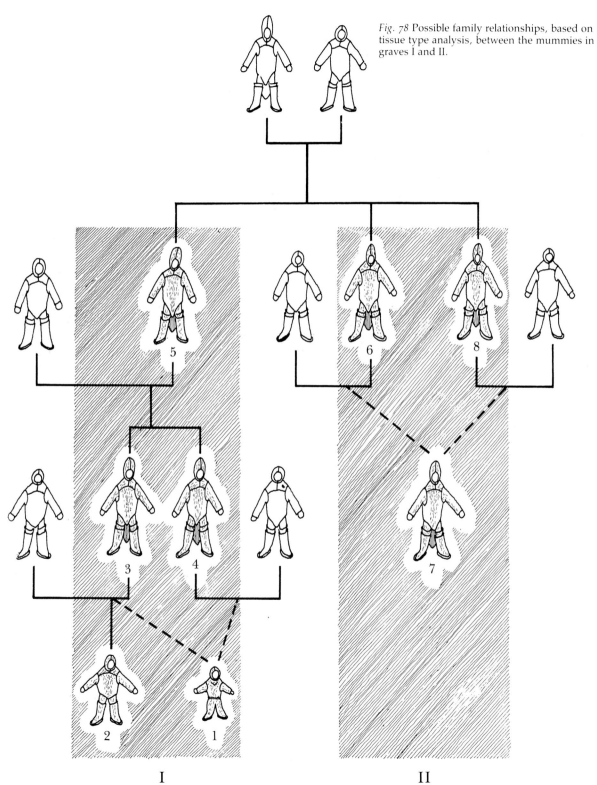

Fig. 78 Possible family relationships, based on tissue type analysis, between the mummies in graves I and II.

I

II

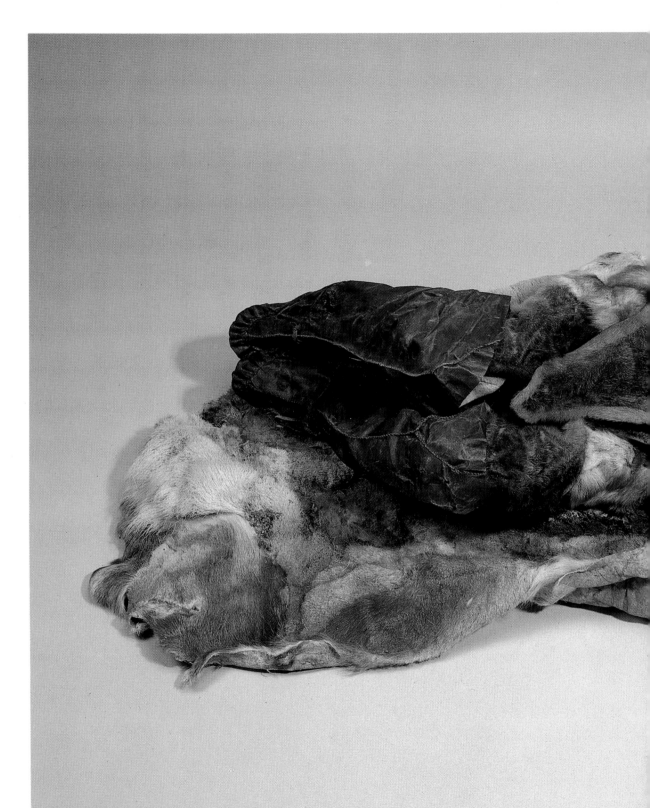

Fig. 79 Mummy II/6, a 50-year-old woman.

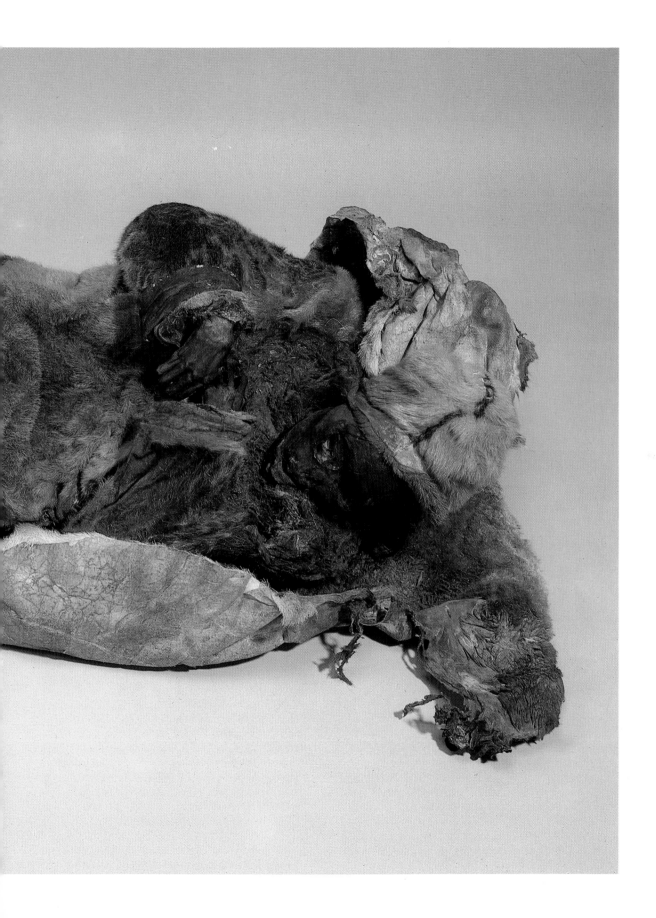

known today must also have been so in 1475. In contrast, there exists only very scattered material concerning the Inuit population groups. The groups studied are quite small and consist of not entirely unmixed Inuit ancestry.

Table II shows a comparison between the frequency of the same HLA factors found among, respectively, the people of Qilakitsoq, 5200 Danes and 182 Inuit of unmixed Greenlandic origins with regard to their parents and grandparents. It is seen that even though the factors HLA–A1, A10, B8 and B17 are rare among contemporary inhabitants of Greenland, compared with Danes, their presence has been established. Thus it is not possible to postulate anything as to what extent European genes were mixed into the Inuit population of Greenland already in the fifteenth century. However, this possibility cannot be rejected in any case.

The results of the HLA-tissue type tests.

Mummy	Age	HLA-type
I/2	3½–4½ yrs	A9, A10; B8, B40
I/3	c. 25 yrs	A9, A10; B8, B40
I/4	c. 30 yrs	A9, A10; B17, B40
I/5	c. 45 yrs	A1, A10; B17, B40
II/6	c. 50 yrs	A10, A28; B5, B40
II/7	18–22 yrs	A28; B5
II/8	c. 50 yrs	A28; B5, B40

BLOOD GROUPS

Blood group determinations (the ABO system) have been attempted on muscle tissue from all the mummies except the infant I/1, since as a result of mummification all blood had disappeared. Several methods were attempted but the findings were uncertain and divergent. The reason for this is probably that the blood group structures are more easily broken down than the HLA structures and often to varying degrees, and that many micro-organisms such as bacteria and fungi can form substances with the same activity as the blood group traits, thus giving rise to false reactions. Continued experimentation in the blood group determination of bone tissue is underway.

The frequency in Danes and Greenlanders today of the HLA-tissue types observed in the mummies.

HLA-type	Danes	Greenlanders
A1	32%	c. 5%
A9	18%	85–90%
A10	10%	1–2%
A28	18%	20–25%
B5	11%	20–40%
B8	24%	3–5%
B17	8%	1–3%
B40	18%	c. 40%

Causes of death

By the term cause of death we mean the disease or condition which directly brought about the termination of life. Today, when a doctor makes out a death certificate he must also state the manner of death; that is, whether death was natural or whether it was an accident, murder or suicide. The cause and manner of death is often clear for many people die in a doctor's care. In uncertain cases an autopsy, examination of the internal organs, is able to clarify the circumstances of death. However, the cause of death of the Qilakitsoq mummies has not been determined for sure in more than one case despite exhaustive examination. Nor has it been possible to ascertain whether they all died and were buried at the same time, or whether they died at intervals of perhaps several years.

The four best preserved mummies (I/1, I/3, I/4 and II/6) were not undressed, since the clothing would have been damaged. Thus it was possible only to examine the exposed parts of the body. They could of course be X-rayed and specimens for scientific study could be taken, namely from a small cut that was made in the back of mummies I/3, I/4 and II/6. The other four mummies which could be thoroughly examined, both externally and internally, were badly deteriorated. Only in the case of mummy II/7 could some of the internal organs be identified and closely studied. A standard autopsy entailing investigation of all the organs was not possible in any of the cases.

Despite these shortcomings the examinations have provided much information. It must be emphasised that there are no signs whatsoever of violence immediately prior to death which could have brought about death. The slight consequences of earlier violence detected by X-rays were in all cases unrelated to the cause of death.

In mummy II/7 it was possible to recognise various internal organs – the lungs, heart, liver, gall bladder, stomach, small intestine and large intestine. These organs were extremely shrunken and could not be detached. To allow for closer study and for subsequent microscopic examination the dry mummified tissue had to be softened. An attempt was made to rehydrate the tissue, with the intention of restoring it to its original size and structure as much as possible with the least damage. After re-hydration the kidneys, urinary organs and sexual organs were still indistinguishable. Microscopic examination of the lung tissue showed considerable deposits of soot, larger amounts than are usually found in a modern city dweller. The explanation is undoubtedly that she had breathed in combustion particles from the blubber lamp, which it was the duty of the Inuk woman to tend every few hours. There were no signs of tuberculosis, a disease which, in later generations at least, has ravaged the popu-lation of Greenland. Her heart was surprisingly well-preserved, for the cavity, valves and coronary arteries could be identified. There were no pathologi-cal changes. The gall bladder was normal and con-tained no stones. The stomach was empty but in the large intestine there were a number of black lumps of faeces. Thus the most detailed examination poss-ible of all the mummies revealed nothing about the cause of death.

The X-rays of mummy II/8 had shown widespread destruction of the base of the skull. This destruction was presumably caused by a malignant tumour. A virtually identical picture is seen today in patients with cancer of the nasopharynx. This form of cancer is especially frequent among people of Inuit origin in Greenland, Canada and Alaska. In fact, its current rate is about twenty-five times as great for Green-landers as for Danes, for example, and several new cases occur each year in Greenland. (It is also quite widespread in certain regions of China and North Africa, although it is rare in Europe.) No doubt both hereditary and environmental conditions play a role in the occurrence of both cancer and a number of other diseases, and this accounts for the relatively high rates of certain types of cancer and low rates of others in present day Inuit.

The tumour in mummy II/8 must have caused distressing symptoms during the last days of the woman's life, with blindness and pain. Changes in her nails, however, indicate that she was able to

work with skins right up to her death. Presumably the tumour was the cause of death, although, of course, it may be argued that a person suffering from cancer may die from entirely different causes. However, in this case that is hardly probable, for the cancer was clearly in its final phase.

X-ray examination also offers certain indications concerning the death of mummy I/2, the four-year-old boy. As mentioned above in the X-ray section, this boy suffered from a serious disease in the left hip joint which must have caused pain and difficulty in walking. Today this disease is treated by relieving the pressure on the hip for years in order to prevent permanent invalidity. Moreover, the shape of the boy's pelvis indicates that he suffered from Down's syndrome, a congenital, non-hereditary condition entailing mental deficiency and various malfor-mations. Other cases have been found among Inuit. The boy must have badly needed support, being able only to limp or perhaps just crawl about, and his mental development was probably low in relation to his age. The reduced calcium content and the position of his bones may indicate that he moved very little. Surprisingly, the soles of the boy's boots were heavily worn, repaired in fact, which seems contradictory to his condition. The explanation, however, may be that he was given another child's boots when placed in the grave. This supposition is supported by the fact that the right and left boots were on the wrong feet. Such a child would have had difficulty surviving in Greenland in the fifteenth century: his resistance to contagious diseases and hunger would have been poor. Also, children suffer-ing from Down's syndrome have a higher death rate than normal children as a result of congenital heart disease and leukaemia. However, no other malfor-mations or diseases could be detected in the boy because of the poor state of preservation of the tissue.

The manner of death of the child mummy could be either natural or non-natural. He may well have died because of congenital or acquired disease and general low resistance. Alternatively he may have been exposed or strangled, as was the custom with child invalids, although no trace of strangulation can be found on the body. However, the possibility that he was exposed cannot be altogether discounted.

Similar considerations apply in the case of the infant, mummy I/1, who seems to have developed normally. Because of his size and incredibly well-preserved condition the child has been left com-pletely intact and no specimens, except for a few

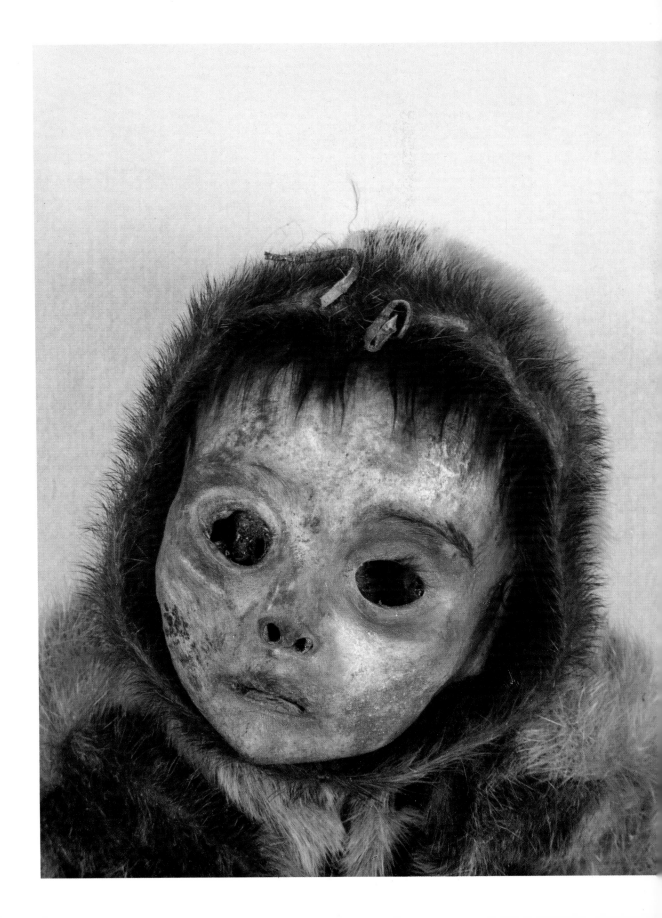

Fig. 81 Microscopic section of the root of the lung of mummy II/7. Windpipe cartilage (darker pink areas) and considerable deposits of inhaled soot (black areas) are visible. Enlarged 25 times.

Opposite Fig. 80 Mummy I/1, a 6-month-old baby.

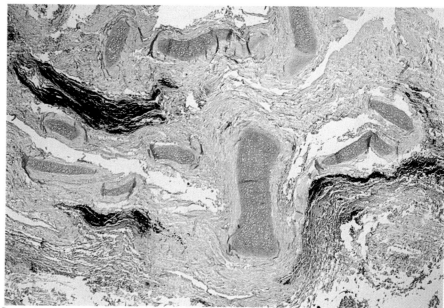

hairs, have been taken for scientific study. Of course, he has undergone X-ray examination. The child shows no signs of injury or disease, but may have died a natural death from some congenital or acquired disease which it is not possible to identify. Alternatively, he may have been buried alive with his dead mother. This was a relatively common custom since, in small arctic societies, it was not always possible to save an infant whose mother had died. Instead of letting the child die gradually of hunger because no other woman could be found to nurse it, the father would immediately put the child to death. Often it was suffocated and buried with its mother so they could journey together to the Land of the Dead, or in other cases the child was buried alive.

Finds made during the examination of mummy I/3 included a kidney stone and a small bone fragment, probably situated in the gastrointestinal canal. This kidney stone may have caused a malfunction of the kidney, but the bone fragment, which must have been ingested with food, was following the natural route of the food through the human body when death occurred. However, it is not altogether improbable that the fragment tore a hole somewhere in the gastrointestinal canal or caused ileus by being lodged in the intestinal passage, both possible causes of death.

In mummy I/4, who was initially thought to be pregnant, there may have been a water cyst, perhaps stemming from an ovary, in the distended abdomen.

This cyst could hardly have caused death, although the possibility cannot be definitely excluded.

Nothing is known about the cause of death of mummies I/5 and II/6.

During the five hundred years which have passed since the deaths of the Qilakitsoq people, the disease patterns in Greenland have changed greatly, especially in the twentieth century when the war against many infectious diseases has become effective. Nonetheless, the disease pattern in Greenland today still differs considerably in some ways from conditions in such countries as Denmark. This can be partly explained by the fact that for thousands of years the Greenland Inuit have lived in relative isolation. In fact, this isolation was really broken only by the Second World War when the military importance of the Arctic increased and its natural resources were further exploited. An admixture of non-Inuit hereditary genes subsequently occurred and living conditions and the environment started to undergo radical changes. In West Greenland today the proportion of European genes is at least 25 to 30 per cent. These changes in heredity and environment are also reflected in the disease pattern, which in some ways is coming to resemble that of Western Europe. For example, the occurrence of uterine cervical cancer, and lung and breast cancer, has grown considerably in recent decades.

One characteristic feature of the unique Inuit pattern of disease is that coronary heart disease is rare.

Fig. 82 Microscopic sections of the eyes of mummy I/2. A. Remnants of the choroid and the lens (asterisk) are seen between two layers of sclera. Enlarged 24 times. B. Lens fibres (by the asterisk). Enlarged 140 times. C. Pigment granules from the retina. Enlarged 560 times. There were no remains of cornea or optical nerve and ophthalmological examination revealed no signs of injuries or illnesses.

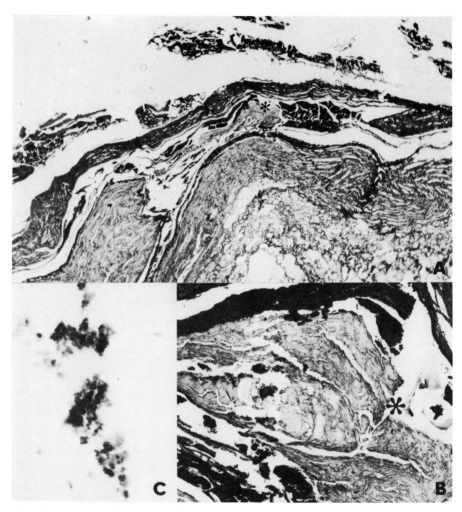

Today this disease occurs six times more often among Danes, for example, than among the Inuit of Greenland. This is no doubt because the blood of Inuit has a poor ability to coagulate; for centuries Greenland Inuit have been known to bleed easily. Today there is proof of a pronounced tendency for nose-bleeding and a relatively high rate of cerebral haemorrhage and haemorrhaging in connection with births. At present, intensive research is attempting to determine whether certain elements in the traditional Inuit diet are responsible, and if so, whether these can be used to decrease the rate of coronary heart disease elsewhere in the world. The occurrence of arteriosclerosis has not been conclusively determined. Diabetes also ought to be mentioned in this respect, for both the type which occurs in young people as well as that which afflicts older people is extremely rare in Greenland.

The bones of Inuit are relatively deficient in calcium, although their bone structure was otherwise quite normal. This fact is known from studies of Inuit skeletons up to fifteen hundred years old from the entire arctic world – Greenland, Canada, Alaska and the USSR – as well as of living persons. However, the vitamin D content, which is essential for the development of the bone tissue, seems to be high. As a result of the high vitamin D content in the diet, rickets is not found among Inuit in Greenland, whereas the low calcium content in the blood creates bones which are deficient in calcium and brittle. The calcium content in the blood of Inuit in Greenland rises when they move to Denmark, for example, probably as a result of their eating dairy products rich in calcium.

Among the possible causes of death, infectious diseases must be given prominence. In the course of time, a great many epidemics have ravaged Greenland, carrying off a certain percentage of the population. Moreover, some infectious diseases are believed to have occurred more or less constantly. Depending upon the intensity of the infectious matter and the resistance of the individual, some of the afflicted survived. The mummies, therefore, may have been the victims of incidental infectious diseases. Laboratory studies of specimens from all the mummies except for the infant were carried out to identify possible infectious diseases but all results were negative, although the possibility of such diseases having occurred is not thus excluded.

The investigation entailed direct growth experiments to determine bacteria capable of germination; also, experiments were made to ascertain traces of bacteria in tissue or traces of each subject's reactions to earlier bacterial infection. Such traces can appear to the extent that the subject forms antibodies against the bacteria. The latter experiment yielded no helpful information, but the direct growth experiment revealed a rich bacteria flora similar to that found in soil. Among the bacteria found in a specimen taken from inside the pelvis were gas gangrene bacteria. These bacteria are found in soil and frequently in the content of the large intestines of healthy humans and animals. Under special conditions this bacteria, like other intestinal bacteria, can be pathogenic. In poorly oxidised tissue the bacteria can cause gas gangrene, which in former days was often fatal. The significance of the find is difficult to evaluate, and it is very likely that it is incidental since gas gangrene does not seem to have been reported in Greenland in historical times.

Other possible causes of death are starvation or freezing. However, collective starvation is unlikely, for the subcutaneous fat was well-developed. Mummy II/7, for example, seems to have been nourished somewhat above the average. Her intestinal content indicated a relatively recent food ingestion and the clothing and extra skins were thoroughly well-preserved, showing no traces of having been gnawed upon: in Greenland when people or their dogs were starving to death, strips of skin were sometimes cut off and boiled; the boiled material was then chewed or fed to the starving dogs to quiet their raging hunger. Despite the lack of such evidence, the theory that the mummies froze to death cannot be left out of consideration, because this cause of death leaves neither external nor internal traces.

Among other misfortunes which could have caused these people to die concurrently are poisoning and drowning. Fatal food poisoning, or botulism, from eating rotten meat was and still is prevalent throughout the Arctic. Fatal mussel poisoning among Greenlanders has also been reported, although fatal poisoning caused by eating plants has never been mentioned.

The theory of drowning was suggested shortly after the mummies were found. The Inuit were thought to have drowned together in the sea near Qilakitsoq. Perhaps a women's boat carrying women and children only capsized on the way to the winter camp when an iceberg calved. The men in their kayaks would have been able to ride the tremendous waves. However, no evidence supporting this theory has been found. Despite exhaustive mineralogical investigations, not a single grain of certain characteristic minerals found in the sand of nearby beaches where the victims could have been dragged up after the accident has been found on the mummies or in their clothing and skins. Joas Andersen from Uummannaq has offered his opinion that the mummies could not have been the victims of a sailing accident:

> There are too many things showing that these people didn't die because their boat capsized. For example, there are no traces of the women's boat and no skins or wood in the grave. The custom of our forefathers was to cover the drowned with the skin of the boat, because boats, kayaks, and tools linked to death could not be used again. Our ancestors believed that if you used the implements of the dead, you too would meet misfortune.

The theory that these Inuit had drowned together led to an exhaustive investigation to determine the content of diatoms in the tissue of the dead. Since the beginning of the twentieth century, the presence of plant plankton, particularly diatoms, in the lungs has been assumed to be proof of death from drowning. In the 1960s this claim was called into doubt when diatoms were found in the liver tissue of people who had not drowned. Subsequently opinion has been sharply divided, with some scientists insisting the presence of diatoms to be an indication of drowning and others claiming that diatoms are worthless as a determinant of drowning.

Diatoms are one-celled plants which are autotrophic, meaning that they can build up organic material from inorganic material with the help of solar energy. They are found most frequently in water (salt, brackish and fresh water) but also appear on the surface of the earth and floating in the air. Material from all the mummies, except for mummy I/1, has been studied to determine the diatom content. Freshwater types were found to occur more frequently than saltwater species. As the mummies were all coast dwellers and probably obtained most of their food from the sea, the relative scarcity of marine diatoms is odd, for the meat of all animals probably contains diatom shells. As a basis of comparison, supplementary studies have been made of the meat of mammals and fish as well as of material from drowned and non-drowned bodies from Denmark. No essential difference was found between the composition of the diatom frequency in the mummies and the frequency determined for eight Danes who died five hundred years later.

Thus the investigation showed not only that the drowning theory could not be confirmed but also the fundamentally significant fact that the content of diatoms in the tissue of drowned and non-drowned persons, respectively, differs too little to serve as conclusive evidence of the cause of death.

As a conclusion, it must be stated that it was not possible to establish for certain either the cause or manner of death for most of the mummies. There are indications that the infant mummy I/1 was buried alive, a practice not uncommon in prehistoric Greenland when a mother died leaving an infant. The four-year-old child, mummy I/2, suffered from Down's syndrome and Calvé-Perthes disease which meant he had a lower resistance to infections and other disorders, a combination of which may have caused his death. Mummy II/8 probably died of a naso-pharyngeal carcinoma.

Did they die at the same time?

As mentioned above, it has not been possible to determine whether the people in the graves died and were buried at the same time, or whether they died from various causes at intervals of perhaps decades.

Conditions in the graves indicate that an initial single burial was made, after which the graves were gradually filled up. It is possible that there were one or two common burials after the simultaneous death of all or most of the women. Grave I, for instance, contained a large, flat, upright stone which must have been put there after the woman at the bottom was buried, since it leaned against a pile of skins which had been buried with her. Perhaps this stone

was to increase the height of the grave for subsequent burials and to prevent it from being too wide when the capstones were set in place. In grave II the bottom woman was at first difficult to see because she was covered by skins and grass. There were numerous small and loose stones around her and, when the top two bodies had been removed, it seemed that the grave had been almost filled with skins and stones after her burial.

Further information that implies more than one burial comes from the first radiological examinations of the four-year-old boy in grave I. Seven milk teeth were found to lie under his back, apparently inside his clothing. They were at first thought to be in a small, partly disintegrated pouch of animal skin. Four other teeth were found, encapsulated in soft tissue, by his throat and behind his left jaw. How-

Fig. 83 X-ray of mummy I/2's rib-cage. A set of teeth and their roots can be seen on a level with the 11th thoracic vertebra; on the right of the picture (the boy's left ribs) two more teeth surrounded by small stones are visible, and more stones are in the clothing on the left of the picture. The teeth belong to the boy and must have fallen out several years after death. The position of the teeth indicates that the body was moved long after burial.

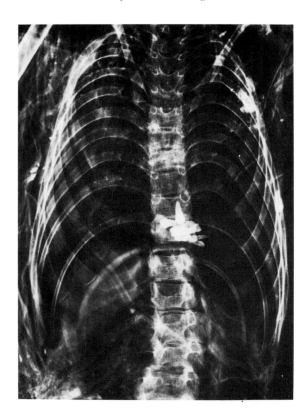

ever, all these teeth, which came from the boy him-self, had roots and so had fallen out post-mortem. His clothing and the skin he lay on were partly disintegrated around his lower back, where the seven teeth lay, and it was discovered that they actually lay beneath his own skin and that there was no skin pouch at all. The teeth were surrounded by mummified soft tissue, indicating that they reached their final scattered position before the process of mummification was complete. The probable reason for the scattered position of the teeth, which presum-ably fell out years after death and burial, is that the body was moved, perhaps to be buried in another grave with his mother or other relatives. The removal of the bodies after the mummies were discovered in 1972 could not have caused the changed position of the teeth.

The carbon–14 method of dating cannot, unfortu-nately, give a definitive answer because the margin of uncertainty is so great; it is estimated to be fifty years either way.

Special studies of the mummies' hair were ex-pected to provide information about the times of death and burial through the detection of identical variations in the concentration of elements along the hairs. These concentrations vary according to diet and if an identical diet is consumed identical varia-tions should be demonstrable in hairs from different mummies. However, no characteristic patterns were found and the results do not answer the question.

The fact that the grave contained only women and children has given rise to speculation. In all that is known about the burial customs of the time, there is nothing to indicate that men and women were buried separately. Nor is there any indication that women were usually buried in common graves and men in single. But one must remember that the graves may have contained only women and chil-dren because the men of the settlement had, for example, perished at sea or disappeared in the mountains; settlements have been known to be provided for by one or very few hunters, and acci-dents have always been one of the most common causes of death in Greenland.

In only one of the mummies was it possible to find the remains of food ingestion, in the form of lumps of faeces in the large intestine. The contents of these indicate that the woman died during the summer in July or August, although the evidence is still ambiguous. If comparison of food remains had shown that all the mummies had died at the same time of year this would have indicated contempor-aneous death. Had it been possible to ascertain that the mummies had all died of the same cause this too would have indicated death at the same time. The question is still unanswered.

5
Tattooing

H. Kapel, N. Kromann

F. Mikkelsen, E. Løytved Rosenløv

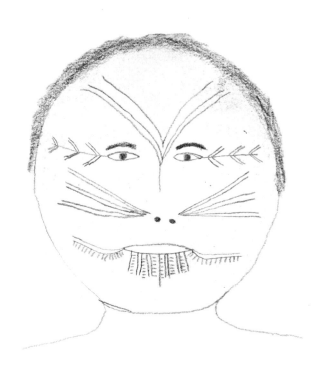

Detection

It was logical to presume that the adult mummies had been tattooed, for historical sources have told of tattooing in Greenland. When the facial skin of the mummies was examined prior to cleaning, no tattoos could be seen, but after cleaning, faint traces did show up. These tattoos must have been distinct when their bearers were alive, but mummification had made the skin very dark and the translucence of dry skin is slight compared to live skin, which has a high moisture content. It was therefore necessary to find a method which could reveal deposits of colour invisible to the naked eye.

A special photographic technique using infra-red light (heat rays) had already been used to make out the tattoos of a frozen, mummified Inuit body in Alaska. Infra-red rays penetrate the skin to a very slight depth, about 0.5 mm, and thus the pigment immediately below the surface of the skin is included in the picture. In the tattooing process, pigment is deposited in the upper dermis. The exact details of the photographic procedure have not been described previously and in the course of the mummy studies a reliable method has been developed; the technical details are given in the caption of Fig. 85.

As the skin could be damaged by cleaning and conservation processes, all exposed areas of skin were photographed beforehand. Several facial tattoos were thus distinguished wholly or in part. After cleaning, a new set of photographs was made, and facial tattoos were clearly distinguished in five out of the six adult women; the exception was the youngest woman, mummy II/7. No tattoos were found on the torsos or limbs, especially not at the joints. However, it must be noted that several areas were examined without cleaning and other areas were covered by

Fig. 84 Left An ordinary and *right* an infra-red photograph of mummy I/4, the latter revealing tattoos. Line drawings of the pattern of tattoos on each mummy are shown in Fig. 86. The infra-red photograph reveals the forehead markings clearly, but the spot above the bridge of the nose is indistinct, as are the cheek markings. The stripes on the chin are clear only on the right side, but presumably there were twelve in total.

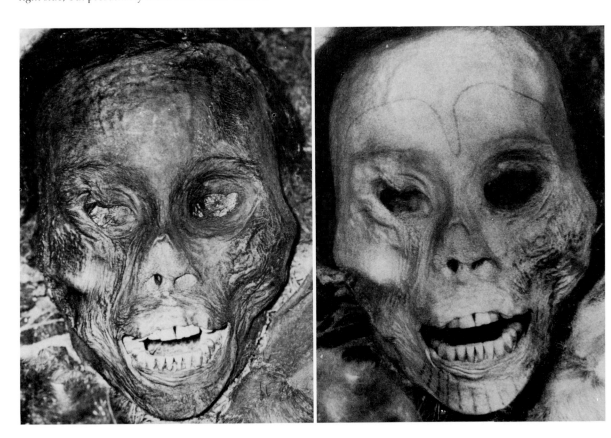

Fig. 85 Infra-red photography. Light source: 2 Osram theratherm infra-red lamps of 220–230 volts and 250 watts. Distance from subject: approximately 50 cm. Film: Kodak High Speed Infra-red black and white negative film. Filter: Kodak Wratten Gelatine Filter number 87c. Exposure: 1/15 secs, f 11.

clothing. The backs of hands and wrists, where tattoos might be anticipated, were examined with particular care.

Each tattoo was black or dark blue and consisted of elegantly formed, usually fully drawn lines with no irregularities. However, in one case there were dotted lines where small marks pricked in the skin at intervals of a few millimetres were distinctly seen, and one, or possibly two, other mummies had a few indistinct dots on the forehead. The width and clearness of the lines was consistent in each individual, and there was, in all cases, symmetry around the central line of the face. All except mummy II/7 had lines tattooed on their foreheads. One had lines at the outer corners of the eyes, and four were tattooed on their cheeks. Three mummies had lines tattooed on their chins; mummy II/8 may have had these lines but her chin is so poorly preserved that it is impossible to tell. All the tattoos are depicted diagrammatically in Fig. 86.

Cultural and historical background

Tattooing exists in virtually all parts of the world. Its origin is unknown but the word tattooing has been used in Europe for about two hundred years only. The word is derived from Polynesian and was first introduced to Europe in 1769 by the English explorer James Cook, who mistakenly transcribed the Polynesian word *tatatau* (meaning 'to strike properly') to the English form *tattow*. In Polynesia tattooing was executed with a fork-like implement with many points which were pressed into the skin with light blows of a club. The Greenlandic language group also has a word for tattooing; in West Greenland it is *kakiorneq*, in East Greenland *kagierneq*, both meaning 'stuck in' or 'drawn by a needle'.

As elsewhere in the world, it is not known how long the custom of tattooing has been in use among the Inuit. The earliest evidence we have is a small tusk figure found in a grave at Point Hope in Alaska. This figure, dated to about 95 BC, bears distinct chin tattoos, closely resembling those of the Qilakitsoq mummies. Another find from Alaska is a blubber lamp of sandstone, the underside of which is shaped like a facial mask with tattoos on the chin, cheeks, temples and forehead. This find, dated to 450 AD, belongs to the Indian-influenced Ipiutaq or Norton culture. This people had a rich and diversified pictorial world with innumerable examples of various kinds of tattoos. The custom was presumably quite widespread at that time. The Dorset people in arctic Canada and Greenland demonstrated a similar artistic urge between 500 and 1000 BC. Many of their

3

4

5

6

8

Fig. 86 The patterns of each tattooed mummy.

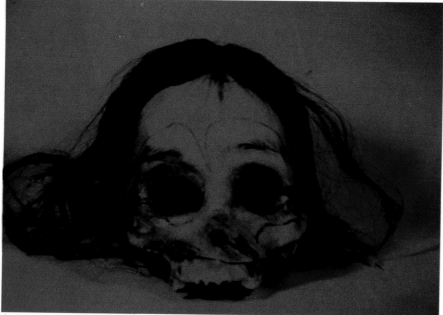

Fig. 87 Infra-red photograph of mummy II/8's tattoos.

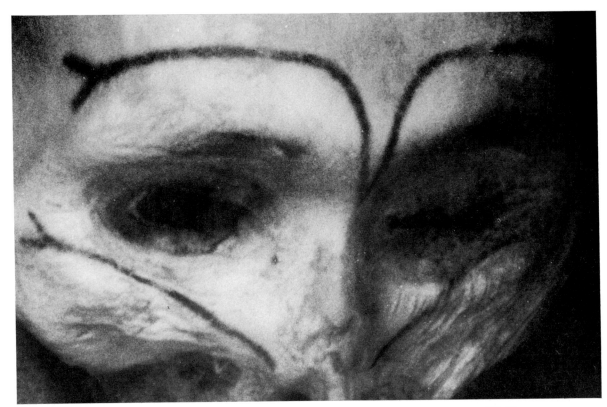

Above Fig. 88 The particularly strong and broad lines of mummy I/5's tattoos. *Below Fig. 89* Mummy II/6. Her tattoos are different from the tattoos of the other mummies, as seen in Fig. 86. All the lines seem to be dotted with traces of pinpricks. Her chin and cheek tattoos are preserved only in part. *Opposite, top Fig. 90* Mummy I/3. *Left* A distinct spot in the middle of her forehead and *right* a horizontal line at the corners of both eyes. *Opposite, bottom, Fig. 91* Forehead and cheek tattoos on mummy II/8.

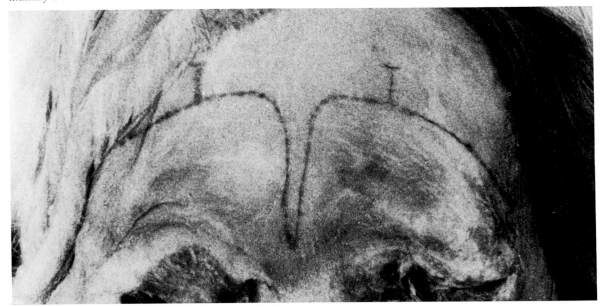

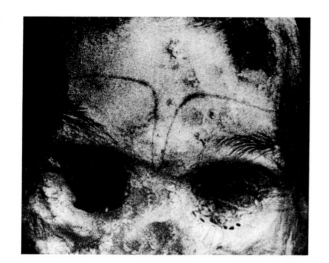

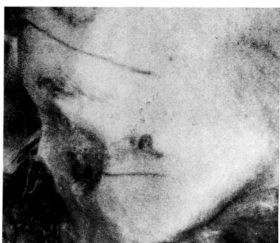

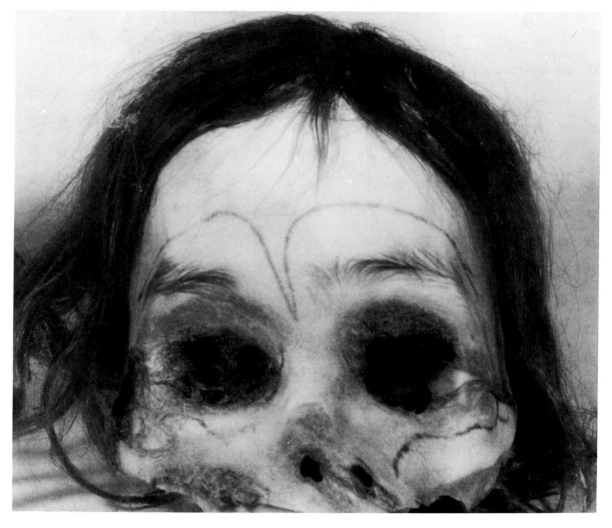

finely carved human figures and face masks are incised with tattoo patterns on the chin and forehead.

Because of the artistic products of these people, we can prove that the type of tattooing found on the Qilakitsoq mummies can be traced back at least to the period around the birth of Christ, although it is probably much older. Even though the people of the Thule culture who, during the following millennium, settled on the coasts of Greenland, have not left behind the same sort of pictorial evidence as the Dorset people, there can be little doubt that tattooing was practised.

The earliest known Danish description of tattooing among the Greenland Inuit is a verse by the priest Claus Christopherssøn Lyschander in his book *Den grønlandske Chronica (The Greenland Chronicle)*, which was published in 1608: 'They cut their faces/and rub upon them/both blue and yellow: and thus they mean/To honour and adorn His creation.'

The earliest European descriptions of Inuit have very few details. They consist of secondhand information characterised by more or less fanciful ideas. The first somewhat reliable account appeared in the middle of the sixteenth century: in 1566 a French skipper from Zeeland brought back two Inuit, a woman of about twenty and her child, who had been captured on the coast of Labrador. The Inuit were exhibited publicly, arousing much attention. The sensational press of the time supplied a picture and gave a brief description of them on a handbill. It is especially interesting in this context because it clearly shows the woman's chin tattoos; the horizontal shading of the cheeks and forehead in the picture is doubtless meant to illustrate tattooed bands or lines.

About ten years later Martin Frobisher, the leader of an English expedition, reported from his voyage to the Baffin Island area that the women here were tattooed with small blue dots on their faces. Fortunately, these observations were illustrated by the artist John White, who participated in the expedition. His watercolour from 1577 shows a series of dots running in a curved line across the woman's cheek. It was Frobisher who re-discovered Greenland during his travels from 1576–8 after all contact with the Norsemen had been lost 200 years earlier.

Apart from the early historical sources mentioned above, our knowledge of tattooing in Greenland is derived mainly from more recent accounts and from individual portraits, which give a good impression of the design and placing of the patterns. After

Above Fig. 94 Left and right Maria of Frederikshaab, South Greenland. She voluntarily left Greenland with a Norwegian priest and stayed in Copenhagen in 1746–7. This painting of her by Mathias Blumenthal (see also Fig. 139) clearly shows her tattoos.

Below Fig. 95 Blubber lamp of the Norton culture, displaying tattoo decoration. Found in the ruins of a house in the Platinum settlement, southwest Alaska, *c.* AD 450. L. 16.2 cm.

Opposite, top Fig. 92 Microscopic examination of soot particles deposited in the dermis of mummy II/8 after tattooing. Enlarged 400 times.

Opposite, bottom Fig. 93 Buckle, carved in walrus ivory from the Near Ipiutak Culture. This serves as testimony of tattooing among Inuit 2000 years ago. Found in a grave at the Point Hope Settlement, northern Alaska. H. 6.5 cm.

the colonisation of Greenland in 1721, the sources became more numerous and more detailed, but at the same time the custom of tattooing was rapidly disappearing in West Greenland.

In his *The History of Greenland* from 1765, David Crantz writes that this tradition had disappeared long before. Nevertheless, in 1771 the priest H. C. Glahn claimed that tattooing in West Greenland was more frequently seen in the south than towards the north. This was attributed to the frequent contact between the inhabitants of the Cape Farewell area and the 'Easterners' from the east coast, among whom the tradition had been kept alive. In fact as late as 1900 a district medical officer, Gustav Meldorf, who had vaccinated the Inuit in this area, reported that ten out of fifteen of the adult women examined were tattooed.

The reason for the relatively rapid disappearance of tattooing in West Greenland is probably that the missionaries considered the custom incompatible with the Christian faith and therefore declared it to be sinful. However, Glahn claimed that the women refused to be tattooed 'so they could more easily catch a Danish man, whom they know takes no pleasure in an embroidered chin'.

Detailed studies of the custom of tattooing in Greenland first appeared in the late nineteenth and first
half of the twentieth centuries. During an expedition
in 1884–5 in a women's boat to Ammassalik Gustav
Holm attempted to find out why people allowed
themselves to be tattooed; and during the fifth Thule
expedition from 1921–4 led by Knud Rasmussen
material was systematically gathered about the various tattoo designs and the conceptual world related
to this practice throughout the Inuit region.

In the eastern Inuit area of Greenland tattooing
was carried out almost exclusively on women. In
1832 W. A. Graah reported from his exploration in
East Greenland that all women, but only a few men,
were tattooed. This is confirmed by Gustav Holm.
The physician Meldorf found out that out of thirty-
eight men, only one was tattooed, and he had no
more than a few dots on his upper right arm.

Earlier sources make no mention of tattooing in
connection with men. However, some scholars believe that previously, certainly before 1721, it was
common among both sexes. In the central Inuit
region in Canada tattooing was also practised mainly

Below Left Fig. 96 Woman with forehead tattoos. Drawn
by Paul Egede in West Greenland, 1788.

Below Fig. 97 Woman with extensive tattoos.
Photographed in East Greenland, 1906.

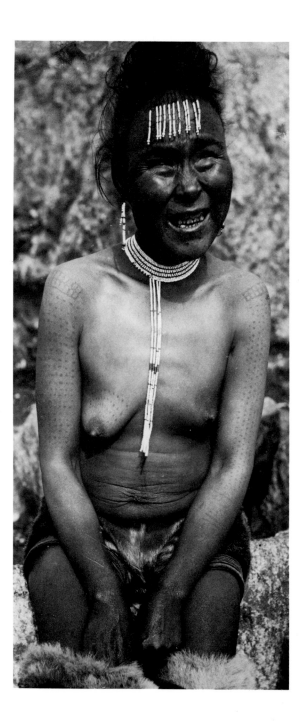

on women. Among certain groups, for example the Copper Inuit and the Labrador Inuit, the tattooing of men has been seen, although usually on the torso or limbs.

The situation is slightly different in the western Inuit area. From both the Bering Strait Inuit and Asiatic Inuit there are numerous reports of the tattooing of both sexes on the face and body. The same holds true of the neighbouring peoples, the Chukchi and the Koryaks of Siberia.

Among all Inuit groups where tattooing existed, facial tattooing was practised. The chin was the part of the face most frequently decorated. The designs here were nearly always lines or bands running from the lower lip down the chin. The number of lines varied from one to about twenty. Among the Bering Strait Inuit, young girls as a rule had only one chin line which was supplemented with extra lines when they married and had children. The most varied patterns were in fact found in this western Inuit region.

Cheeks were the next most frequently tattooed part of the face. Here the diversity of patterns was greater, although the most frequent designs were straight or curved lines running from the root of the nose. In Greenland, only this simple form is known whereas in Canada the lines were double or multiple, and sometimes formed lens-shaped figures. The greatest variation was found far to the west, where there was a distinct influence from the Chukchi in Siberia with their complex patterns with circle and spiral elements.

Tattooing of the forehead is found among many groups, although it is clearly more rare among the western Inuit. Most common are straight or slightly curved lines forming a V-shaped figure running from the root of the nose. However, there are several variations. Whereas in the central Inuit region the pattern usually consists of double or multiple lines, only single lines are seen in Greenland.

Along with these three most normal areas for tattoos, the chin, cheeks and forehead, some Inuit also tattooed the corners of their eyes, often with arrow-shaped figures, which in Canada are compared to a larch tree. Only in the western Inuit region have tattoos at the corners of the mouth been seen, and these usually consisted of a double-lined Y-shaped sign, called the 'whale tail motif'.

The tattooing technique employed determined to some extent the design, and the 'sewing technique' was more common than the 'dot technique'. The former procedure has been described several times,

Fig. 98 Tattooed mask of driftwood. East Greenland, 1900.

perhaps in greatest detail by Captain G. F. Lyon, a member of W. E. Parry's expedition to the Hudson Bay area in 1824. During a visit to the Iglulik Inuit, Lyon himself was tattooed. His description is as follows:

Having found a small needle, she took a piece of caribou sinew, which she blackened with soot. She began the work by sewing a rather deep but short stitch in my skin. When the thread was drawn beneath the skin, she pressed her thumb on the spot so as to press in the pigment. The next stitch commenced where the previous one had ended. The work went slowly, for she broke a needle while trying to press it through my flesh. When she had sewed forty stitches and the stripe was about two inches long, I felt that it was enough. The operation ended with my skin being rubbed with whale oil.

Lyon remarked that he could vividly imagine the suffering which a young woman had to endure for the sake of beauty.

The technique of dot tattooing was more limited geographically. It was used by the Inuit of the Pacific and the Aleutian Islands as well as by certain groups in Canada. Although the method had not been observed in Greenland there can be no doubt that many of the tattoos which were seen and photographed by Johan Petersen in Ammassalik around the turn of this century were made in this way. Petersen was the Greenlandic assistant of the Inuit expert W. Thalbitzer, and later became the first factor of East Greenland. The mummies of Qilakitsoq are further proof that the dot technique was used in Greenland. From 1921 to 1923 Therkel Mathiassen, a Danish archaeologist on the fifth Thule expedition, had the opportunity to study the procedure among the Netsilik. The method entailed pricking a hole in the skin with a metal needle equipped with a handle. A thin wooden needle dipped in soot was then inserted into the hole. When the needle was removed the colour was kept in by the pressure of a fingertip.

Tattoos were blue or black on the whole. The most frequently used colouring matter was soot, found, for example, at the bottom of a cooking vessel. Some of the many other pigments used were graphite, ashes, the juice extracted from certain types of seaweed, and even black gunpowder. Only one source, namely Lyschander in his *Greenland Chronicle*, mentions another colour when he claims that 'both blue and yellow' were used. The reason that the tattoos appeared blue (when the colouring matter was black) was probably that the black pigments deposited deep in the skin appear to be blue, whereas the natural colour of the pigment is seen only when the pigment is deposited directly beneath the surface.

Illustrations of the tattoos of the five Qilaktisoq mummies are in schematic drawings (Fig. 86). Decoration of the forehead was clearly a common fea-

Fig. 99 Tattooed woman of the Netsilik Inuit tribe, Canada. Drawn in 1922.

ture. However, the tattoos are not identical, and it is worth noting that in mummies I/5 and II/8 the lines at the temples terminate in a Y-shaped split. Mummies I/3 and I/4 seem to have one or two dot tattoos above the deep V-shaped depression at the root of the nose. This is proof that these Inuit practised dot tattooing. On mummy II/6 there is a T-shaped figure running from the line of the forehead approximately over the middle of each eye.

Cheek tattoos could be seen on four of the mummies, except mummy I/3. The designs were basically identical, although the curve of the lines differed slightly. In each case, there was a single line ending at the temple in the same Y-shaped division as seen in the forehead tattoos. On mummy II/6 the line is nearly dotted, as the individual pin-pricks are distinct. There is also an extra dot both over and under the middle of the line.

There were only three cases in which chin tattoos were determined with certainty. (Mummy I/5 had no tattoos here, and the skin on mummy II/8's chin was extremely poorly preserved.) However, it was not possible to ascertain whether the number of lines was the same in all three cases, although otherwise, the tattoos appeared to be identical.

Lastly, the tattoo at the corner of mummy I/3's eye should be noted – this was a horizontal line, a few centimetres long, running from the outer corner of the eye.

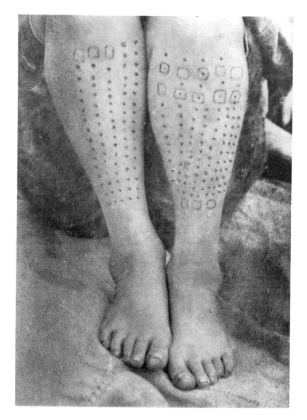

Left Fig. 100 Dot tattoos on a woman. Photographed in East Greenland, about 1900.

Above Fig. 101 In 1654 a Danish expedition captured four Inuit from the Godthaab Fjord area. An unidentified artist painted this, the oldest picture of Inuit from Greenland. The tattoos have a striking resemblance to those of the Qilakitsoq mummies.

The tattoos of each individual are quite similar in breadth of line and quantity of colour. However, there are notable differences from person to person, with the exception of mummies I/5 and II/8, whose forehead and cheek designs are identical. Judging by their tissue types, these women may have been sisters which may account for the identical tattoos.

Although the tissue type of mummy II/6 is such that she too could be the sister of mummies I/5 and II/8, her tattoos are quite different in both technique and detail. In fact, her tattoos are so unique that she may originally have belonged to another tribe or community.

In comparing the overall impression of these five tattooed faces with the tattoos known from elsewhere in the Inuit region, it is immediately apparent that the closest parallels are found among the central Inuit inhabiting the Hudson Bay area. However, certain features diverge markedly from the familiar patterns, and indeed are not found among other Inuit groups.

The most striking difference is the course of the forehead line. As mentioned above, the forehead tattoos of the central Inuit territory consist of double or multiple lines, usually in a V-shape. In some groups, this type of tattoo has survived only as two extremely short lines at the root of the nose. The refined curve seen on the mummies of Qilakitsoq with the characteristic sharp bend before the descent to the nose cannot be called a V. However, there is a remarkable similarity between the course of the forehead line and the hanging flaps of a fur of an outer parka. As neither the T-shaped additions on mummy II/6 nor the dots of mummies I/3 and I/4 are seen elsewhere in the Inuit region, they must be viewed as characteristic of West Greenland.

Tattoos at the outer corners of the eyes have in recent times been described only in relation to part of the central Inuit region, namely among the Copper, Netsilik and Iglulik Inuit. The single lines seen on mummy I/3 do not resemble the 'willow' or 'larch tree' motifs found among these groups.

Cheek tattooing is similar in this regard to forehead decoration – the harmonious curves have no direct parallels in the neighbouring regions. Here there are most frequently straight or slightly curved lines which are double or multiple. The unilinear pattern on the chin, however, is more widespread, appearing as it does not only in Canada but also in the western Inuit region. Even among the Siberian Chukchi a similar pattern is found.

Finally, one small but significant detail must be mentioned – the Y-shaped division of lines of the forehead and the cheek. This division is found in the Hudson Bay area, but here it is always part of strict geometrical patterns, usually on the arms and legs. However, there does seem to be a connection between cheek tattoos such as those seen on a woman from Southampton Island (Sallermiut) (see Fig. 103) and those which must be called character-istic of the Qilakitsoq women. One of the oldest sources from Greenland, and most reliable, is the well-known work from 1656 by Olearius, *Beschrei-bung der muscowitischen und persischen Rejse*, which mentions this detail, and the description includes a number of points of similarity with the tattoos of Qilakitsoq:

> Following the American custom, the adult women paint [tattoo] their faces with blackish-blue stripes, from the lower lip to the extremity of the chin and below it. One woman had thirteen and another woman fifteen stripes, thick as coarse thread and thicker, in a row. At the top of the nose, between the eyes, there runs a stripe which divides into two on the forehead and extends over the eyebrows to the temple, where it ends in two points like a fork. They had the same sort of lines under their eyes. These stripes are said to be made with a sewing needle and thread, rubbed with soot and drawn through the skin . . . They regard as beautiful that which is hideous in our eyes. They have them made when they are considered nubile. This is the reason that only the two adults had them, but not the child of thirteen.

This description concerns the four Greenland Inuit who were captured in 1654 by Dannell in the Nuuk area. It is accompanied by a painting of the same year by an unidentified artist which depicts the four captives.

Why were these people tattooed, and upon what concepts were these traditions based? This question has been asked by many people in the course of time, but unfortunately it was often asked when the practice was dying out or had been abandoned entirely. However, there was clearly a certain magi-cal significance in most tattoos.

Fig. 102 Implements used by the Netsilik Inuit in Canada for tattooing. Collected in 1922. Actual size.

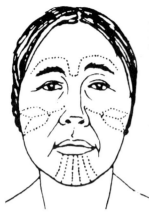

Fig. 103 Tattoo pattern of women from Southampton Island, Hudson Bay, Canada, *c.* 1898.

The Copper Inuit in Canada believed that tattoos prevented labour pains, whereas the Siberians felt that they helped cure childlessness. A hunter from the Cape Farewell region in Greenland related that he had himself tattooed so that he would not be recognised and pursued by a shark which he had once harpooned. A common belief among both women and men was that tattoos made one skilful at domestic tasks and lucky in the hunt. The East Greenland Inuit tattooed dots or lines on their wrists in the belief that they could thus harpoon better. From Hans Egede, the first missionary and coloniser in Greenland in 1721, we learn of the belief that if a woman's forehead was not elaborately tattooed, her skull would be used as a whale oil lamp beneath the blubber lamps in the Land of the Dead. Other beliefs from Canada are that after death an untattooed person will not end in 'The Land of Happiness' but instead in 'The Land of the Gloomy', whose inhabitants sit listlessly with heads hanging low and live on butterflies which flit by.

There are other, more practical explanations for tattooing. These marks could quite simply have indicated tribal or family relationships. Also, among most Inuit, chin tattoos were linked with a young girl's puberty or marriage, two events which often coincided. From the western Inuit region accounts relate that after her first menstruation a woman was tattooed with a single stripe, and the rest of her chin lines were added when she married. In Greenland, chin tattoos were linked to marriage. Perhaps the reason that the young woman, mummy II/7, was not tattooed is that she was unmarried. The fact that tattoos on various parts of the face were often made at different times may also explain why they appear with varying degrees of distinctness in the photographs. The tradition of displaying one's sexual and marital status was maintained in Greenland until the twentieth century. Such details as the colour of one's boots and hair ribbon and the fashion of one's clothing or beadwork ornaments were also clear indications to those who could interpret them.

Finally, some tattoos bestowed status upon their bearers. In the whale-hunting cultures on the Bering Strait and in northern Alaska it was common for men to mark their catch with a tattooed sign, a line or a dot. Other Inuit are said to have indicated a murder by drawing two horizontal lines across the nose.

Without doubt many of the original reasons for tattooing were forgotten in the course of time, and to a great extent the custom was practised as a matter of habit. Also, man's urge to beautify himself has always existed. Perhaps the often grotesque attempts seen today to emphasise physical advantages and assets or conceal one's lack of them is basically not so different from the tradition of tattooing which Inuit have practised for thousands of years.

Fig. 104 An approximately 90-year-old woman from the inland Inuit west of Hudson Bay, Canada. Tattoos of this type were drawn until about 50 years ago.

6
Clothing

T. Ammitzbøll, M. Bencard, J. Bodenhoff

Rolf Gilberg, A. Johansson, Jørgen Meldgaard, Gerda Møller

Rigmor Møller, E. Svejgaard, L. Vanggaard

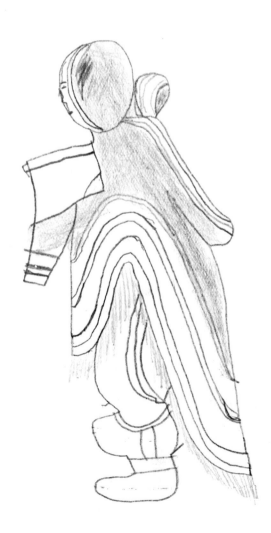

Development of Inuit clothing

To face the harsh climatic conditions of the Arctic, warm protective clothing was, and is, required. An Inuit hunter's attire has to meet particularly rigorous standards and is therefore directly related to his physiology. It has to provide insulation from the cold while the hunter stands or sits, waiting motionless, and to allow for sudden, energetic and precise movement when the game comes within range. The transition from motionless waiting to sudden activity increases the body's heat production by several hundred per cent and the body must rid itself of this heat without sweating, thus the clothing must be able to breathe.

The clothing from Qilakitsoq reveals surprisingly few functional differences from the clothing commonly worn up to the twentieth century. This is obviously an important fact, confirmation that Inuit had, quite early on, developed a dress form that met the demands of insulation and freedom of movement. The optimum had been achieved, and neither the opportunity nor the need existed for any further development. Even the introduction of iron and fire-arms, which led to a revolution in hunting methods, caused no basic functional changes in clothing. Europeans could provide nothing comparable with Inuit clothing, and it was not until polar explorers such as Charles Francis Hall and Robert Edwin Peary began to use Inuit garments and methods of transportation that it was possible to achieve the results for which they became famous.

Physiologically the clothing of the Qilakitsoq mummies provides no new information, although it does emphasise the high technological level and the extent of specialisation which were essential for survival in arctic societies.

Fig. 105 Inuit hunting walrus. Drawing from W. E. Parry's expedition to Arctic Canada, 1823.

Fig. 106 From left to right, Polar Inuit Ole, Kutsikitsoq and Inoterssuaq on a sledge voyage from Greenland to Ellesmere Island across Smith Sound. All three wear reindeer anoraks with collars of bluefox tail. Kutsikitsoq wears reindeer trousers which he replaced with bearskin trousers when he reached Ellesmere Island after a fortunate polar bear hunt. Photographed by Christian Vibe, March 1940.

The traditional fur garments of the Inuit were composed of only a few basic pieces. The tailoring of these was similar to that of the costumes of other peoples, and can be traced back to some basic primitive types.

The skin jacket, or parka, was a further development of the poncho, a very simple garment which was a free-hanging skin or piece of cloth with an opening for the head. The practical value of a skin poncho depended upon the size of the animal, and often it was advantageous to use two skins, sewn together at the shoulders, though still with an opening in the middle for the head. Many Indian tribes adapted the two-skin poncho by sewing the skins together at the sides and adding sleeves in order to make a sort of skin shirt. By adding a hood to this skin shirt, we have the basic pattern of the Inuit parka.

Outer skin trousers were another essential part of the Inuit costume and were worn by both men and women. The cut indicates that they were developed by sewing together a pair of the long leg coverings used by many Indian tribes. In some Inuit regions, trousers were long and loose; elsewhere they were worn short and tight, especially by women. Since about 1850, Greenland Inuit women have worn extremely short outer trousers suited to their high boots. These trousers were low-waisted and tight at the hips and buttocks.

All Inuit wore inner trousers. At home and in the summer the women wore no outer trousers, and so the cut and decoration of the inner trousers were important. In nineteenth-century West Greenland these trousers were often like shorts, tight and ornamented with leather bands or coloured leather mosaics. This tradition apparently dates back to the mummy costumes of the fifteenth century.

Footwear, like the rest of the Inuit costume, always consisted of two layers. Unlike the trousers, there was no kinship with the footwear of the Indians of the northern forests who wore soft moccasins, even in the winter snow. The kamik, a combination of a skin stocking and a boot, had a separate sole and seems to have originated from the sewing together of a sandal and a skin stocking. The skin of the sole wrapped around the foot, where it was folded into tiny pleats painstakingly sewn to the boot. Women's kamiks particularly included many different designs; during the nineteenth century in West Greenland the most popular type was one that stopped high above the knee and fitted quite tightly around the leg. The Qilakitsoq find now reveals the early form

Fig. 107 Costume fashion in two Inuit tribes. Drawings from W. E. Parry's expedition to Arctic Canada, 1823.

of this West Greenland boot.

The Inuit costumes which have been either described or brought to museums by Europeans over the last few centuries show that most regions, from Alaska to Greenland, developed costumes with local variations. Some of the changes and additions were functional: adaptation to conditions such as the cold, snow and ice, or to a warmer, more humid climate, or to a specialised life in which for example, the catching of sea mammals along ice-free coasts was the basis of subsistence. Other changes and new features were based upon considerations of style, the wish to make a beautiful or remarkable garment. Thus both highly practical considerations as well as fashion-conscious ideas and the chance to model the uniqueness and solidarity of the tribe were the main factors determining the design of the costume, even in the most extreme climatic conditions. Often these intentions could be realised at the same time in one style which was both practical and fashionable to a degree. For example, emphasis could be placed upon elegant tailoring (by sewing in light or dark strips of skin) or form (by adding edging and fringes).

Fig. 108 Women of the Umingmaktormuit, or Copper Inuit, tribe in Canada. Photographed on Knud Rasmussen's fifth Thule expedition, 1922.

However, fashion sometimes seems to have been of primary importance, especially with women's clothing. For example, parkas may have had extremely tight waists or hoods, or long, flapping skirts; boots were possibly over-sized; or sleeves and trousers were short to expose arms and legs.

The find of the costumes at Qilakitsoq has shown how style and fashion five hundred years ago were combined with the necessary requirements for warm clothing which could be worn for working and travelling.

Clothing production

PREPARATION OF THE SKINS

The seal was the Greenland Inuit's most important game animal. There are twenty-one different species of seal, five of which are found off the coasts of Greenland. Every part of its body was put to use: the flesh, intestines, blubber, bones and skin. The inhabitants of Qilakitsoq had made their garments out of sealskin (as well as the skin of caribou and birds). Because of the seals' thick layer of blubber and sensitive temperature regulation, it is able to maintain the same body temperature as a human, even in northern arctic waters. It has a warm, protective fur consisting of overhair, often called guard hair, and wool, and numerous sebaceous glands

keep the fur constantly covered with oil. The seal moults during the breeding season; some species in the same way as land mammals, and others, including the Greenland species, shed both the epidermis and hair in large sections, after which new fur grows. During these moulting periods the skin has no practical value for man.

The five harp seal species, starting with the largest, are the bearded, hooded, harp, common and ringed seals. Of these, the skins of the bearded, harp and ringed seals are most commonly used for making clothing.

The bearded and harp seals migrate over great distances in the sea. They give birth to their young on ice floes off Newfoundland and Jan Mayen. The ringed seal remains in the fjords of Greenland and gives birth to its young in a hole dug into the snow just above the ice of the fjord. The young of these three seal species are born with a long, woolly fur which is shed within the first month, before they begin to swim. After this, during the first years, they alter appearance each time they moult. The Inuit, with their knowledge of the life and ways of seals, have special terms for the animals at each stage. There is a great difference in the appearance of the fur of the male and the female, and there are wide individual differences in colour and markings from seal to seal.

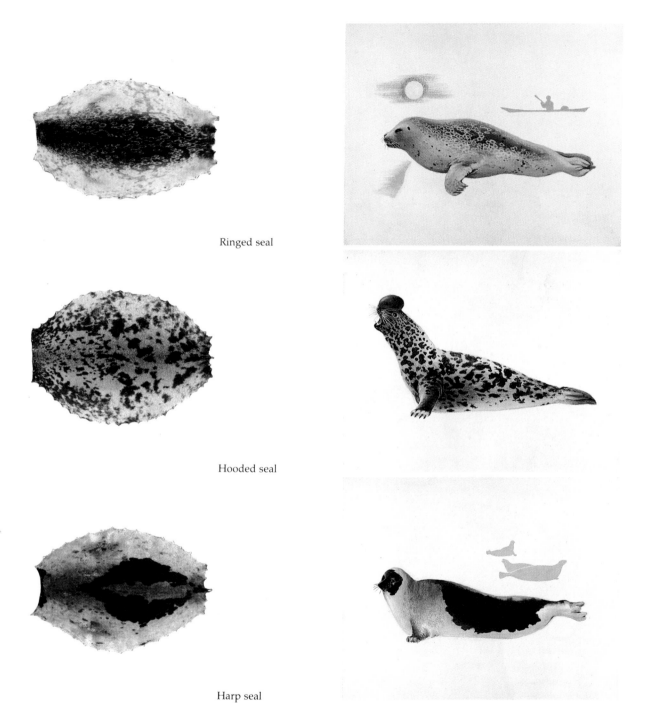

Ringed seal

Hooded seal

Harp seal

Fig. 109 Skins from these three seal types were the most important in the manufacture of Greenlandic furs.

Fig. 110 Fat being scraped off a harp sealskin. Egedesminde, West Greenland, 1918.

Right Fig. 111 Sealskin stretched out to dry. Nuugaag settlement, 1909.

The adult bearded seal is silvery- or bluish-grey, with black-spotted markings which can vary a great deal. The female is lighter in colour than the male, with less striking spots. The male may grow as long as 3.5 m, whereas the female is slightly smaller.

The harp seal ranges in colour from white to yellowish-grey, with a black saddle-shaped marking along its flanks, which merges above the shoulders opposite the front flippers. Its head is black. The markings of the female are less pronounced, and may, in fact, be lacking altogether or be replaced by black dots. The markings are not completely distinct until the animal is about five years old. The male can be up to 2 m long, and the female can be almost as large.

The ringed seal, which is the most important seal for the Greenland Inuit, has a wide range of colour combinations, running from light yellow to dark brown to black. All ringed seals have a light, whitish-grey underside, and characteristic dark spots surrounded by irregular light rings on their backs and flanks. This is the smallest seal species, measuring from 1.3 to 1.4 m in length.

In West Greenland it is a man's work to hunt seal. The work which follows, flensing, preparing the skin and so on is a woman's work. When she flenses the seal, she removes the skin and the blubber in one step and then cuts the blubber from the skin. The last bits of blubber are scraped off the skin as much as possible. This is hard work and much experience is needed to avoid damaging the skin.

To make the clothing, three different types of skin are used: ordinary skin (with the fur preserved), water skin (with the fur removed), and white skin (with both fur and epidermis removed). Ordinary skin is used for clothing, as the fur ensures good insulation. Water skin is virtually waterproof, and is used for summer clothing and kamiks. White skin is used primarily for embellishment, for example, as an ornamental edging. The entire outer jacket and

the kamiks may be made of white skin for festive occasions.

Ordinary skin is rinsed in water after the blubber has been cut away, scraped with a blunt ulu, and soaked in human urine for about twenty-four hours, which is supposed to remove the last traces of blubber. Today soapy water is used for this purpose. The skin is rinsed in water again and small holes are cut around the edges with an ulu. It is then laid out to dry, either stretched out in a frame or pegged out on the ground. When the skin is to be used, it is moistened on the flesh side, folded to make it flexible and then rubbed and stretched until completely soft.

In preparing water skin, the preliminary steps are the same, except that the skin is soaked in urine for a longer time, from three to five days. When it is removed, the hairs are plucked out with a blunt knife; ashes or sand may be sprinkled in the fur to provide a better grip. Today a detergent with enzymes is used instead of urine, and scouring powder instead of ashes, but the procedure is just

as demanding. After the preparatory stage the skin is scraped and rinsed, sometimes in salt water, and then stretched out to dry in the same way as ordinary skin. Skin which has been stretched on snow becomes the softest.

The Greenlandic word for plucking the hairs out is *erisaq*, 'the plucked'. The hair may also be cut off, in which case the word is *salisaq*. The stubble which remains makes the skin rough, which is an advantage when the skin is used for such things as kayak mittens. An alternative method of removing the hair is to place the skin in a skin bag containing blubber. After about six months the hair has loosened and can be brushed off.

The third type of skin, white skin, is at first treated like water skin, but when removed from the urine bath, the skin is dipped into hot water, after which the hair and epidermis are scraped or pulled off. The skin is then scraped with a blunt ulu, washed in urine and scraped again until all blubber has been removed. It is then soaked in water, which is

Fig. 112 Aleqasina softening skins from kamik soles. Thule district, 1909.

Right Fig. 113 Kamik ED 14 made of watertight sealskin from which all the fur has been removed.

changed regularly for a few days until it is clean and clear. The skin is then stretched out to dry.

The preparation of skin is an arduous, time-consuming task for the woman, and demands both skill and experience which has been passed down from generation to generation. There are many indications that this same procedure was used in the fifteenth century, from which we have examples of ordinary skin, water skin and white skin. For example, the crescent-shaped marks made by the ulu in the fine-cutting process when the Qilakitsoq skins were soaked, are clearly visible, and many of the unsewn skins had stretch holes along their edges, indicating that they were pegged out to dry.

SEWING

The tools which the fifteenth-century Inuit women used to flense, prepare, cut and sew skin consisted of an ulu, a needle, a needle case, a thimble and an awl. Various kinds of hooks, furrow bones, stone scrapers and pumice stones were also used.

The ulu differed somewhat in design from region to region in Greenland. However, all ulus had a crescent-shaped or slightly curved blade and a handle made of tooth, bone or wood. The ulu used for flensing, fine-cutting and tailoring skin was sharp; the ulu used for scraping and stretching was blunt.

Sewing needles were made either of iron, bone (such as bird-bone) or tooth. Before the Inuit came into contact with Europeans, the iron used for both men's and women's implements could sometimes be obtained in the northern part of West Greenland from iron meteors or from local iron. This iron was either cold-hammered or ground to the desired form. Needles were stuck into a piece of skin inside the needle case, which was usually made of walrus ivory. The awl, made of bone, was used for making holes in the skin.

A piece of skin worn as a ring was used as a thimble. The thimble and sinew-thread were kept on an anchor-shaped double hook. The furrow bone

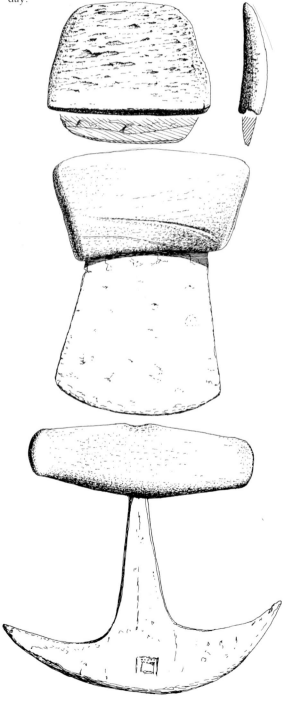

Fig. 114 Ulus, women's knives, from the Uummannaq district. *Top* A stone blade and whalebone grip, perhaps dating from the 15th century. *Middle* Large iron blade, used in the 17th and 18th centuries. *Bottom* Sickle-shaped iron blade, used from the 19th century to the present day.

was used to gather the tiny pleats at the toe and heel of the kamik.

When cutting out the skin, the women cut it from the flesh side diagonally against the hairs, which were not cut off but instead often used to cover the seam.

The thread used was made from the sinew of caribou, dolphin, narwhal or seal. The sinews were cleaned in sea water to wash off the blood and then scraped with an ulu. They were then soaked in sea water once again until completely clean. Next, they were split and hung to dry. Before use, they were moistened again and split further to the desired thickness. The women smoothed the threads by drawing them across their teeth. After being moistened with saliva, the sinews were twined by the woman rubbing them against her thigh or cheek. The end of the thread which was to be pulled through the eye of the needle was made very thin. To keep the thread flexible while sewing, the woman would pull it through her mouth now and then.

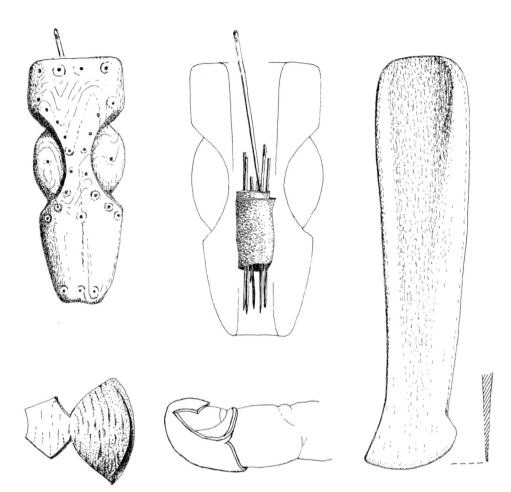

Fig. 115 Sewing implements. *Top left* A needle case, carved in walrus ivory and used from the 13th to 15th centuries; the needles lie in a piece of leather inside the case. *Bottom left* The thimble is leather and is worn round the fingertip. *Right* The boot-shaped bone knife is a furrow bone for working on the kamik. All from the Uummannaq district.

THE FINISHED GARMENTS

The outer parka is made of sealskin and consists of a front, back, shoulders, hood and sleeves.

The front is made of one sealskin with the dark skin of the seal's back running down the middle. The skin is cut off level with the woman's chest which, on a seal is just below the earholes, where the skin is narrowest. The entire width of the skin is used. The light-coloured fur of the belly is used for the sides of the parka. The armholes, which are extremely wide, are cut into the front of the parka, where the flippers of the seal were cut off. The skin is then cut off at the sides at the woman's waist and it tapers down the front into a narrow, pointed tail, reaching to about the knees.

The back is divided into three sections, with a narrow middle section made of the dark skin of the back of the seal. This tapers down into the back tail, which is longer and slightly wider than the front tail. At the top a deep U-shape is cut into the centre of the skin to allow for the hood. The sides of this U-shape continue in two narrow straps over the shoulders either side of the hood. The two side pieces of the back are made of light-coloured belly skin. Together with the shoulder pieces they form the back part of the armholes. They are connected with the front by a seam along the sides.

The two shoulder pieces are made of light-coloured belly skin. One end of each is joined to the front, and from there they go over the shoulders to the middle of the shoulder blades, where they meet the side pieces and the dark middle section of the back. The shoulder pieces are at their widest on the shoulders, where the width is further increased by the addition of a crescent-shaped piece by the sleeve. The two pieces are sewn together at the middle in the front after which they are joined to and divided

Fig. 116 Woman rolling sinew-thread on her cheek. Kronprinsens Eiland, Disko Bay, 1918.

by a chin piece. Together with the main front section, they form the front part of the armhole.

The hood is composed of two symmetrical halves of light-coloured skin joined at the middle by the insertion of a dark fur band about one centimetre wide. These skin pieces are cut to fit into the U-shaped neck opening of the back, and thus create a striking ornamental effect. In front the side pieces of the hood are elongated by two gussets which together form a U-shaped chin-piece. This is joined to the shoulder pieces. The hood is edged with a dark band of fur, the fur against the skin, which also edges the uppermost side of the chin-piece. The hood is quite high and remarkably narrow, especially in relation to the neck piece, where it must have left at least half the neck exposed.

The sleeves are made of the back skin of the seal and composed of two, three or four sections. They are extremely wide at the armhole, which is cut deep into the front and shoulder pieces, and makes the garment extremely narrow at the chest – only 22–25 cm wide. The large crescent-shaped curve at the top of the sleeve makes the underneath of the sleeve shorter than the top. There is a band at the wrist with an inset of light-coloured belly skin at the front forming part of the cuff.

The inner parka is made of bird-skin and is cut to the same pattern as the outer parka. However, in some instances the same basic elements are made up of innumerable small pieces of skin, such as that of the female eider. In other instances, larger, entire skins from various birds have been used. The Inuit clearly recognised the insulating effect of a number of layers of feathers, and bird-skins are used with the contour feathers intact. The inner parka closely duplicates the front and back pieces of the outer parka; both have tails in the front and back, shoulder pieces, hoods and sleeves. All free edges are set with bands of caribou skin.

The trousers are made either of caribou skin or sealskin with the fur turned outwards. The legs are either short or half-length. The trousers are made with two symmetrical halves joined by a centre seam. Most trousers have a waistband, and some have a belt at the waist to be tied at the back.

The kamiks, or boots, are made entirely of water-proof skin and consist of a leg and sole. The sole turns up around the sides of the foot and is gathered and joined to the kamik leg at the heel and toe. Along either side of the foot there is an ungathered area about 6 or 7 cm long. To the front of this area on both sides an eye is cut for a strap. In some instances this strap is attached. The leg of the boot has either one front seam or a seam both at the front and back, and there may be various pieces of skin attached both at the top and bottom. It seems as if the kamiks were made of left-over pieces of skin, for right and left ones are rarely identical. The front seam sometimes runs straight to the sole with no ankle piece; other times it runs to the sides of foot. The kamik leg may go straight up and end in a band with a facing and strap which is laced at the back; or it may widen towards the top and end in a band without a strap; or it may end without a band altogether. Some kamiks are very carefully sewn, with front and back gatherings which are small works of art; others are very loosely sewn.

The kamik stockings are made either of sealskin or of caribou skin, worn with the fur side inward. The pattern is the same as for the kamiks – the sole is turned up and gathered at the front and back, but the pleats are larger and fewer here than on the kamik. There may be a casing at the top with an

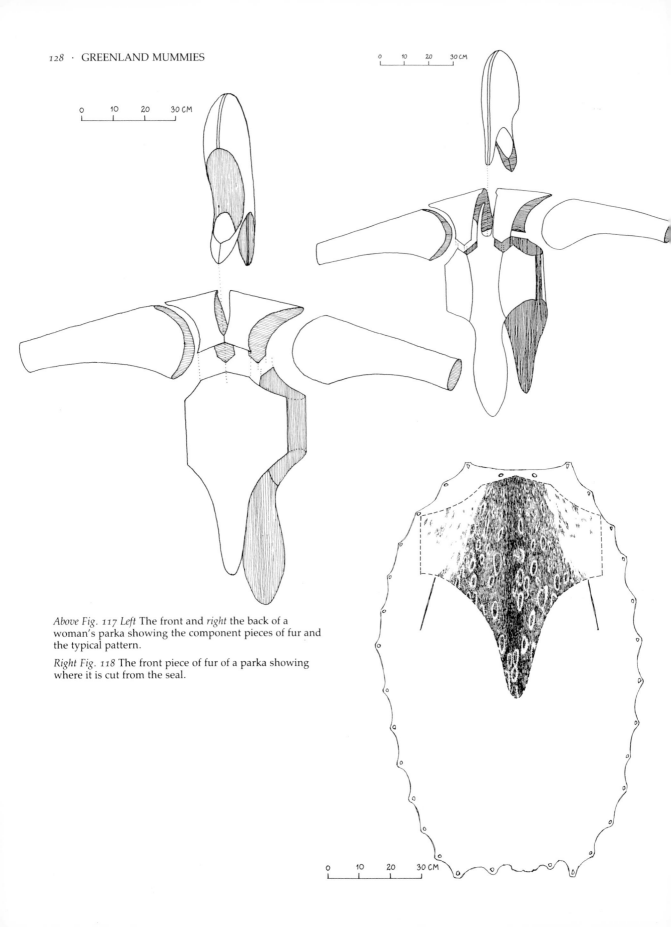

Above Fig. 117 Left The front and *right* the back of a woman's parka showing the component pieces of fur and the typical pattern.

Right Fig. 118 The front piece of fur of a parka showing where it is cut from the seal.

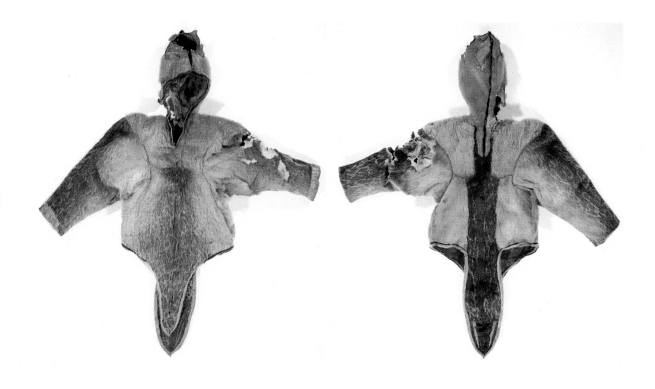

Above Fig. 119 Left The front and *right* the back of a parka ED 28.

Below Fig. 120 Trousers ED 13 of reindeer skin.

Right Fig. 121 Top The front and *bottom* the back of a pair of short sealskin trousers ED 12. Symmetrical halves are sewn together in the middle and each comprises ten different pieces of fur, for decorative purposes.

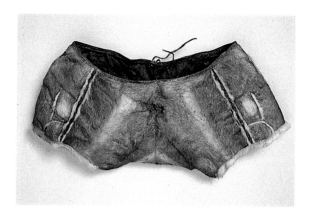

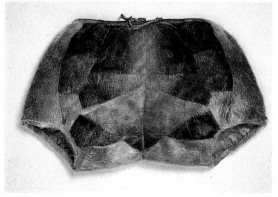

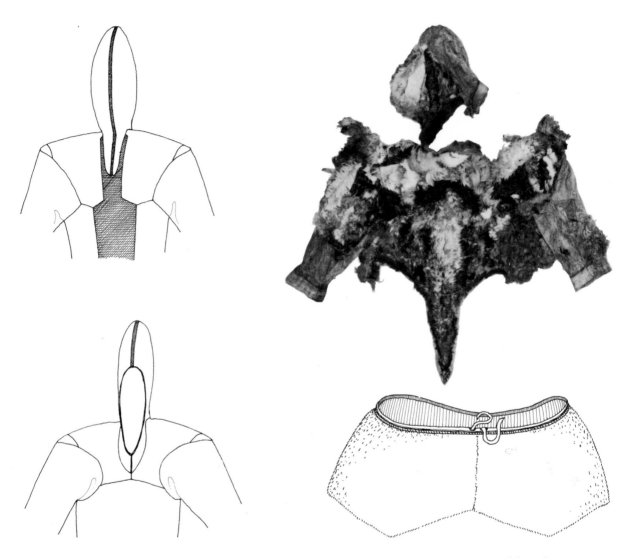

attached strap; or a band of inward-facing fur terminating either with or without a band. The leg is joined to the sole either at the front or both at the front and back. Stockings sewn of sealskin always have the back of the skin towards the back of the stocking and are shaped to the calf of the leg. The sole is nearly always made of light-coloured belly-skin with the fur pointing to the front.

Above, left Fig. 122 The back, *top*, and front, *bottom*, sections of a parka illustrating the particular cut that allowed freedom of movement – large armholes and a small chest section.

Above, top Fig. 123 Mummy II/7's inner parka of bird-skin. Compare with Fig. 125.

Above Fig. 124 Basic type of short trousers.

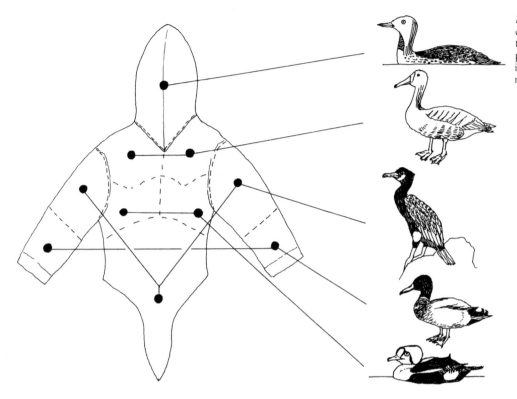

Fig. 125 The five different birds and their corresponding positions in the inner parka of mummy II/7.

Table of all the articles of clothing.

Type of clothing	Mummy I/1	I/2	I/3	I/4	I/5	II/6	II/7	II/8	No. of garments	Loose garments	Total
Parkas											
outer	*	*	*	*	*	*	*	*	8	7	15
inner		*	*	*	*	*	*	*	7	1	8
intermediate								*	1		1
Trousers											
outer	*	*	*	*	*	*	*	*	8	3	11
inner						*			1		1
Footwear											
kamiks		*	*	*	*	*	*	*	14	5	19
stockings		*	*	*	*	*	*	*	14	7	21
Half sleeves										2	2
Total									53	25	78

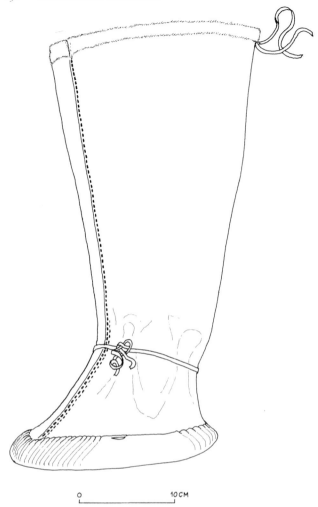

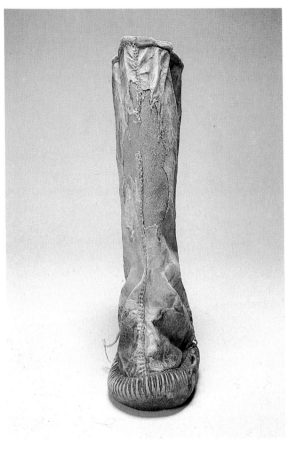

Fig. 126 Left A typical kamik. *Right* Kamik ED 15 made of furless sealskin.

Conservation

On preliminary examination, the Qilakitsoq find revealed little. The clothing and skins were dry, stiff, extremely dirty and thickly covered by mould. It was impossible to measure and describe the garments and to determine absolutely the skin types used, although most of the clothing seemed to consist of sealskin and bird-skin. The conservation process therefore had not only to keep the material from perishing but also to straighten out the skins by soaking them, cleaning them thoroughly and drying them without shrinkage. This was an enormous and most difficult task for the conservation experts, and the first time material of this sort had been treated. Thus, prior to the conservation itself a number of

studies had to be made to ascertain the condition of preservation and to determine whether or not the skins had been tanned. The experiments made were to lead to a method of treating the skins to make them soft enough to work with.

Like human skin, animal skin consists of the epidermis (the outer layer), dermis (the inner layer) and subcutaneous fatty tissue. The dermis consists mainly of collagen and a semifluid ground substance. Collagen is made of thread-like fibres, composed of protein. These fibres make the skin tough and strong. Between the fibres is the ground substance, which binds water and lies like a gel between the fibre bunches. This ground substance makes the skin soft and supple. Specimens of the skin clothing were biochemically investigated to determine the content of collagen and ground substance. This investigation was made to ascertain whether the five-hundred-year-old skins had been treated in the same way as modern skins from the Uummannaq district, that is, whether they had been scraped, washed and dried. Another question was whether biochemical methods could reveal how well the finer structures of the skins were in fact preserved.

Comparison of the skins found in the graves with specimens of new skins of the same seal species which had been treated in the Uummannaq district by scraping, washing, stretching and drying, showed that both old and new skins had an identical content of collagen and ground substance, thus indicating that the old skins had been treated in the same manner as the new ones. The results of the investigation also revealed that the skins were dry when they were placed in the graves, and that they remained dry until they were discovered five centuries later: as long as skin is kept dry, its collagen and ground substance levels remain unchanged, and its appearance is preserved with intact fur, a light colour on the flesh side and a flexible consistency. If skin gets damp, the ground substance deteriorates first, and the collagen later and the skin does not preserve well: it becomes thin and dark, with loose fur or no fur at all, and the consistency is brittle.

A preliminary analysis of the skins from the graves showed that they were all untanned. Such untanned skin is well suited to the dry, cold, arctic climate. Although untanned skin usually becomes hard and stiff when it dries after having been wet, the Inuit knew how to care for their skin clothing to keep it soft and supple.

It was decided to tan the skins with alum, a method which gave the finest results. The skins were placed in solution baths which made them supple. It was then possible to clean the skins and stretch them, and the best preserved areas thus regained their original elasticity. After the skins had dried no shrinkage could be ascertained. However, a certain modest shrinkage must have occurred during the five hundred years in which they lay in the graves. After tanning, which restored, preserved, and softened the skin, facilitating examination, it was possible to measure most of the garments and describe them. After they were restored, the best preserved garments were mounted on dummies.

However, unlike the separate pieces of clothing, the costumes which the mummies were actually wearing could not be soaked and tanned. The fluid used to clean this apparel softened the skins and coatings. The tractable skins could then be straightened out and cleaned, after which they dried, without shrinkage.

The skins of different animal species evince characteristics: the thickness of the skin, the nature of the fur, and the strength and suppleness of the dermis. Biochemical investigations of the collagen and the ground substance of the untanned dermis showed that the ringed seal and the harp seal, two closely related species, had small but marked differences in their chemical composition. Electrophoresis, a special study of the ground substance, provides a sort of fingerprint which can reveal whether an untanned, unhaired sealskin is from one of the two seal species. This method may perhaps be developed to allow for the general identification of untanned, unhaired skin.

The amount and composition of the collagen of the dermis also vary from species to species, although less characteristically than the ground substance. Biochemical examination after tanning showed that the ground substance is washed out in the tanning fluids used. Collagen, which is in fact the material which is tanned, does not change in composition. Thus after tanning it is not possible to utilise studies dealing with ground substance to determine the animal species.

Fig. 127 Sealskin fur ED 78 prior to softening and conservation.

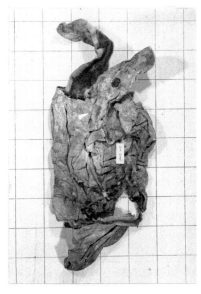

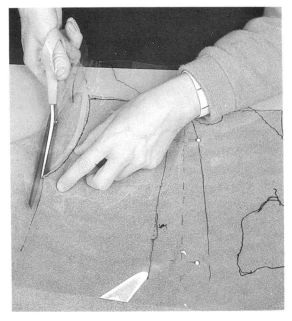
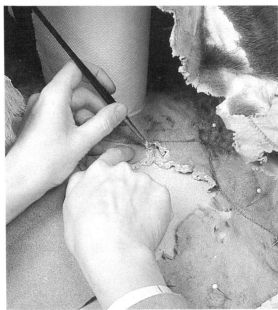

Above Fig. 128 After restoration of the sealskin fur, the missing parts are reproduced and added.

Left Fig. 129 Parka ED 27 before and after restoration.

RADIATION

As mentioned above, it was not possible to tan the clothes worn by the mummies, and so once they were cleaned no more examinations were to be carried out. But preventative measures had to be taken against the micro-organisms such as fungus and bacteria which continued to decompose the mummified material. In France, the mummy of Pharaoh Ramesses II (who died in about 1225 BC) had been cleansed of micro-organisms by irradiation, and so it was decided to carry out a similar treatment on the four best preserved, dressed mummies which are now on exhibition in the Greenland National Museum.

Gamma radiation, ionising radiation emitted from the artificial isotope Cobalt 60, was the chosen method because for a number of years it has been used for conservation and sterilisation (mainly of pharmaceutical products such as disposable hypodermic syringes). This particular method has no danger of making the irradiated object radioactive because the energy of the rays is so small that they are not strong enough to convert the atoms of which the material is composed to radioactive particles. Therefore, the material can be handled after irradiation with no risk whatsoever.

Before the actual irradiation of the mummies was made, a number of irradiation experiments were made on specimens of the poorly preserved mummy skins and sealskin. After irradiation any changes in colour and consistency which may have occurred were to be evaluated. But none of the specimens showed signs of change after having been irradiated, and so it was decided to irradiate completely the four mummies.

Before being irradiated, the mummies were carefully packed in cheesecloth, plastic bags and cardboard boxes. The irradiation process itself took place in a gamma radiation plant used for irradiating pharmaceutical products and laboratory equipment. In one special section of the irradiation room it is possible to irradiate extremely large boxes. Here there is a sort of surplus irradiation from the ordinary irradiation of the products themselves. The gamma rays have an extremely high penetration capacity, which is utilised particularly in the sterilisation of pre-packed products. This penetration capacity made it possible to irradiate the mummies in their packaging, as the rays go through both wrappings and bodies.

The amount of radiation which an object receives is called the *dose*, and it is measured in units called

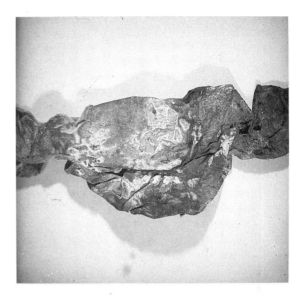

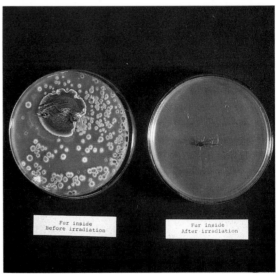

Above, top Fig. 130 White, fungal coatings were found on the exposed body surfaces, clothing and skins.

Above Fig. 131 Left A petri dish with pronounced growth of fungal organisms from a piece of fur prior to radiation. *Right* Fungal growth from an irradiated piece of fur, evidence of how such growth ceases after radiation.

rad (one million rad = one Megarad). On the basis of the irradiation of Ramesses II and preliminary experiments with specimens of mummy skin and sealskin it was decided to operate with a dose of about two Megarads. The irradiation time necessary to give the dose mentioned was determined prior to the actual irradiation, so that no part of the mummies was irradiated more or less than intended.

After irradiation the mummies, still in cardboard boxes, were placed in wooden boxes and sent to Nuuk. Here, at the Greenland National Museum, the mummies were unpacked in conditions as free from bacteria and germs as possible, and then put into bacteria-free exhibition cases.

Other mummy finds in Greenland

Along the west coast of Greenland, graves containing mummified corpses with partially preserved clothing had been found before the Qilakitsoq find, but none contained nearly as well-preserved garments for adults. The graves found earlier seem to date from a later period than the Qilakitsoq graves, ranging from one or two hundred years after the sixteenth century up to the introduction, at some time in the eighteenth century, of the Christian burial custom which decreed that the dead be buried in the ground in a coffin and covered with earth or pebbles. No radiocarbon datings of these graves have been made.

Two of the more notable mummy finds were made in rock caves in South Greenland. On the island of Uunartoq, just north of Nanortalik, local inhabitants knew of caves containing the bodies of many adults and children. Legend had it that these dead stemmed from the time when there were still Norsemen in the country: when the Greenlanders on the island heard that the Norsemen planned to attack them, those who could fled in umiaks and kayaks; the rest hid in the caves behind the settlement of Qerrortut, where they starved to death. In 1930 an American anthropologist, Martin Luther, visited the area. Luther had received a telegram from the Danish National Museum permitting him to open ancient graves and take a few skeletons to Harvard University. Unfortunately, he discovered the caves at Uunartoq, of which there were three, and removed most of the mummies.

In 1934 the Danish archaeologist Therkel Mathiassen arrived at the same site. Mathiassen described the three caves and the finds which were left. Two of the caves were really just small shelters below boulders, quite similar to Qilakitsoq, whereas the third was a much larger cave with several rooms and passages. Although the finds had been disturbed, it was evident that they were burials. There were remains of stone graves and traces of at least seven bodies. Some grave goods, including implements and ornaments, indicated that some of the

dead had probably been buried in the sixteenth century.

Very few items of clothing were left in the caves: some kamiks and pieces of seal, caribou, dog and bird-skin. However, one single grave was completely intact. This consisted of an oval stone circle (50 × 40 cm), placed on a boulder, which contained three small sealskin bundles. The remains of a child's kayak lay by the grave. When the bundles were unpacked at the National Museum in Copenhagen, they proved to contain three infants, all of whom were just a few months old. Because of the poor state of preservation, it was possible to ascertain only that one child was dressed in a hoodless sealskin parka, the second wore a bird-skin parka and sealskin stockings, and the third a gut shirt with a hood.

Fig. 132 Three child mummies wrapped in sealskins. Found in a cave near the settlement of Qerrortuut on Uunartoq Island, South Greenland.

The second notable cave find with mummified corpses was made in the Nuuk area. Beneath the steep Pisissarfik mountains on the Kapisillit Fjord lies the settlement of Iffiartarfik with the ruins of a Norse farm and an Inuit settlement. A great many graves lie on the mountainside, among fallen boulders. These graves were visited and partially investigated by the Danish National Museum in 1945 and 1952.

Here too, local tradition links the graves to the conflicts between the Inuit and the Norsemen. As late as 1952, Old Jacob, an Inuit from the salmon river at Kapisillit related:

Up there in the caves you can find Norsemen who were buried after the last fight, which took

Fig. 133 The steep rock face of Pississarfik, near Godthaab, at the foot of which are some mummy graves. Woodcut illustrating the outcome of a contest between a Norseman and an Inuk – the Norseman lost and fell over the cliff. Cut by Greenland artist and seal hunter Aron of Kangeq, 1859.

place at the foot of Pisissarfik. It's also said that the troubles began here. One man from each side, good friends and good bowmen, were up on top of the mountain, competing to see who could hit a stretched-out sealskin down by the shore of the fjord. The Inuit won and pushed the Norseman over the edge of the mountain, for they had agreed that to be the fate of the loser. That's why this place is called Pisissarfik, which means 'the shooting place'.

However, the graves were actually Inuit. One of them contained three children, all less than a year old. Another resembled in some ways those at Qilakitsoq and consisted of a large heap of stones topping a small burial chamber (1.1 × 0.65 m), containing two women and two children. On a soft matting of grass and twigs lay three caribou skin bundles, one on top of the other. The bottom bundle was partially disintegrated, and the skull of an old woman with badly worn teeth lay on the ground. Apart from fragments of skins from seal, caribou and bird, only the toes of the kamiks remained.

The other two bundles were opened at the National Museum in Copenhagen. The middle bundle, which was the largest, proved to contain a young woman and a child. The woman lay with her knees folded up to her chest. Only at her head and limbs were her garments fairly intact. The head shows that she had originally worn both an inner and an outer parka of sealskin. The hood was high and had a narrow band of black sealskin sewn into the centre seam. The shoulders were wide. The outer trousers of sealskin were very long and quite unusual: their lower edge hangs below the knee to the upper edge of the stocking, where they seem to have a bag hanging down between the kamik and the stocking. This costume may have been identical in type to that which we see in the painting of four Inuit captured in the Nuuk area in 1654 (see Fig. 138). The only difference is that the women in the painting are not wearing long outer trousers. It was probably this type of trouser which the priest and historiographer Lyschander described in 1608 in his *Greenland Chronicle*: 'And many pairs of Stockings they wear/And Knife, Needle, and Thread they do

keep there/And other things they wish not to leave behind.' These trousers are similar to those which until recently were worn by Inuit in central arctic Canada, and which had a baggy part at the knee where small implements were stored.

Inside the skin wrapping of the young woman there lay two children's parkas made of bird-skin and a smaller skin bundle containing a child barely a year old. The outer parka is made of sealskin, the inner one of bird-skin, and the trousers are of long-haired dog-skin, drawn down over a pair of long caribou-skin stockings.

The small skin bundle which lay uppermost in the grave also contained a child, between eight and ten months old, who wears an outer parka of caribou skin with front and back flaps. The inner parka is made of caribou skin, but a bird-skin parka was

Above Fig. 135 Kamiks on the young woman in the graves at Pississarfik, excavated in 1952.

Above, left Fig. 134 Child from the bundle of skins which also contained a young woman. From the graves at Pississarfik, excavated in 1952.

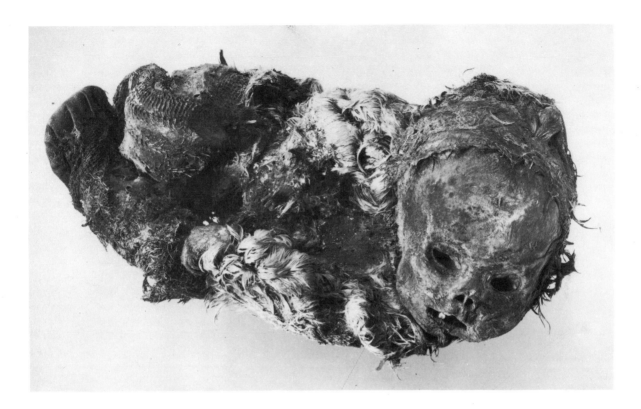

Fig. 136 Child dressed in furs and kamiks of bird-skin. From the graves at Pississarfik, excavated in 1952.

placed over the legs as an extra layer of clothing, a sort of undershirt. One trouser leg is short and the other long, and they go down to, respectively, a knee-length caribou-skin stocking and a short caribou-skin shoe.

These mummified corpses at Pisissarfik were buried without grave gifts which could have revealed the time of the burial. No carbon–14 dating has been made, but the graves are probably from the sixteenth or seventeenth century. They are definitely pre-Christian, and so earlier than 1749, the year in which Whitsunday services were held at the foot of the Pisissarfik mountain.

Dress in later times

The first known drawing of an Inuit dates from 1539, when the Swedish archbishop Olaus Magnus published a learned work in Latin, *Carta Marina*, which included a woodcut showing an Inuit fighting with a European (see Fig. 7). The picture shows a bearded 'pygmy' with a wide-brimmed hat, uncharacteristic of an Inuit, facing a large European; the background is a map of Greenland. Apparently the artist had only an old report of the small pygmy-like Skraelings (the Norse term for Inuit) on which to base his picture.

In the sixteenth century, a century after the era of the Qilakitsoq mummies, the first fairly naturalistic depictions appeared in Europe. The oldest of these is the picture of the woman and child who were captured on the coast of Labrador in 1566. This woodcut, printed on a handbill in Augsburg, Germany, advertised an exhibition of the two Inuit, who had apparently already been displayed in Holland and France. The text printed on the picture describes the capture, which was most dramatic. The woman was said to be twenty years old and the child seven when captured by Frenchmen in August 1566. The woman's costume was apparently 'made of sealskin, as shown in this picture'. Comparison with the clothing of the Qilakitsoq women reveals similar features such as the high hood, the parka with long flaps and the large kamiks.

A few years later Greenland was re-discovered by an English expedition led by Martin Frobisher. In

1576 Frobisher sailed past South Greenland, continuing west in his search for the Northwest Passage. In 1577 he returned and explored the coast of southwest Greenland by ship, meeting the inhabitants of the country along the way. The expedition then continued on to Canada, where, after fighting with the Inuit on Baffin Land, a man and a woman were captured. In England in 1577, these Inuit were portrayed in naturalistic, coloured drawings made by John White, a respected contemporary artist and a member of the expedition (Fig. 137).

White's picture shows a mother and child, the child looking out through the hood opening from its position in a bag on its mother's back. The band under the woman's breast holds the jacket together and the bag and child in place. The woman has tattoos on her face. Her parka has features similar to the Qilakitsoq clothing, particularly the short front flap and the long back flap extending all the way to the heels. The brownish-red colour of the jacket indicates that it is made of caribou skin. The kamiks are long, and the skin stockings reach a little further up the thighs.

After the English had reached Greenland in 1576, the Danish king Christian IV reacted by sending out expeditions in 1605 and 1606 to claim sovereignty over the old Norwegian–Danish possessions in the North Atlantic. On returning to Denmark, the navigator of the expedition reported encounters with Inuit, 'five of whom we captured with their boats and kept in our ship'. But in total, nine Greenland Inuit were brought to Denmark. One of these was selected for study by the chancellor and historian Arild Huitfeldt; others were dressed up with rapiers and hats with ostrich feathers to serve as popular entertainment, 'quite as if they were the grandees of Greenland'. However, these Inuit soon died of various causes: some perished because of 'homesickness'; one while attempting to return home to Greenland in his kayak; another while pearl-fishing in Kolding Fjord; and the last from 'grief'.

Lyschander wrote a description in verse of these Inuit in which their clothing is mentioned. We learn that the costume was made of grey sealskin with hoods and wide flaps, and many pairs of stockings were worn. Some of their garments, made of gut, sealskin and bird-skin, were given, together with a kayak and hunting implements, to the Ole Worm Museum in Copenhagen, but the remaining clothing has since vanished.

The best source of information about Inuit dress in Greenland in the seventeenth century is the painting made in 1654 of the four Inuit from the Nuuk area (see Fig. 138). In 1652 King Frederik III had re-established connections between his kingdom and Greenland. The king granted special permission to a Danish trading company to sail to the country which 'for many years had been unused and unknown', and to 'enjoy and use everything with which the Lord has blessed this land'. This monopoly was to be valid for thirty years, but only three summer voyages were in fact made, between 1652 and 1654 with David Dannell as captain. The expedition traded with the Inuit of the west coast, thus acquiring such prized items as skins, and walrus and narwhal ivory. Ethnographic objects were also collected for the king's cabinet of curiosities, and some of these hunting implements are still preserved at the National Museum in Copenhagen.

It was during the last voyage that the Inuit were captured. On the way back to Denmark the ship called at Bergen in Norway where the painting was probably made. Although the artist has not been identified, it must have been one of the very competent portrait painters of the day. The costumes seem to be depicted precisely and realistically. Of course, in studying the painting for comparison with the mummy clothing, it might be wished that some important details were shown more clearly, but who can reasonably demand instructive sewing patterns of the first artist to portray the legendary Skraelings from Greenland? In Bergen the Inuit were probably still remembered as having been the bane of the Norsemen between 1300 and 1500.

Their faces are peaceful but full of character, and the tattoos of the women are carefully depicted. All four are dressed in summer clothing. The man wears only his inner jacket, the fur of which is worn against the body; he stands with his bladder-spear for hunting seals from a kayak, and a bow and arrows for hunting caribou. The woman in the foreground is wearing a parka which is almost identical with those of the Qilakitsoq mummies. The hood is particularly characteristic. The trousers, however, present more of a problem: they are unusually short, and even if one imagines the wrinkled boots pulled up over the knees, a good part of the thighs would still be left bare. The explanation must be that these are inner trousers; perhaps the outer trousers were lost during the voyage, or perhaps the women were led aboard ship on a warm summer day, leaving their outer trousers behind in the tent.

During the voyage from Bergen to Copenhagen, the Inuit man died of disease. The women were

immediately sent on to the king in Flensburg in the southernmost part of Denmark: a plague was ravaging Copenhagen that year, and the king preferred to hold court as far away as possible. He sent the women on to the Duke of Gottorp, where the learned and well-travelled Adam Olearius was staying. Olearius' studies of the Greenlanders resulted in a whole new chapter in a new edition of his *Beschreibung der muscowitischen und persischen Reise*

from 1656. Here we find the first detailed depiction of Greenland Inuit in general, their customs, means of subsistence, language – and dress. The text describes the Inuit dress thus:

> As for their clothing, it is made of sealskin and caribou skin, the fur of which is turned outward, as seen among the Samoyeds.
> They are lined on the inside with birdskin,

Opposite Fig. 138 Four Greenland Inuit captured in the Godthaab Fjord by a Danish expedition led by David Dannell in 1654. Artist unknown.

Fig. 139 Maria of Frederikshaab, South Greenland. 1747. See also Fig. 94.

mainly that of swans, wild geese, ducks, and seagulls. In the summer they also wear the feathers outwards.

Men and women are dressed nearly alike. They have close-fitting trousers and jackets, as well as foot-length shirts or tight shirts which extend about to their posterior.

At the top there is a neck opening and a hood (as on a munk's robe). However there is one difference: the man's hood fits the head closely, whereas that of the woman continues about one foot higher, because they fix their hair

elaborately, and their topknot sticks up in the air. The woman's jacket has a long flap in front and back reaching all the way down to the knees, a flap which the man does not have, as seen in the engraving.

The men's trousers go to their knees and sometimes lower; in contrast, the women's end uppermost on the thigh, and hardly cover the buttocks. From the trousers down to the boots which only go up to about a handsbreadth below the knees, they are quite naked.

Their shirts, cut out of tanned sealskin and beautifully sewn, barely reach their rear end. These shirts are called *Kapissil*.

Olearius added a copperplate etching of the four Inuit in the middle of his text (Fig. 140). This etching was made from a drawing which in turn was based on the painting. The figures are posed in the same way but have been moved around, and the woman with the high hood has been turned so that her back is partly visible. Olearius' intention was to display the details of the costume, and here he can show that there is also a long hanging flap in the back. Apparently he also wished to show a special feature of the kamiks which the painter had not noticed (if these are in fact the same boots): there seems to be a triangular extension of the top edge of the kamik. A modern version of this element has been found among Canadian Inuit west of the Hudson Bay. In Olearius' picture it looks like this point can be pulled up and tied at the knee, perhaps to the trousers. The trousers in the etching, incidentally, are longer than in the painting; perhaps the women told Olearius that they ought to be properly dressed, with outer trousers as well. However, there is some discrepancy between Olearius' illustration and text.

Olearius, a humane scholar, remarked in his work that it was the king's intention to send the women back to Greenland once they had learned the language and teachings of the Christian religion. However, no more ships sailed to Greenland during the reign of the king. The Inuit lived in Copenhagen for some years until they died of typhus fever. By then, says another source, 'they had learned Danish well and had become well-behaved'.

King Frederik III felt that the four Inuit were so interesting that he had them portrayed in sculptures of gold and silver. These figures were set on a goblet and a drinking mug, two superb pieces of craftsmanship, which undoubtedly attracted much attention at the royal table. The objects are kept in the Royal Collections at Rosenborg Castle, Copenhagen.

Both the goblet and the tankard can with great probability be attributed to Jacob Jensen Nordmand, a royal craftsman. Although Nordmand probably knew the three Inuit women, his figures were clearly inspired by the picture in Olearius' work. However, Nordmand did not pay heed to the text regarding the difference between male and female dress.

The figure on the goblet is the woman Kuneling, the Gunnelle of the painting, with the characteristic finger pointing downward, who here appears as a hunter with the bow of the man Jhiob. The spear in Jhiob's left hand has been replaced by the tooth of a unicorn (narwhal), one of Greenland's most prized treasures. The sides and the lid are made of this material which, according to contemporary belief, prevented attempts at poisoning the drink in both the goblet and the tankard. The figure is also furnished with a quiver, a new and undoubtedly naturalistic addition. Both the quiver and the costume bear distinct dark spots, an indication that the skin was that of a ringed seal. This figure allows us to see the back of the costume, with the long tail and the way the hood was seamed with a seemingly darker strip of skin – identical to the garments of the Qilakitsoq mummies. The enamelled gold sculpture is only 8 cm high, but the artist has managed to reproduce many characteristic details.

The tankard is mounted with gilt silver. The Inuit is the piece by which the lid is lifted, and sits with a fish (as in the painting from 1656). However, the most important accessory is a unicorn tooth, and the three legs of the tankard are shaped like unicorns. This is again a man dressed in female clothing with a high hood and short inner trousers which the three women wore to Europe. Nordmand took this artistic liberty, although in the silver plate on the lid of the same tankard he copied and engraved the man and the woman on the right of Olearius' picture.

Despite the confusion of male and female elements, these figures contribute to our knowledge of the history of dress in Greenland. Engraved in the gold plate with the figure on the lidded goblet is the monogram of Frederik III and the date, 1663. Both the artist and the king could compare the sculpture with the live models, and no doubt they desired a naturalistic representation of the costumes.

In early colonial times of Greenland, after Hans Egede had come to Greenland in 1721, Inuit dress was often mentioned by missionaries and merchants, and a few small, rather simple drawings of women's clothing have been preserved. However, the best illustration is once again a painting, showing a Greenland woman who lived in Copenhagen. This woman had voluntarily left Frederikshaab in South Greenland to accompany a Norwegian priest to Denmark and Norway. She was in Copenhagen in 1746, where she served as a valued assistant to Hans Egede's son, Poul Egede, in his work of compiling the first dictionary of the Greenlandic language. In

Opposite Fig. 140 The four Inuit depicted in Fig. 138. Engraving by Adam Olearius in 1656, accompanied by a description of the costumes.

Kleider der Grünländer.

Ihre Kleidung betreffend / seynd dieselben aus Seehunden Fellen vnd Renthieren Häuten gemachet / vnd daß rauche / gleich der Samojeden / heraus gekehret; Inwendig seynd sie mit Vogel Fellen / sonderlich von Schwanen / wilden Gänsen / Enten vnd Meven gefuttert / des Sommers kehren sie auch die Federn heraus. Männer vnd Weiber gehen fast über ein gekleidet / haben enge Hosen vnd LeibRöcke / als wie Futterhembde / oder enge Köller / gehen kaum biß ans Gesesse / oben ist Halß vnd Haube dran (wie an den Münche Kappen) bey welchen doch dieser Unterscheid: Den Männers lieget die Haube plat auff dem Kopffe / den Weibern aber gehet sie fast eine hal=

Der Kleider unterscheid.

be Elle höher / vnd solches wegen ihrer Art die Haare auffzubinden / welche mitten auff dem Kopffe in die höhe stehen. Den Weibern henget an dem Leib= Rocke hinten vnd forne ein langer Zippel / biß zu deu Kniehen herunter / welches die Männer nicht haben / wie in der Figur zu sehen. Der Männer Ho= sen gehen biß zu den Kniehen / auch etlichen drunter; der Weiber aber hören weit über den Kniehen am dicken Fleische auff / also / daß sie kaum das Gesesse darinnen bedecken können. Von den Hosen an biß zu den Stieffeln / so auch nur eine Handbreit biß vnter das Kniehe gehen / seynd sie gantz bloß.

Hembde.

Ihre Hembden seynd von auffgeschnittenen vnd gedrögeten Därmen der Sehlhunde gemachet / welche Riemenweise subtiel zusammen genehet / gehen auch kaum biß ans Gesesse / heissen Kapissil.

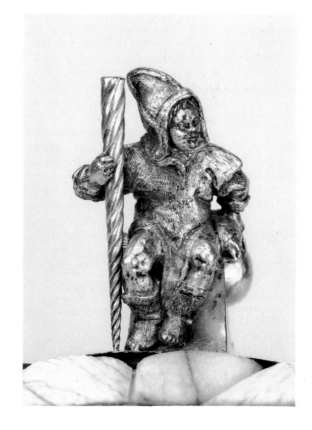

Fig. 143 The lid of the mug in Fig. 142. It is a circular, gilded silver plate engraved with two of the Inuit, and is inspired by Olearius' engraving.

1747 this woman, Maria, was painted by Mathias Blumenthal. The details are set forth in a painted text on the back of the painting at the Danish National Museum, signed by Blumenthal in 1753. The first version of the painting has disappeared.

The painter has obviously taken pains to make a realistic portrait of Maria. Her tattoos are carefully depicted, as described in chapter 5. The characteristic topknot is tied up with a red hairband. For the first time there is evidence of the way women indicated their status, as described by Europeans in early colonial days: widows wore black ribbons, married women wore blue ones, unmarried women with children wore green ones, and red ribbons indicated virgins such as Maria.

Maria's elegant costume includes an unusually long jacket with tongue-shaped flaps and very wide shoulders. This style more closely resembles cos-

Pages 146, 147 Top, left and right Fig. 141 Cup made of narwhale ivory and gold. The subject of the enamelled gold figure is one of the four Inuit brought back by Dannell in 1654 from the Godthaab Fjord (Fig. 138), and is based on Olearius' engraving (Fig. 140). Engraved date 1663. H. 33 cm.

Page 147 Bottom, left and right Fig. 142 Mug made of narwhal ivory and gilded silver. The mug and the cup display the oldest European sculptures of Greenland Inuit. The seated figure is a man dressed in a woman's costume, again inspired by Olearius' engraving. Date unknown. H. 19.6 cm.

tumes which have been preserved from the nineteenth century. The rather tight-fitting jacket and the narrow kamiks have evolved far from the old voluminous clothing worn by the Qilakitsoq women and the three women in the painting from 1654.

The earliest preserved woman's clothing (Fig. 144) from West Greenland was registered at the National Museum in Copenhagen in 1844 as 'An ordinary female costume'. However, such an extraordinarily richly ornamented costume as this one, with both the parka and trousers made from caribou skin, from the Attu settlement near Egedesminde could hardly have been owned by every woman. The front of the parka, which has been divided by a centre seam for ornamental reasons, continues up over both shoulders to the back section. There are thus no shoulder pieces, as in the Qilakitsoq parka. The complicated back section consists of a centre panel and narrow side panels. The cut and the seams are emphasised by sewing in strips and small squares of white and brown skin, and the distinct edgings emphasise the elegant shape of the flaps, which are here reduced to modest tongues. The sleeves are shorter, as seen in women's dress of later times.

The trousers and kamiks are long and narrow. In the kamik, a triangular or tongue-shaped knee piece has been inserted, an element which became popular all along the coast up to the present. Several explanations have been offered for the inclusion of this knee piece, called *serquaq* in Greenlandic. As a rule it is emphasised by an edging made of a light piece of skin. One scholar suggests it to be an element in the ancient skeleton ornamentation, intended to distinguish the knee and the soul which inhabits this joint. Another possible explanation is that this knee piece was included for practical reasons, because this part of the boot is easily worn and ought to be easily replaceable. However, this latter explanation is obviously a European one, as it does not take into consideration the fact that the Greenlandic hunter's wife rarely kneels when she works; the typical working position is sitting or standing with knees extended. Perhaps the explanation of the origin of the knee piece is found in the Qilakitsoq kamiks: one of the kamiks is cut in a V-shape above the knee and has a gusset extending downwards which could very easily develop into an ornamental knee piece.

Finally, the most recent woman's costume which can shed light on the Qilakitsoq clothing and the history of dress in West Greenland is a sealskin costume which illustrates the long and vigorous

it is for ornamental reasons only that the skin has been cut in half and sewn together again with a strip of skin mosaic. The front is connected by means of the shoulder section to the back, which consists of three parts: a narrow middle part of dark skin, which extends downwards into a flap and divides into two branches at the top which enclose the root of the hood. Sewn to the centre panel there are two broad side panels, which meet the shoulder pieces at the armholes. This cut was also used by the people of Qilakitsoq, and it is preserved in some Canadian Inuit jackets. Perhaps this type of parka may be regarded as the original type, going back a thousand years in the history of Greenland dress, to the first Inuit who migrated with the Thule culture from Canada to Greenland.

Left Fig. 144 The oldest woman's costume from West Greenland. From the Attu settlement near Egedesminde, about 1840.

Below Fig. 145 The cut on the back of a woman's costume. This costume displays the same basic traits as the costumes of the Qilakitsoq mummies, despite the time lapse. West Greenland, about 1880.

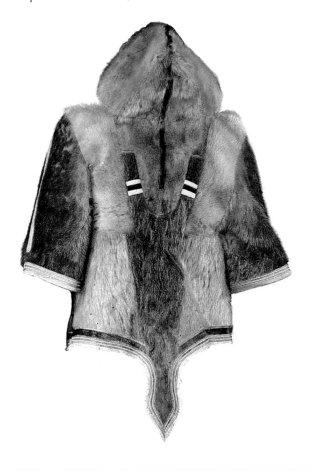

tradition of this type of clothing (Fig. 145). This outfit was acquired by the National Museum in 1884. The most interesting element is the parka. At first, this rather short jacket with its short sleeves and narrow shoulders seems to have very little in common with the clothes of the mummies. But with an examination of the cut, similarities emerge. The front is divided in the centre, like the Qilakitsoq parkas, but

7
Living Conditions

J. Bresciani, W. Dansgaard, B. Fredskild, M. Ghisler

P. Grandjean, J. C. Hansen, J. P. Hart Hansen, N. Haarløv

B. Lorentzen, P. Nansen, A. M. Rørdam, H. Tauber

The mummy find at Qilakitsoq offers us many opportunities to learn about the living conditions of the fifteenth-century Inuit of Greenland. The people themselves, their clothing and the skins of which they were made, the fragments of plants and stones which have been found, combined with the information about the climate derived from the inland ice – all these factors contribute to form a picture of the inhabitants of Qilakitsoq, their living conditions, environment, daily life, game animals, diet, use of plants and much more.

Climate

Climate is important to all, but to the people of Qilakitsoq it was of exceptional, in fact decisive, significance. In speaking of the climate in North Greenland at the end of the fifteenth century, one might think immediately of the climate further to the south, where the last traces of the Norse culture died out with the disappearance of the East Settlement at this time. One of the explanations suggested for the extinction of the Norse community is a poor harvest due to climatic deterioration.

The basis of life, both for the Inuit of Qilakitsoq and the Norsemen of the East Settlement, can better be understood by studying the climate, which in Greenland varies more and plays a greater role in determining living conditions than in most other regions. It is essential to keep in mind that the basis of subsistence of the Inuit society differed from that of the Norse: Inuit lived mainly from hunting sea mammals, which thrive where there is much sea-ice, whereas the Norsemen were predominantly dependent upon cattle- and sheep-breeding. The early Norse community took advantage of the long, mild summers and abundant rainfall. A change in the climate with lower temperatures and thus greater quantities of sea-ice would therefore presumably have strengthened the basis of the Inuit subsistence while impairing that of the Norsemen.

What do we know about the climate of Greenland in the fifteenth century? We can derive much information from the inland ice: the snow which falls on the surface of the ice-cap does not melt away and accumulates through the year, an alternation of summer and winter snow, one annual layer on top of another. The weight of subsequent layers compresses the snow into ice, but each layer preserves its characteristic composition, for example the concentration of a heavy oxygen isotope (with an atomic weight of 18 (O^{18})) in the water molecules. This concentration has proved to be greater when the snow crystals are formed at a higher temperature. Consequently the concentration of this particular oxygen atom is high in summer snow, low in winter snow, and higher in snow from climatically warm periods than in snow from cold periods.

This relationship is useful in a number of ways. Measurement of the O^{18} concentration along an ice-core is obtained by drilling through the alternating

Fig. 146 Areas on Greenland's icecap from which cores of ice have been drilled for investigation into climatic variations. Ice west of the dotted curve is slowly moving towards Greenland's west coast; the rest is moving east or north.

Hans Tausen

Camp Century

North Site

North Central

Summit

Milcent   Crête

Camp 3

Dye 2

Dye 3

South Dome

500 km

summer and winter layers of the inland ice. This yields an O^{18} versus depth relationship which reveals the age of any given layer; the amount of precipitation year by year; and long term temperature changes as far back in time as the ice-core dates. Fig. 00 shows a concentration curve of this kind measured from 256 to 283 m deep below the snow surface at Station Milcent on the inland ice, on approximately the same latitude as Uummannaq. High values (on the right) denote summer layers, low values (on the left) winter layers. By counting the summer peaks from the surface down to a depth of 283 m shows that the uppermost dark summer layer in the figure corresponds to the summer of the year 1499, and the bottom one to the summer of 1450. (This method is quite similar to the determination of the age of a tree by counting its annual rings inwards from the bark.) This figure also shows the thickness of an annual layer, which corresponds to the total precipitation for the year in question.

The annual precipitation at Station Milcent over the last 800 years is shown by the two curves in Fig. 148, after the removal of all oscillations shorter than 30 years and longer than 120 years. Over this long period of time, the precipitation has remained surprisingly constant. Even the least smooth curve contains only one deviation of more than ten per cent from the overall mean, namely around 1200 AD. Of course, this does not mean that there were no individual years or short series of years with greater deviations. For example, the annual precipitation at Station Milcent in the three year period from 1471–3 was only 43 cm of ice in contrast to an average of 57 cm in the 1460s. Current investigations of a new ice-core extending to the bottom of the inland ice at Dye 3 in South Greenland suggest that the precipitation changes there were of the same magnitude as further north.

Overall, the ice-core investigations suggest that in the fifteenth century the climate on the west coast of North and Central Greenland was warmer than the average for the last seven hundred years, in fact almost as warm as in the present century. As for South Greenland, preliminary studies suggest considerably lower temperatures here in the fifteenth century than today, as was probably the case in England and Iceland (see Fig. 150).

However, even if these findings are confirmed by future research, the fate of the East Settlement cannot be completely explained solely by a poorer harvest due to a colder climate. The harvest depends first upon the amount of precipitation, which does

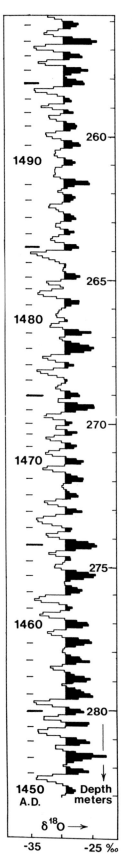

Fig. 147 Seasonal changes in the isotopic composition of precipitation that fell at Station Milcent in the last half of the 15th century. The dates to the left of the curve are based on the summer peaks (black areas) counted down from the surface of the ice. The distance between the two extremities of the curve are a measure of the precipitation of the year in question. This distance can be read on the depth scale to the right of the curve.

Fig. 148 Annual precipitation at Station Milcent every year for the last 800 years, expressed as a percentage deviation from the medium value, which is 54 cm of ice per annum. Oscillations above and below 120 and 30 years respectively have been removed. The amount of precipitation has been very constant.

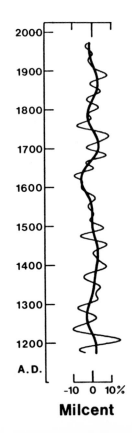

Milcent

Left Fig. 149 Top The drilling of a 2073-metre-deep core of ice from the inland icecap was begun in May 1979. The 4-metre-high building from which this operation was managed was erected 600 m away from the American radar station Dye 3, seen in the background. *Bottom* The drilling station was virtually buried under the snow when the drilling stopped in August 1981.

Below Fig. 150 Variations in temperature in Greenland over the last 1400 years, taken from deuterium measurements at all investigated ice-cores in North, Central and South Greenland. This is not a temperature graph since temperature does not vary as much or in the same way in all areas of Greenland. For instance, systematic observations show that from 1890 to 1935 the 30-year mean temperature rose 1.4°C in Ivigtut, and 2°C in Upernavik. The climate in the 15th century in northwest Greenland was probably a little warmer than today, while that of South Greenland was slightly cooler.

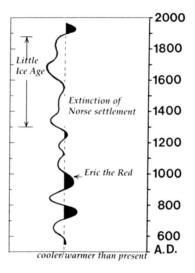

not seem to have been less than today, and next upon the length of the growth period, which is not shortened by a temperature fall as much as might be thought. If we consider the fact that the growth period of the Greenlandic grass species lies during the summer when the average temperature for a twenty-four-hour period exceeds 2°C, then a temperature drop of one or two degrees will shorten the growth season by 8 or 15 per cent respectively, given the present climatic conditions in the East Settlement; a notable but not necessarily catastrophic difference. Considering that the climate of South Greenland in the fifteenth century was hardly much colder than now – and probably warmer in the fourteenth century, when the West Settlement died out – the weather could only have destroyed the Norsemen's annual husbandry by one or a few years of extreme weather conditions. This possibility cannot be ignored; nor, on the other hand, can it be confirmed by the ice-core investigations. In all cases a temperature fall would have strengthened the Norsemen's alternative means of subsistence, namely the hunting of sea mammals. Thus the extinction of the Norse settlers is still a riddle.

Natural resources

ROCKS AND MINERALS

In attempting to gain an impression of the Qilakitsoq people in the area surrounding the settlement, a mineralogical study has been made of the many pebbles and fragments of rocks which were found in the clothing, skins and wrappings. Sand and gravel washed out of the skins and wrappings during conservation has also been examined. As a basis of comparison, modern specimens of the rocks found near the graves have been examined, as well as samples of sand from the bay below the graves, the cove slightly to the west, the large mouth of the river Kuukassak and the settlement of Qilakitsoq itself.

If one sails from the west along the north coast of the Nuussuaq peninsula in through the fjord which

Fig. 151 Microscopic photograph of mineral grains washed out of hides from the graves. The light mineral is a cluster of incomplete magnetic iron crystals. They consist in part of a skeleton only, because the grains formed a lava that hardened so fast that the grains were never completed. These grains are so special in form that they must derive from the formation of basalt in western Nuussuaq. The skins were probably stretched out in that area when the grains lodged in the hairs. These grains are testimony to the migration of the people of Qilakitsoq. Enlarged 220 times.

Fig. 152 Banded gneiss, the most common rock type. The light strips are made up of quartz and feldspar while the grey parts contain dark mica and amphibolite. The green spot of verdegris proves the presence of copper.

Fig. 153 Microscopic view of a sample of beach sand from the bay below the graves. The individual grains are angular, not particularly worn, and so have not moved much. The colour and shape of the grains indicates the type of mineral. Most of the dark green ones are amphibolite of local origin, but some grains are not local and have been transported by wind, ice and sea currents. Enlarged 75 times.

leads to the heart of the Uummannaq district and Qilakitsoq, one first passes to the west massive black volcanic mountains which consist of basalt. Further into the fjord one comes to the Archaean rock with older, sharp-edged, crumbling mountain formations consisting mainly of gneiss. The material studied in the skins proved to be mostly of local origin, neither basalt nor gneiss. However, minerals were also found which were neither fallen material nor beach sand, but which can definitely be traced to rock types in west Nuussuaq. It is thus seen that man moved throughout the entire Uummannaq district, both in the basalt areas to the west and in the gneiss areas to the east. There are traces probably from the settlement of Tupersuatsiaat on Storøen, for a find was made of a single grain of a rare mineral known to occur at this very place but otherwise only at a few virtually inaccessible spots in the district.

PLANTS

Together with the mummies, a number of plant remains were found, both kamik grass (which was used to line the kamiks) and the heather which lined the graves and upon which the dead were laid. In most cases, a certain plant was preferred, Lyme-grass for example, but of course parts of other plants growing at the same place were invariably mixed in when the favoured plant was picked.

Kamik grass can be formed as insoles in kamik stockings or it may constitute an insulating layer between the stocking and the kamik. Because grass used thus is exposed to much wear, a type with a well-developed strengthening tissue is needed. The best-suited grass in these regions of Greenland is Lyme-grass, which is common on sandy and stony ground by the shore and in river valleys, as well as on manured ground at settlements and bird cliffs from Cape Farewell northwards to Svartenhuk about 100 km north of Qilakitsoq. Lyme-grass is very robust with long runners and stems. The leaves are 20–30 cm long with a flat or slightly involuted blade.

In some cases the grass found in kamiks was so worn that only the ribs were left. Often totally worn-out blades of grass lay together with new ones; old inlays were not always replaced with new ones but merely supplemented with new material when necessary.

Perhaps in the course of time the use of kamik grass contributed to the spreading of plants. When an Inuit needed new insoles in his kamiks, he would sometimes throw the old insoles away. Evidence of this is the discovery of the seeds and fruits of at least five species of flowering plants, and fragments of at least twelve species of moss together with the kamik grass. Recently Lyme-grass was found near a settlement on Ellesmere Island in northern Canada, almost 1000 km north of the known northern limit of the plant. The explanation may be that its fruits were carried over this long distance in the kamik grass or other clothing of the Inuit.

Lyme-grass constitutes the main part of the kamik grass. In some cases, however, another grass predominates, namely Alpine Foxtail. This is a widespread arctic grass which is found in West Greenland southwards to Sisimiut (Holsteinsborg). Alpine Foxtail grows scattered in bogs and along rivers; it is not particularly tall. However, as this grass, like Lyme-grass, favours manured soil, it is quite common at settlements and bird cliffs, where it can develop into a thick grass with stems up to 30 or 40 cm high. If one sails along the coast of Greenland in

Fig. 154 Inner sole of kamik grass.

the summer it is often possible to see old settlements from a great distance because of the strong green colour of the luxuriant vegetation of Alpine Foxtail and Lyme-grass. One sample contained the flower of a species of Alkali-grass, probably the Sheathed Alkali-grass which, like Alpine Foxtail, is extremely common at inhabited sites between the Disko Bay and Thule.

Together with the grasses named, small bird feathers which were probably part of the soles, were found in many cases. In addition there were incidental fragments of various plant species, including the leaves of willow, either Arctic Willow or Northern Willow, of Crowberry, Arctic Blueberry, White Arc-

Fig. 155 Lyme grass (*Elymus mollis trin*) is often used for insoles, that is, as kamik grass. The blades, sheath and underside are smooth while the topside is rough with ribs 0.2 m thick and small thorns. These characteristics are evident in the mummies' insoles. *Left* Enlarged 1.8 times. *Right* Enlarged 12 times.

tic Bell-heather and Mountain Avens, as well as the seeds of Crowberry and Alpine Chickweed.

In the graves, the dead were placed on a layer of plant material, which consisted in one case of Lyme-grass and in another of heather, mainly White Arctic Bell-heather, but also some Crowberry. White Arctic Bell-heather is the predominant dwarf-shrub in North Greenland, where it forms extensive heaths at places which are well covered with snow in the winter. To the south, it is found down to Nuuk fjord, although here it usually grows at fairly high altitudes on northern slopes. It is widely used as fuel because of its large content of resin, enabling it to burn even when wet. It has a very spicy fragrance, but counteracting the stench of decomposition can hardly have been the main reason for using it to line the graves. More probably it was used simply because it grew abundantly on the north slope around the cave.

The seeds of White Arctic Bell-heather mature under the snow during the winter and are not dispersed until the following spring. Thus the presence of many capsules on the plants gives no hint of the season during which they were gathered. However, one shoot was found with a flower whose bell-shaped corolla was missing but which had two anthers still hanging on their filaments. This suggests that the plant was picked in July or early August, when the flowers wither. However, this proof is not conclusive as investigation of a very large collection of pressed plants at the Copenhagen University Botanical Museum has revealed examples of anthers which have hung on throughout the winter.

Crowberry is just as common as White Arctic Bell-heather in these regions of Greenland, and was also widely used as fuel. In addition, in August this plant can be covered with tasty black fruits which are eaten by both man and animal.

The layer on which the mummies were laid was found to contain the remains of at least ten species of flowering plants and twelve mosses, all of which are common in the area today.

Personal health

Diet

The Inuit diet depended upon game animals and vegetation. In only one of the mummies was it possible to find traces of food in the internal organs: the lower part of the large intestine of mummy II/7 contained the black lumpy remains of faeces. These lumps contained extremely small pieces of partly digested muscular tissue of indeterminate origin, hairs of seal, caribou and alpine hare, and feathers and down of ptarmigan and little auk. There were also large amounts of plants, lichens and pollen of many plants, such as grasses, Dwarf Birch, White Arctic Bell-heather, Crowberry, willow, and Mountain sorrel. Small fragments of wood, both charred and uncharred, as well as many grains of sand and some lice were also found besides some microscopic soil-living animals and fungi.

It was surprising to find so many pollen grains. Assuming that after death the faeces were not contaminated with soil, there are two possible explanations. The pollen can either have been filtered out of the inhaled air in the nose and subsequently swallowed, or else it was ingested as a contamination of the food or part of a food. The first explanation seems improbable because there was no pollen from Cotton-grass, Sedge or other plants of the Sedge family, which are widespread all over Greenland. The fifty-five species of this family are all wind-pollinated, and their pollen are very common at the bottom of every Greenland lake and pond. One would therefore expect such common pollen to be among the other types found in mummy II/7's intestine.

Above, left Fig. 156 Lyme grass, still in use today, at Iniffik, east of Qeqertarssuaq.

Above Fig. 157 Alpine foxtail (*Alopecurus alpinus Sm.*) was often used as kamik grass.

Left Fig. 158 White Arctic Bell-heather (*Cassipe tetragone (L.) D. Don.*). The mummies' graves were lined with this plant.

Fig. 159 Mountain sorrel (*Oxyria digyna (L.) Hill*). This was a delicacy in Greenland, eaten by the people of Qilakitsoq.

As mentioned small fragments of wood were also included in the intestinal content. Some were charred, indicating that driftwood which could not be used as timber was burned together with local fuel. As known, there are no coniferous trees in Greenland, but it is impossible to determine whether this wood came from trees which grew in Siberian, North American or perhaps Norwegian forests.

It is most logical to assume that the contamination of the intestinal contents happened before death and consists mainly of soil, in this case from a heath of White Arctic Bell-heather, a common vegetation type at Qilakitsoq. The contamination may have been caused directly, during preparation of the food outdoors or from earth falling from the turf walls during cooking and eating. Also, cooking utensils and the cook's fingers may have helped contaminate the food. Characteristically most of the grass pollen came from Alpine Foxtail, which is in fact extremely common in Inuit settlements.

Fig. 160 White Arctic Bell-heather (*Cassipe tetragone (L.) D. Don.*) found in the mummies' graves.

It was hoped that the examination of the intestinal content might indicate the season during which mummy II/7 died. However, only one piece of evidence points to summer as the time when she had her last meal: Mountain Sorrel. This plant is common all over Greenland and is wind-pollinated; therefore its pollen is found in the sediment of almost any lake. Most of the nineteen pollen grains of this plant found in the intestine were clearly immature, and consequently it must have been eaten with hardly opened flowers, a factor which suggests July or

August as the time of death. However, Mountain Sorrel is a favourite treat in Greenland, and can be conserved in seal oil, therefore the presence of its pollen is not conclusive evidence that death occurred in July or August.

It must be kept in mind that part of the food may have come from the stomach contents of an animal. For example, the stomach contents of a freshly-killed caribou was once regarded as a special delicacy. However, some of the plant structures are believed to be too well-preserved to have been broken down by digestive juices twice, first in the stomach of an animal and next in the gastrointestinal system of a human, unless the animal was killed immediately after eating the plants.

As mentioned in chapter two, studies of the carbon atoms of tissue specimens have provided vital information about the Inuit diet, and particularly about whether the food came from the sea or from land plants and animals. Because of the vast natural circulation system shown in Fig. 34 it is possible to distinguish the origins of the carbon compounds. When green land plants absorb carbon dioxide from the atmosphere in the process of photosynthesis, by which inorganic material is converted to organic material, the plants are able to absorb all three forms of carbon dioxide, containing, respectively, carbon -12, carbon-13 and carbon-14, but the plants do not absorb these three forms in the same proportions in which they occur in the atmosphere. Green plants absorb slightly more of the light carbon dioxide molecules with carbon-12 than of the heavier molecules with carbon-13 and carbon-14. Thus green plants on land obtain a characteristic ratio between the carbon isotopes, a ratio which differs from that found in the atmosphere. This characteristic ratio is passed on to animals and humans who eat the plants growing on the land.

Changes also occur when carbon dioxide is dissolved in sea water, but here the types of carbon dioxide which are absorbed preferentially are the heavier ones with carbon-13 and carbon-14. In the photosynthesis of plants in the sea there again occur changes, which are passed on to the marine fauna. In this way the various carbon compounds in living things attain a characteristic content of the three carbon isotopes, which reveal their origin almost as clearly as a fingerprint. Naturally this also applies to carbon compounds in the human skin and muscle tissue, which acquires a slightly different composition depending upon whether the food of the individual in question derives mainly from the sea or from land animals and plants. However, a certain variability in the ratios found must always be allowed for due to small differences in the metabolic processes from person to person.

Because the content of carbon–14 in the carbon compounds changes slowly in the course of time the isotopes used to characterise the isotope content of the carbon compounds are primarily the stable ones, carbon–12 and carbon–13. This is done by measuring the ratio of the number of carbon–13 and carbon–12 atoms. Subsequently it is calculated how much this value diverges from the corresponding isotope ratio in an international standard. This standard has, in fact, the same ratio between carbon–12 and carbon–13 as that found in carbon dioxide in sea water. Carbon compounds from marine animals normally contain 1.0 – 1.7 per cent less carbon–13 than the standard, whereas carbon compounds from land animals usually contain 1.8–2.5 per cent less carbon–13 than the standard.

The ratio between the number of carbon–13 and carbon–12 atoms in samples from Qilakitsoq, expressed as the deviations from an international standard (PDB standards).

Grave I		Grave II	
sealskin	−1.41%	caribou skin	−1.90%
sealskin	−1.36%	caribou skin	−1.88%
caribou skin	−1.97%	sealskin	−1.88%
human skin	−1.48%		

The values found in samples of sealskin and caribou skin correspond exactly to findings from other marine and land animals. It is interesting that skin tissue from the four-year-old boy contains approximately the same amount of carbon–13 as marine animals. It is thus certain that the main part of his diet came from the sea. Because of the natural scatter of such carbon–13 values, however, it is difficult to say exactly how large a part of his food came from the sea. In this question, information provided by carbon–14 measurements can be useful. With our knowledge of the difference between the carbon–14 content of carbon compounds in materials which came from the sea and the land, and of how much carbon–14 there was originally in the boy's skin tissue (see p. 48) respectively, we can calculate how many of the boy's carbon atoms must have come from food from the sea and the land. The result is

that 75 per cent, give or take 7 per cent, of his food came from the sea, probably in the form of seal, walrus and fish, while 25 per cent came from caribou and other land animals and plants.

PARASITES

A parasite is an organism which derives its nourishment from other living organisms, and it can be found everywhere. In material which is over a thousand years old, the well-preserved remains have been found of both internal and external parasites stemming from humans and animals, or their waste products. This is because of the solid, durable, chitinous structure surrounding worm eggs, which is included in the skeleton of a number of parasites. In contrast, infectious matter such as bacteria, viruses and pathogenic fungi are rapidly broken down and often lose their characteristic appearance.

Among the parasites found in man, lice have a prominent position. Lice are found everywhere on earth, and are not infrequent in Greenland today. They were widespread in Greenland already at the beginning of the colonial period. Hans Egede writes: 'And not least of all is that one is badly afflicted by lice, of which the Greenlanders have many, and which they can pass on to others in abundance if one comes too close to them.' Lice occur most frequently wherever hygienic conditions are poor. They are transferred by contact with people who are infested with them, or whose clothing, particularly headwear, scarves and fur outer garments bears them, and they live on human blood.

The two most important, widespread types of lice are head lice and body lice. The former type is the more common. Body lice thrive especially well on people with poor body hygiene. In his natural history written in 1780 Fabricius writes that lice 'thrive most abundantly on the heads and clothing of the Greenlanders. . . . They are eaten by the Greenlanders and considered delicious [ut delicatus]'. A third type of lice is the crab louse or morpion, which is rarely found among the Inuit.

Lice can be irritating in general because by sucking blood from the scalp or body they create itching and small sores. But lice can also be dangerous as carriers of infectious matter from one person to another. The best-known example of this is the role of lice in disseminating typhus fever. Lice can also convey other, less dangerous diseases.

The hair on the heads of all of the mummies of Qilakitsoq was infested with lice. Lice eggs were found attached to the hairs at varying distances from

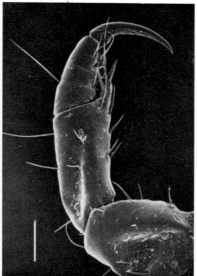
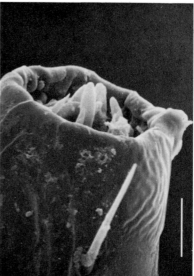

Above Fig. 161 Electron microscopic pictures of a mummified head louse (*Pediculus capitis de Geer*) found in a pair of sealskin trousers. *Left* Underside view, showing it to be female. Scale 1 mm. *Middle* Front leg. Scale 0.1 mm. *Right* Tip of one of the antennae, the one further forward in underside view. Scale 0.01 mm.
Below Fig. 162 Top Remains of a mite and *bottom* a louse found in the intestinal contents of mummy II/7. Enlarged 50 and 100 times respectively.

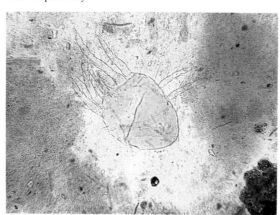

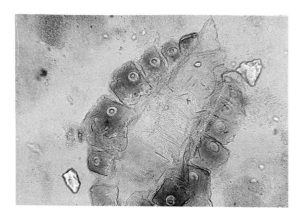

the scalp, on some hairs as much as 18 or 20 cm from the root of the hair. As lice always attach their eggs directly at the hair roots, and as hair grows from 5 to 10 mm per month this indicates a long-lasting, permanent 'cohabitation'. Mummy II/7 in particular was badly infested, with lice eggs on every third or fourth hair. Numerous mummified lice were also found on her scalp. In a few loose half-sleeves in grave I and in some sealskin inner trousers in grave II there were many lice and especially lice eggs on and between the hairs of the sealskin. In some places the quantity of lice eggs was so great that the skin took on the brownish colour of the eggs. All the lice were head lice. No body lice, or crab lice were found.

In the present century, both head and body lice have been found among the inhabitants of Greenland settlements, so it was not surprising to find them on the mummies. However, the great degree to which mummy II/7 was infested suggests an extremely low hygienic standard, and perhaps, to some extent also, low resistance to the attack of lice. The occurrence of lice in this woman's faeces indicates that the observation which Fabricius made in 1780 was accurate.

The lice found on the mummies are remarkable for being so well-preserved, because they had been mummified. Recently head lice were found on three mummies dating back four hundred years from the Aleutian Islands, and body lice have also been found

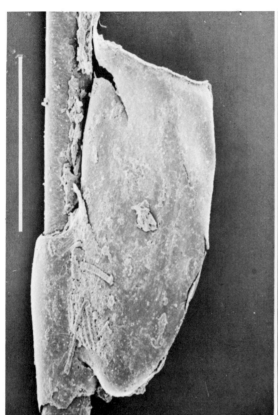 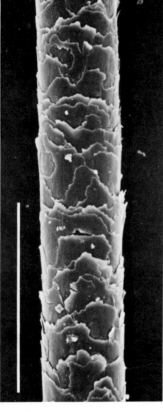

Fig. 163 Left Electron microscopic picture of an egg container of a head louse fastened to a hair of mummy II/7. Scale 0.5 mm. *Right* Hair in greater magnification. Scale 0.1 mm. Both hair tips are turned upwards.

at the Norse farm of Sandness at the head of the Ameralik fjord in the Nuuk district which date to 1000–1350 BC. However, none of these lice are as well-preserved as the lice from Qilakitsoq.

Trichinae, parasitic worms found in the intestine, cause the disease trichinosis in animals and humans. The worm is a few millimetres in length and lives in the intestines once it has sexually matured. Here it breeds and its larvae bore into the intestinal wall, from which they are carried through the body with the lymph and blood. They settle and are encapsulated mainly in muscle tissue. Such encapsulated muscle trichinae are found primarily in masticatory muscles and in the respiratory musculature, that is, in the muscles of the pectoral wall and the throat as well as the diaphragm. The worm is transmitted when infected meat is eaten, and is released during the digestion of the meat. The spread of trichinae can be avoided by cooking the meat to a certain heat, or until it is grey.

Trichinosis is found among wild animals such as boars, foxes, bears, polar bears and also walruses and seals, who sometimes eat the flesh of other animals. Among domesticated animals trichinosis is particularly frequent among pigs. Even today, it is still a serious problem, particularly among arctic hunting peoples. Presumably part of the population of modern Greenland has encapsulated muscle trichinosis to a certain degree: since 1947 at least five hundred cases of trichinosis have been reported. Major outbreaks of the disease have occurred in the Disko Bay, Upernavik and Thule districts. About 24 per cent of all Greenlandic polar bears and 1 per cent of all walruses are known to be infected, and they are the only source of this infection for Greenlanders.

As the danger of trichinae infection has no doubt existed for thousands of years, an exhaustive study has been made to find trichinae in the muscle tissue of the mummies. Muscle tissue from the pectoral wall, the diaphragm and the masticatory muscles has been examined, but all results have been negative. It ought to be mentioned that this study would hardly be able to reveal an incipient trichinae infection but on the other hand, no evidence has been found to indicate that the mummies died of trichinosis. With our knowledge of more recent epidemics of trichinosis in which a large part of the arctic population groups have been infected, it is in fact strange that it was not possible to determine trichinae in the Qilakitsoq people as well.

The common intestinal worms, roundworms and whipworms, are extremely hardy and turn up frequently in archaeological material such as mummies and the calcified remains of faeces. However, in only one Qilakitsoq mummy was it possible to examine the intestinal content, and in this case many pinworm eggs (oxyurus vermicularis) were found. This worm can live in the distal part of the large intestine and may cause itching around the anal opening. Most often, however, there will be no symptoms.

Pollution

The organs of humans and animals reveal the environment in which they live. Thus analyses can reveal both pollution and the occurrence of the necessary tracers, the so-called micro-nutrients, which exist in very slight quantities in the organism. In recent decades there has been a growing interest in systematic measurements to determine, in particular, the extent and distribution of pollution of such things as heavy metals. As it is not possible to take specimens of all types of tissue, and as tissues vary in their concentration of elements, interest has been focused on tissues and body fluids which are easily accessible and well suited for analysis.

As for heavy metals, there has been much interest in using hair for analysis, both because metals are concentrated in greater quantities in hair than in other tissues, and because hair is easy to obtain, send and preserve. Its easy preservation allows for comparison between different chronological periods, which is usually not possible otherwise, because other tissues change. Comparison of this sort over a period of about five hundred years is made possible by this mummy find, for the heavy metal content of the mummies' hair can be compared with the content of the hair of present-day Greenlanders. Moreover, the content of heavy metals in the fur of the game animals from the time of the Qilakitsoq people can be compared with the occurrence of heavy metals in the game animals of the Uummannaq district today.

Prior to analysis, all samples were washed to remove external pollution. The hair was subsequently dissolved and its organic material broken down by pressure-treatment with nitric acid. Determination of the metal content was done either with X-ray fluorescence in the United States, or by atomic absorption spectrophotometry in Denmark. The X-ray fluorescence method reveals the content of calcium, lead, mercury, bromine, zinc, copper, iron and manganese; atomic absorption spectrophotometry determines the content of mercury, cadmium, lead, copper and selenium.

Both methods of analysis yielded similar results for lead, mercury, and copper. The X-ray fluorescence method permits lengthwise analysis of the hair, providing information about changes in concentration and thus changes in living conditions during the growth period of the individual hair. (It was hoped that changes in the concentration of the various elements along the hairs would help reveal whether the mummies had died at the same time by showing a similar pattern of change during the final phase of their lives. However, no characteristic pattern could be discerned, so this investigation could not support the theory that the individuals had died contemporaneously. On the other hand, the margin of uncertainty of this method is such that this negative finding cannot exclude the possibility of synchronous death.) Some of the results of this investigation are shown in Fig. 164. Here we see the concentration in modern Greenlanders who have not been exposed to abnormal amounts of pollution from working or living close to highly polluting industries. These concentration values thus represent modern normal values.

It is most relevant to examine mercury contamination in Greenland because people in arctic regions, with their great dependence upon food from the sea, are known to have a higher contamination of mercury than other population groups. This is because of the spread of mercury through food chains in the sea. However, whether the relatively high contamination of today is simply the result of the natural effect of the food chain or whether it is a consequence of human pollution has not yet been determined.

It is true that in both animal and human hair an increase in concentration has occurred in the course of time. This increase could be considered a reflection of human pollution, since the use of mercury has been known since prehistory. Global consumption of mercury has increased throughout history, particularly in the industrial age. However, this is not the sole explanation for this demonstrated rise as it is also known that throughout the ages major changes have taken place in the natural background

Mean concentration of elements in hair from the mummies and their hunting animals (seals) compared with the concentration in hair from present-day Greenlanders and seals. The unit is microgram/gram.

Element	Qilakitsoq specimens		Present-day specimens	
	Humans	Animals	Humans	Animals
Mercury	3.1	0.6	9.8	2.6
Cadmium	0.5	0.3	0.4	0.8
Lead	0.7	0.4	6.0	1.9
Copper	8.8	15.1	16.5	10.0
Selenium	2.8	2.3	0.8	2.4

occurrence of mercury, caused by such factors as volcanic activity.

This study cannot therefore explain the reason for the increasing concentration of mercury. However, the findings do indicate that in the arctic regions, already before the industrial age, there was a relatively high contamination from natural causes. This high contamination is reflected in both the human and the animal hairs. The mercury concentration is lower in the animal hairs reflecting the fact that seals are consumed by humans, who are on a higher level of the food chain.

Cadmium is the metal pollutant which, after mercury, has caused the greatest amount of concern in modern times. Calculations of the probable daily intake of cadmium in Greenland, based on analyses of food animals and interview surveys of eating habits have confirmed that in sealing districts in Greenland the maximum cadmium content in food, as recommended by the World Health Organisation, is exceeded significantly. However, the available findings show that there is no difference in the cadmium concentration in the Qilakitsoq people and in modern Greenlanders. In both the historical and contemporary samples, the cadmium values lie within the normal range. Thus analysis of hair cannot show that the abundant cadmium content in the Greenlandic hunter's diet has any effect.

On the other hand, a moderate increase in the concentration has been found to have taken place through the five centuries. This indicates that food animals today are more contaminated by cadmium than previously. The fact that this rise has not affected man is perhaps because, through the food chain, cadmium is bound in a form which is not easily absorbed from man's intestinal tract. A possible explanation for cadmium in animals showing only a moderate increase is that this metal has only been used in technology for about seventy years, so that general global cadmium contamination is not as pronounced as that of lead and mercury, metals which have been known and used for thousands of years.

About 95 per cent of the body's lead content is found in the bone system. This is fortunate for our purposes because it allows us to measure the lead content of well-preserved skeletal parts and obtain an impression of how much lead the individual in question was exposed to during his lifetime.

Comparison with the bones of mummified bodies from the Nubian desert in northern Sudan has shown that the modern Dane contains between ten and twenty-five times as much lead as the Nubians of five thousand years ago. We also know that in the Middle Ages Danes and Faroe Islanders were exposed to a great deal of lead from, for example, pewter plates, lead glazes and medicaments. The lead content of medieval bones can be up to ten times as large as that of today.

Bone tissue from the Greenlandic mummies has also been examined, and the findings are extremely similar to those of the studies of the Nubians. The Inuit had virtually no direct possibility of lead contamination to any notable extent. They lived in an almost lead-free environment at a time when lead poisoning was already a widespread illness and probably also a cause of death in large parts of Europe.

Of all the metals which are injurious to health, it is lead which shows the greatest increase through time in both human and animal hair. The lower concentration in animal hair is due to a lower step in the food chain. The hair of the mummies had a lead content which was considerably lower than that found in unexposed population groups today.

Fig. 164 Comparison of the concentration of elements on the head hairs of the mummies and seals from the 15th century and those of inhabitants and seals in Greenland today. Unit 1 on the vertical line is the start measure and corresponds to the concentration found in Qilakitsoq (white areas). The blue areas indicate contemporary levels. The lead level in human hairs has clearly risen the most, to more than eight times that of the 15th century.

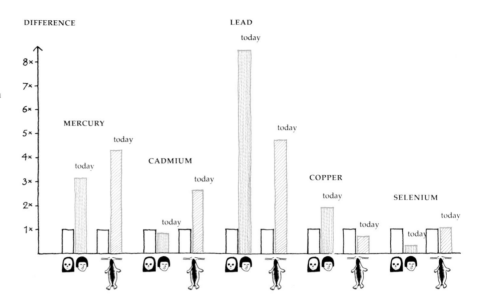

Surprisingly enough, modern Greenlanders have a lead content identical to that of, for example, Danes today. The use of lead as an additive to petrol is believed to be the major source of lead pollution in industrialised societies. The find of relatively high concentrations of lead in present-day Greenland along with the determination of low concentrations in the mummies, supports the theory that in the course of history a steady increase of lead contamination has occurred in the northern hemisphere.

Copper, in minute amounts, is a necessary nutrient. The investigation has not shown differences in the copper concentration found in humans and animals. The same holds true of calcium and zinc in human hair. The concentration in the old sample lies, as in the new ones, in the normal range corresponding to a sufficient supply in the diet. However, the concentration of zinc has shown a very slight increase in the course of time, possibly because fish constitutes a relatively smaller part of the daily diet today in comparison with earlier times. And fish contains only very small amounts of zinc.

A very small amount of selenium is also a necessary part of the diet. The examinations show that there is no difference in the occurrence of selenium in old and fresh animal hair. Thus no changes have occurred in the quantity of selenium available in the food chain. In the mummy hairs the occurrence is normal, but in the course of time it has diminished, so that modern hair specimens contain smaller quantities of selenium, still within the so-called normal range but at the bottom of it. This decrease is not because of a diminished supply through food from the sea animals per unit of weight, but is rather to be considered the reflection of changed eating habits in recent times. Increasingly, imported foods which are low in selenium have replaced the traditional Greenlandic diet, even in sealing districts. It is also possible that the same amount of selenium is ingested but that mercury contamination has risen; for selenium and mercury can be bound to one another in compounds which cannot be converted in the organism, and which are deposited in the organs, particularly the liver. Selenium is therefore detoxicating for the damaging effects of mercury. This binding would decrease the amount of selenium which can be converted in the human body, resulting in a small concentration in the hairs.

However, this explanation is less likely, for in East Greenland a positive connection has been found between the occurrence of mercury and selenium in hair corresponding to the fact that the two elements are absorbed from the same source, namely food from the sea. It is therefore most likely that the difference is ascribable to the changed diet. This theory is reinforced by the finding that the content of iron as well as bromine has decreased. Both of these elements are supplied through food from the sea.

It is also possible to determine the heavy-metal content of plant material. Specimens (of Lapland cassiope, mosses, and kamik grass) were therefore taken from the bottom layer of both graves and from the kamiks, along with samples of fresh Lapland cassiope growing directly east of the graves.

No noteworthy differences were found between the old and the fresh samples. However, there was a generally lower content of heavy metals in the fresh plant material than in the samples from the graves, especially with regard to manganese. This difference is probably ascribable to changed growth conditions caused by variations in the local rock and soil types and drainage patterns. As for the contaminating metals such as mercury, lead and cadmium, nothing in the findings of the analyses indicates that the contamination of the atmosphere has increased in modern times. The reason for this apparent discrepancy in the findings of the investigation of the plant material and those of the material from humans and animals is that the latter are affected by a marine environment, where contamination is possibly more noticeable than in organisms found only on land. Moreover, in contrast to plants, humans and animals are affected by the transport of the elements through a long food chain.

In conclusion it must be emphasised that these investigations provide no definitive answer to questions concerning the actual contamination by heavy metals in Greenland, although they do shed light upon several aspects of the matter. It is still not known how much of the present mercury contamination is man-made pollution. However, it has been shown that a considerable amount of the contamination must be ascribed to the natural passage of the elements through the food chain, for as early as the fifteenth century, before mercury was used in technology to any significant extent, there was already a relatively high mercury concentration. The study made also supports the theory that naturally-bound cadmium is not absorbed in the human organism.

The extremely low lead values in fifteenth-century human and animal hair show, in comparison to the present, that most lead influences found today have been caused by pollution. The question of the mechanism of distribution over vast distances has not yet been clarified.

The decreasing absorption of the essential element selenium is alarming, as selenium is believed to play an important role in preventing a number of diseases.

The process described here, in which essential micro-nutrients are ingested in smaller amounts and poisonous pollutants in larger amounts, indicates that modern technology on a worldwide level and changes in the Greenlandic cultural pattern tending towards a European way of life can in the long run influence health conditions in Greenland. Ongoing scientific surveillance of the environment is therefore important. Many other elements besides those studied here may have undergone changes which can be revealed through continued investigations of the old mummy and animal hair. When all these investigations have been made, the Qilakitsoq find will have made its contribution to the creation of a most valuable reference material from the fifteenth century which can aid our understanding of contemporary and future living conditions.

Appendix

Rolf Gilberg, Gerda Møller

The six women

In all, the material treated comprised sixteen sealskin parkas, seven bird-skin parkas, a caribou parka, twelve pairs of trousers, nineteen kamiks, twenty-one kamik stockings, and two sleeves. The graves also contained numerous extra, loose skins, probably used to cover sleeping platforms or for tents, which were either wrapped round the mummies or used as padding together with various crumpled garments.

These seventy-eight items of apparel were both well- and poorly-preserved. Some of them can provide us with much information, others with virtually none, but together they form a picture of the costume of the Inuit women of the day with all its advantageous features, and apparently some of its drawbacks, for life in the arctic climate.

With cleaning and a detailed examination of the mummies it was possible to see how the costume was worn and what items of apparel it included. With some exceptions, the costume consisted of a bird-skin parka worn next to the skin with the feathers inward, and of inner trousers of sealskin. Outermost, the woman wore a sealskin parka with the fur turned outward, half-length trousers of sealskin or caribou skin with the fur to the outside, kamik stockings of sealskin or caribou skin with the fur inward, and kamiks made of water skin.

All the mummies wore trousers starting from their hips. Some trousers had an attached belt tied at the back. The half-length trouser leg went to just below the knee, and the kamiks and kamik stockings ended slightly above the knee. Kamik grass was used both inside the stockings and between the stockings and the kamiks. Both the inner and outer parkas were waist-length at the sides and probably fitted quite snugly. In contrast, the armholes and the shoulders were very roomy. The position of the hood on the head could not be ascertained precisely because in some cases the hood had slid back and in other cases it was partly missing.

If we study the various garments and their cut, a number of characteristic, basic types emerge. These models were then given individual character with regard to size, ornamentation, and the attachment of pieces of skin for extra warmth. It was determined that the parkas and trousers were made only of either bird- or caribou skin, or of ringed seal. Sewn to some garments were light strips of the skin of unborn or newborn seal. The dark, sometimes nearly black, decorative skin strips may be from the head

or back of the harp seal or from the back of a very dark ringed seal. The stockings are made of caribou skin, apart from two pairs of ringed seal skin.

The loose skins were perhaps intended for making clothing and are mostly ringed seal skins. However, there are also some harp seal skins and a piece of skin consisting of a number of newborn seal skins sewn together.

The garments were sewn together with sinew-thread. Two kinds of stitches, running and overcast, were used. For running stitch, the edges of the two skins to be joined were placed one on top of the other and the needle was drawn up and down through both layers. To make the overcast stitch, the skin edges were placed against each other and sewn together.

Exhaustive study and description of the individual garments in this substantial find have turned up a number of recurring features which must be assumed to be typical of their time. For example, it seems to be characteristic that the new clothes were carefully sewn with small, regular stitches. Also, the costume was not only practical but also demonstrated a consciousness of fashion, as seen in the beautiful ornamental patterns made with light and dark skin, as well as the tall, narrow, open-necked hood of the parka and its long tails. Frequently, for extra warmth pieces of skin were sewn at the hips, cuffs were sewn at the wrist and knee, and short trousers were lengthened. These additions were apparently meant to be attached and removed rapidly, for they are sewn on with long stitches and thick, sometimes braided thread.

When a garment had worn thin, it was patched, sometimes with pieces of skin from another garment. The repairs are not of the same quality as the original tailoring, and over-long, somewhat uneven stitches and often thick thread were used. It was common to reuse old clothes, for example, by inserting a gusset if an old garment was too narrow. Nothing went to waste. In some seams there are narrow bands of newborn or unborn seal skin which seem to serve no practical purpose. However, like the attachment of a piece of bird-skin to the inner side of a parka they may have had magical significance.

Mummy I/3 This young woman, about twenty-five years old, wore an outer parka, inner parka, short trousers, kamiks and stockings.

The outer parka, made of sealskin, has a missing hood. This area around the neck and shoulders as

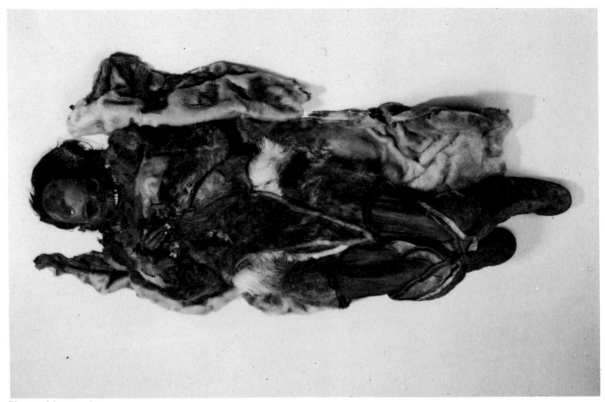

Fig. 165 Mummy I/3.

well as the uppermost part of the back has deteriorated, with much loss of hair. The back tail is about
45 cm long with two fur bands; the inside one is
dark and the outside one, along the edge of the
parka, is light. These bands are not sewn together.
The front tail is about 35 cm long and also has fur
bands, the light one again on the outside edge of
the parka, and a narrow dark one next to it. The
sleeves have no wrist bands, but there are light
inserts of skin about 11 cm wide.

The inner parka, made of bird-skin, also lacks a
hood. The back tail is about 40 cm long and the front
tail about 30 cm long. At the hips the caribou-skin
edgings of the parka are wider than normal, with
fur about 15 cm wide forming a light border which
would have shown below the outer parka.

The short trousers, of sealskin, are about 20 cm long,
edged with a dark fur band which is turned in. At
the top there is a waistband with an unattached belt
tied at the back. A triangular gusset is inserted at
the top of the front.

The kamiks are beautifully sewn from seal skin with
fine, regular gatherings at the toe and heel. The leg

is about 45 cm long and has a band of white skin 1.5
cm wide at the top. Each kamik is sewn together on
the front with an inset gusset and overcast stitching.
The gusset seems to have been added later, because
the kamiks were originally sewn together with backstitch. The gusset also goes up over the band. The
right kamik has a triangular piece of skin sewn on
at the front of the foot.

The stockings are made of caribou skin and have a
band of turned-in sealskin at the top.

Mummy I/4   The costume of this woman, who was
about thirty years old, is somewhat deteriorated,
with a loss of hair around the neck and upper back.
Her clothing includes an outer parka, inner parka,
half-length trousers, kamiks and stockings.

The outer parka is made of sealskin. The back tail is
about 45 cm long and the front tail about 30–35 cm
long. Both tails have light turned-in fur bands, which
also edge the parka along the sides. At the lower
sides pieces of skin about 18 cm wide have been
attached; these go from the middle of the front to
the middle of the back tail, and thus cover the hips.

These skin pieces are made of sealskin with the fur turned inward, and they are sewn on with braided sinew thread in long crude stitching. The sleeves have inserts of light pieces of skin and a turned-in fur band at the wrists. The hood is detached.

The inner parka is made of bird-skin with a tail at the front and back.

The half-length trousers are made of light sealskin and reach the middle of the knee. They have a turned-in fur band at the top.

The kamiks are composed of various pieces of skin, but they are carefully sewn. The leg of each boot is about 32 cm long and ends at the top in a white edging 1.5 cm wide. The leg is sewn together in front with a single row of backstitch which becomes double at the outer side of the foot. The soles are attached to the leg with very regular and finely-made gathers. A sealskin strap 1.5 cm wide is tied round the right ankle.

The stockings, which are made of sealskin, terminate at the top with a turned-in fur band. This band on both stockings has been trimmed with a piece of sealskin, 10–11 cm wide, pieced together of several skin fragments. This skin has been sewn on with long crude overcast stitching. The fur side faces in and the stocking goes above the knee, so that it covers the trousers.

Above Fig. 166 Mummy I/3's kamiks.
Below Fig. 167 Mummy I/4.

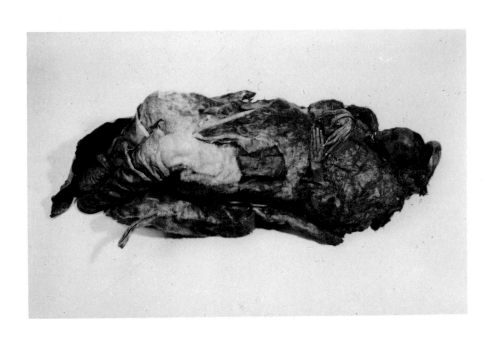

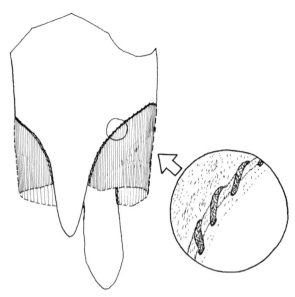

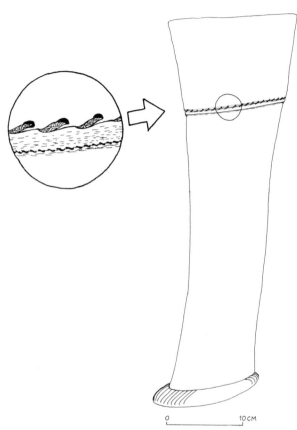

Above Fig. 168 Left Leather additions to the parka of mummy I/4, which have been crudely sewn on with pleated sinew-thread. *Right* Later additions to the stockings.

Below Fig. 169 Mummy I/4's kamiks.

Mummy I/5 The costume of this woman, who was about forty-five years old, is quite poorly preserved, especially at the back. It consists of an outer parka, an inner parka, half-length trousers, kamiks and stockings.

The outer parka, which is made of sealskin, is cut like the other parkas, with a tail in front and probably one originally at the back too, although it is not possible to be certain because most of the back is missing. However, this parka clearly once had the characteristic marking at over the shoulder blades. The hood is edged with a dark, turned-in fur band which also follows the outermost rim of the chin-piece. At both sides in this band there are the remains of a string, made of braided sinew-thread and ending in a knot. This shows that the hood and the chin-piece could be drawn together. The sleeves are edged at the wrist, where there are light-coloured skin inserts.

The inner parka, made of bird-skin, is edged with caribou skin.

The trousers are made of caribou skin – perhaps caribou calf – and are very poorly preserved, hence

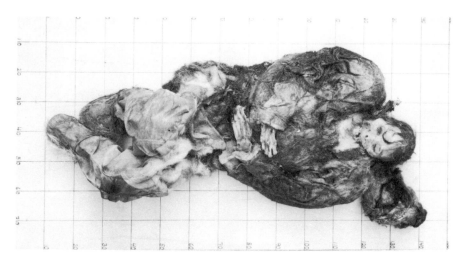

Fig. 170 Mummy I/5, a 50-year-old woman.

most of the back is missing. They are about 40 cm long from the waistband to the bottom of the trouser-leg, which ends just above the knee. There is a fur band at the top with an attached belt to be tied at the back. The trousers appear to have been made symmetrically with a right and left half, each of which is composed of various pieces of skin, and the play of light and brownish tones makes for a striking ornamental effect.

The kamiks have well-preserved legs, but the soles are generally missing. The legs are about 50 cm high and go up over the knee. There is a front seam running from the instep towards the inside edge of the foot; another seam runs across the toes. The sole is finely and regularly gathered to the leg at the toe. The remains of a strap lie on the instep. The leg goes straight up at the back, but in front it runs upward diagonally, so that at the top it measures 30 cm. The fur was cut off the skin, a procedure which left stripes of short hair which clearly show that the hair ran vertically downward on the left kamik but horizontally on the right one.

The stockings are made of thick caribou skin. The legs are well-preserved, in complete contrast to the feet. The stockings are 50–55 cm long and sewn together both at the front and back. They have been widened by additional pieces of skin sewn in at the top.

Mummy II/6 This woman was about fifty years old, and is dressed in a very well-preserved costume consisting of an outer parka, an inner parka, outer and inner trousers, kamiks and stockings.

The outer parka has a piece of skin sewn on the bottom of the sides and running from tail to tail. It is widest at the back, where it measures about 6 cm. It differs in character from the piece tacked onto mummy I/4's parka. On mummy II/6, the piece is sewn on unusually well and must be considered a decorative border. Both the front and back tails are edged with a light-coloured fur band, which also edges the side of the parka. The sleeves are edged, first with caribou skin and next with a light fur band. The hood of the outer parka is stuck to the head, somewhat misshapen.

The inner parka, made of bird-skin, is edged with caribou skin.

The outer trousers are made of caribou skin with sealskin trouser legs sewn on. The caribou trousers must have originally been made as short trousers. They are most ingeniously cut, pieced together with various skin fragments of beige, brown and whitish tones. However, no clear pattern is evident. The sealskin trouser legs were worn under the kamiks.

When the outer trousers were cleaned, the woman was seen to be wearing a pair of sealskin trunks underneath.

The kamik legs are about 45 cm long, ending above the knee. The kamiks are sewn together in front with fairly loose overcast stitches. At the top this seam divides and runs to the sides, leaving room for an extra piece of skin. The soles are quite roughly gathered at the toe and heel; they are sewn to the leg with overcast stitching. Beneath the soles there are traces of both wool and guard hair. Both kamiks have a strap wrapped round the ankle and knotted at the front.

The woman appears to be wearing stockings inside the kamiks, but it has not been possible to uncover them enough to describe them.

Fig. 171 Mummy II/6 and
below a detail of her kamiks.

Mummy II/7 The costume of this woman, who
was between eighteen and twenty-two years old,
consists of an outer parka, an inner parka, trousers,
kamiks and stockings.

The outer parka is extremely worn and much
mended. In the grave it disintegrated further, particularly at the back, where only the bottom part of
the tail and a detached piece of fur at the middle of
the back are preserved. The front tail is about 30 cm
long and edged with light-coloured skin, which also
borders the fur at the side. At the bottom on both
sides pieces of skin about 20 cm wide have been
sewn on; these pieces extend from the middle of the
front tail along the side and to the back, where they
were sewn onto the back tail. These skin pieces are
made from the flippers of newborn seal, placed with
the fur inwards. The pieces are bordered at the
bottom by a band. The stitches, made with braided
sinew-thread, are long and crude.

The sleeves are very worn. They were mended on
the lower side and at the armholes with patches
roughly sewn on with large stitches. The sleeves
have light fur bands by the wrists. Below these
bands 10-cm-wide cuffs of sealskin, pieced together
out of skin scraps, are roughly stitched on with
braided sinew-thread. In the seams of one of the
pieces a narrow woolly strip of newborn seal skin is

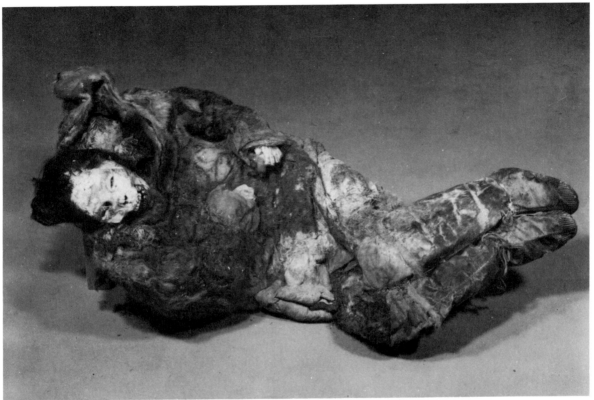

Fig. 172 Above Mummy II/7 and *below* her parka viewed from the front.

set in. This piece sticks out about 5 cm beyond the cuff. In the middle of the sleeves, 19 cm from the shoulder seam, smaller, light skin pieces are sewn in. The pieces on both sides run into the underside of the sleeves with a gusset.

The hood is edged with dark turned-in binding, which also edges the chin-piece. This binding is tacked with a piece of sealskin, fur turned inwards, about 5 cm wide. As with the other additions, the stitching here is made with braided sinew-thread and is crudely done.

The inner parka of bird-skin is missing most of the back. However, the front, sleeves and hood were in such good condition that it was possible to identify what types of bird-skin had been used (see Fig. 125). All skins have contour feathers intact and are placed to best advantage in the garment: skins with short, dense plumage are used where warmth is most important (for example, female eider covering the loins), and more open-feathered skins are placed by the wrists and neck opening to let heat out. This is the ideal thermal suit. The mid-front panel is made

Fig. 174 Mummy II/7's sealskin trousers.

Fig. 173 Detail of a sleeve of mummy II/7's parka with a cuff sewn on.

of the skin of a young cormorant. The front tail forms the neck, and the anus can be seen just under the cut-off point at the chest. There are side pieces of female eider, possibly king eider. The two chest pieces, which are joined to the chin-piece at the neck, are made of whitefronted goose, whose loose feathers allow body heat to escape. The chest pieces continue round the back, interrupted by a transverse shoulder piece made of cormorant. The hood is composed of two red-throated diver skins. This bird has dense short feathers which fit the head closely and allow unhindered movement without disarranging the feathers. The sleeves are made identically of cormorants, probably both young and old, running upward, and the skin of a female mallard is used at the wrists. The edgings are caribou skin.

The trousers are half-length and made of sealskin. They have deteriorated to some degree, with occasional loss of hair; they are also badly worn and much-mended. The trousers are about 52 cm in length, with the legs ending 12 and 6 cm below the knee. There is a piece in the back of the trousers which runs down the inside of the right leg. This piece consists of three 10-cm-wide skin scraps joined

together. The right trouser leg is thus 10 cm shorter than the left. The skin scraps are lined along the edges and appear to come from another garment. A strip of woolly newborn seal skin, 0.3 cm wide, has been sewn between the additional pieces and the original trousers. The long irregular overcast stitches used here are done with thick sinew-thread. Originally the trousers were sewn with very neat, regular stitches. At the bottom, on each inside leg, light-coloured skin pieces measuring about 20 × 10 cm have been sewn in.

The kamiks are well-preserved. The legs are 36 cm long and sewn together in front with regular back-stitching. At the top there is a sealskin casing with an attached strap to be tied at the back. The sole is attached to the leg in regular gathers at the heel and toe. Although there are eyes for a kamik strap at the sides of the soles, both kamiks have a strap round the ankle which is tied in front with many knots. On the left kamik this strap is placed under the heel; on the right kamik, just above it. In the two kamiks and the stockings, the heel was located higher up the leg than normal. There are traces of wool and guard hair under the soles.

The stockings are both in good condition. They are made of caribou skin, with extra pieces at the top of the legs and above the front part of the foot. The legs are 33–35 cm long and seamed in front and at the back. At the top they are edged by a fur band. Tacked onto this band is an edging of sealskin, about 15 cm wide, with the fur turned inwards. Sewn into the right edging is a woolly band, 0.3 cm wide, made of newborn seal skin.

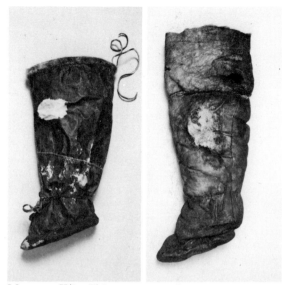

Mummy II/8 This woman, who was about fifty years old, was the first to be buried in grave II and so she lay at the bottom. Her outfit, which was very poorly preserved, consisted of an outer parka, an intermediate parka, an inner parka, trousers, kamiks and stockings. She is the most poorly preserved of all the mummies.

The outer parka lacks the back entirely. There is much loss of hair on the front and sleeves, but the remains of the garment show that the fur was of the same type as the other outer parkas. In the middle of the front, in the seam connecting it with the shoulders, a loop has been sewn in. The sleeves have a band of light skin at the wrist.

The intermediate parka, which is made of bird-skin, completely lacks the back and the left arm. What does remain is formed of the front of a skin with the neck of the animal at the bottom, and of thick dense skin across the shoulder with the neck of the animal towards the sleeve. The chin-piece and edgings are made of caribou skin.

The inner parka is made of caribou skin with the fur worn against the body. Only parts of the front are preserved with the hood and tail and these are very well sewn. An impressive ornamental pattern has been made with areas of dark and light skin, and narrow bands. Two white flaps corresponding to the chest area have seen set in, and a narrow white stripe runs down the centre line. The tail has a band made of skin scraps whose hair acts as a border, and a narrow dark stripe just within this. In the middle a small tail has been sewn in. This tail is encircled, and thus emphasised, by dark skin strips in which the fur has been trimmed to the same length. The hood is made of light skin edged with dark, turned-in fur binding. Running back from the forehead, two furless pieces of skin measuring about 25 × 5 cm have been tacked on. These pieces are fastened to the outer side with just a few stitches. There is a very fine pattern at the nape of the neck, made by an inlay of dark and light pieces of fur.

Above Fig. 175 Left One of mummy II/7's reindeer kamiks. *Right* One of her reindeer skin stockings.

Right Fig. 176 Mummy II/8, a 50-year-old woman.

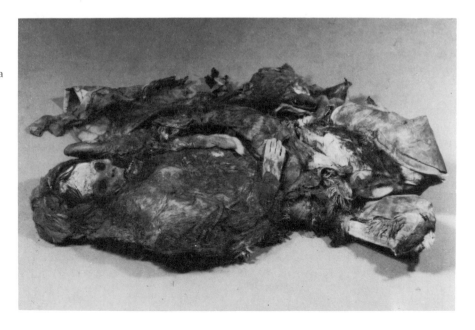

Fig. 177 Mummy II/8's reindeer stocking.

The trousers are very badly preserved, and the entire seat is missing. They are made of sealskin and reach the knee, measuring about 42 cm. There is a turned-in fur waistband at the top.

The kamiks are also poorly preserved, especially the right one, the back and right side of which have rotted away. The legs are about 50 cm long, with a front seam. This seam divides into two directions at the instep. There are triangular piecings both at the top and bottom. The sole is attached to the leg with regular gathers, and there are eyes for a kamik strap at the sides. At the back the leg goes straight up; at the front it widens to about 30 cm at the top.

The stockings are made of caribou skin with very thick, coarse fur. The left stocking is well-preserved. The leg is 53 cm long, with many extra pieces sewn on the inner side. The leg is edged at the top by a turned-in fur band of caribou skin, and sewn together in front with a set-in slipper heel. The sole is gathered at the toe and heel and attached to the leg by two narrow strips of skin which run all the way round the foot.

The right stocking is poorly preserved but matches the left one quite closely. The leg is *c.* 50 cm long.

The children

Mummy I/1   The child, about six months old, is dressed in a sealskin parka and trunks.

The parka is made of sealskin which is dark on the front and back; the sleeves are somewhat lighter. It has a sewn-on hood made of light-coloured skin with a dark turned-in fur band and an attached strap to allow the hood to be drawn together across the child's face and tied above the forehead. A sewn-in skin band joins the two halves of the hood in the middle. This band is dark in the middle, with a light stripe on either side. The hood has disintegrated somewhat at the back, but it appears that the band ran down over the back of the head. The parka is waist-length all way round. In the middle of the front there is a little skin bag sewn together at the bottom and side and fastened to the parka with a sinew thread.

The trunks are made of soft skin, with the fur worn next to the body. They seem to have been cut in two symmetrical halves and sewn together in the middle. Around each ankle there is a strap tied in front.

Mummy I/2   The skin costume of the four-year-old boy consists of an outer parka and inner parka, both hooded, trousers, kamiks and stockings. Much is missing.

The outer parka is made of sealskin with the fur turned outward. It is decayed around the bottom, especially at the front where much is missing. The back and the hood are cut out of one piece. The dark fur of the back of the seal is in the middle, probably cut off just below the earholes where the skin is narrowest. Thus, both the back of the parka and the back of the hood are dark, whereas the sides of the hood are light. The front of the hood has a short decorative stripe of skin, the rear part of which is dark, cut out in one piece with the hood; the front part is an insertion of light skin. There is a casing round the face opening of the hood. The front is made of one piece of dark skin with an inset chin-piece, joined with the back by light shoulders. At the bottom of the parka there is an edging, 5 cm wide, which goes down to a broad point in the front and back. The sleeves are straight.

The inner parka is also made of sealskin, but the fur is worn inwards. It is as decayed as the outer parka. The back and the hood are, again like the outer parka, cut out of one piece, but here the tailoring is somewhat more complicated. The short skin strip to the front of the hood is divided into three, one dark

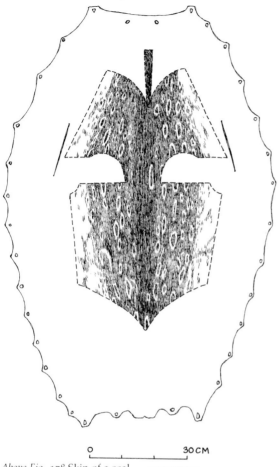

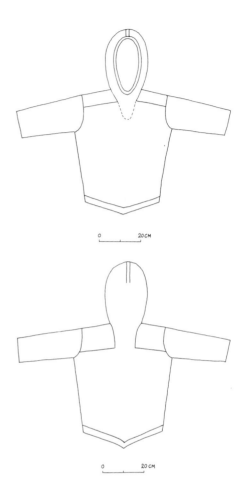

30 CM

20 CM

20 CM

Above Fig. 178 Skin of a seal showing where the back and hood of a parka are cut from.

Above right and right Fig. 179 Line drawing of mummy I/2's parka seen from the front, *top*, and back, *bottom*. *Right* Photograph of the front and back of the same parka.

stripe in the centre with two light bands at the sides. The hood has a dark casing round the face opening. The shoulders have a gusset inserted at the front. The front is made of one piece. The sleeves are straight, but with the insertion of a triangular gusset towards the shoulders. Like the outer parka, the inner parka has an edging, but it is only half as wide.

The trousers are half-length, with the fur turned outwards. They have deteriorated badly at the top, with a loss of hair both in front and on the seat. They are made of two halves, sewn together in the middle. Both trouser legs are made of two pieces of skin with an inner seam between the legs and a side seam turning in to the back of the legs. There are triangular pieces of light skin at the bottom and a waistband at the top. This band has a lacing of about 2 cm at the back. The trousers are very badly sewn, clumsily and roughly-done, with loose ends, large knots and long stitches.

Fig. 180 Mummy I/2's trousers.

The kamiks, in contrast, are well sewn but extremely worn, with scratches on the legs and patches on the bottom of the soles. The left kamik is composed of two pieces of skin and the right is made of one piece; both are seamed in the front. From the instep the stitching runs towards the outer edge of the foot. The sole is attached to the leg with very regular gathers at the front and back. At the sides of the soles there are eyes for a kamik strap, and an attached strap. Traces of stitching indicate that there was originally a band at the top of the legs.

The stockings, made of sealskin, are equally well sewn and preserved. Each of them is made of two pieces of skin with another piece at the top of the leg. The seam is in front. The legs are 27 cm long and terminate at the top in a fur band.

Fig. 181 Mummy I/2's kamiks.

Garments found loose in the graves

The dead were given a number of garments as extra apparel for their journey to the Land of the Dead. The garments are labelled ED.

Outer parkas Seven of these were found in the graves, five of which have a basic cut identical to the parkas worn by the six women, although each parka demonstrates interesting features. The other two parkas (ED 30 and 78) are cut quite differently.

ED 25 is a parka of ringed sealskin. The parka is only partly preserved, consisting mainly of the right sleeve, the shoulder with the neck opening and much of the back. It has many holes and cracks and is extremely worn, with patches sewn on the back and right arm. The parka is sewn together with sinew-thread, using overcast stitching, and consists of many small scraps including a piece of bird-skin sewn on the inside above the bottom band. Braised sinew-thread has been sewn along seams in the sleeve, the armhole and at the bottom by the edging. The sleeve is curved and there are several pieces sewn on at the wrist.

Fig. 182 Mummy I/2's parka ED 26, front, *left*, and back, *right*.

ED 26 is very dilapidated: most of the fur is worn off at the front, the back is much torn and the sleeves are cut off just below the armholes. In the edging on the sides there are long, crude stitches, made with thick sinew-thread, which go from the middle of the front tail to the middle of the back tail. At the right side are the remains of a fur which had been sewn on but was subsequently torn off. Skin scraps seem to have been tacked on later, just as with the parkas of mummies I/4 and II/7. The garment was otherwise well-sewn.

ED 27 is made of ringed sealskin, seamed with regular overcast stitching. It is a splendid parka in both colour and tailoring. The dark panel in the middle of the back seems almost black. The parka has been lengthened with additional pieces on the hips, about 5 or 6 cm wide, added as a decorative border. One of the most interesting features is sewn to the inner side of the front flap, about 22 cm from the bottom. It is a piece of black bird-skin, the head of an alcidae in fact, measuring about 3.5 x 2.5 cm, and tacked on with sinew-thread. It was probably an amulet.

ED 28 is another beautifully made parka of ringed sealskin. The central section of the back, which includes the tail, is very dark, and this is the only parka to have two white decorative skin bands sewn on at the bottom. The point of the back flap has a loop of braided sinew-thread holding a small piece

Fig. 183 Skin from the head of an Auk bird which was sewn on the inside of skin ED 27. Perhaps it was an amulet.

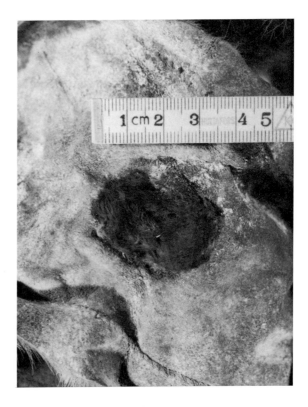

Fig. 184 Pattern for parka ED 15. The drawing is a poster produced by the Greenland National Museum.

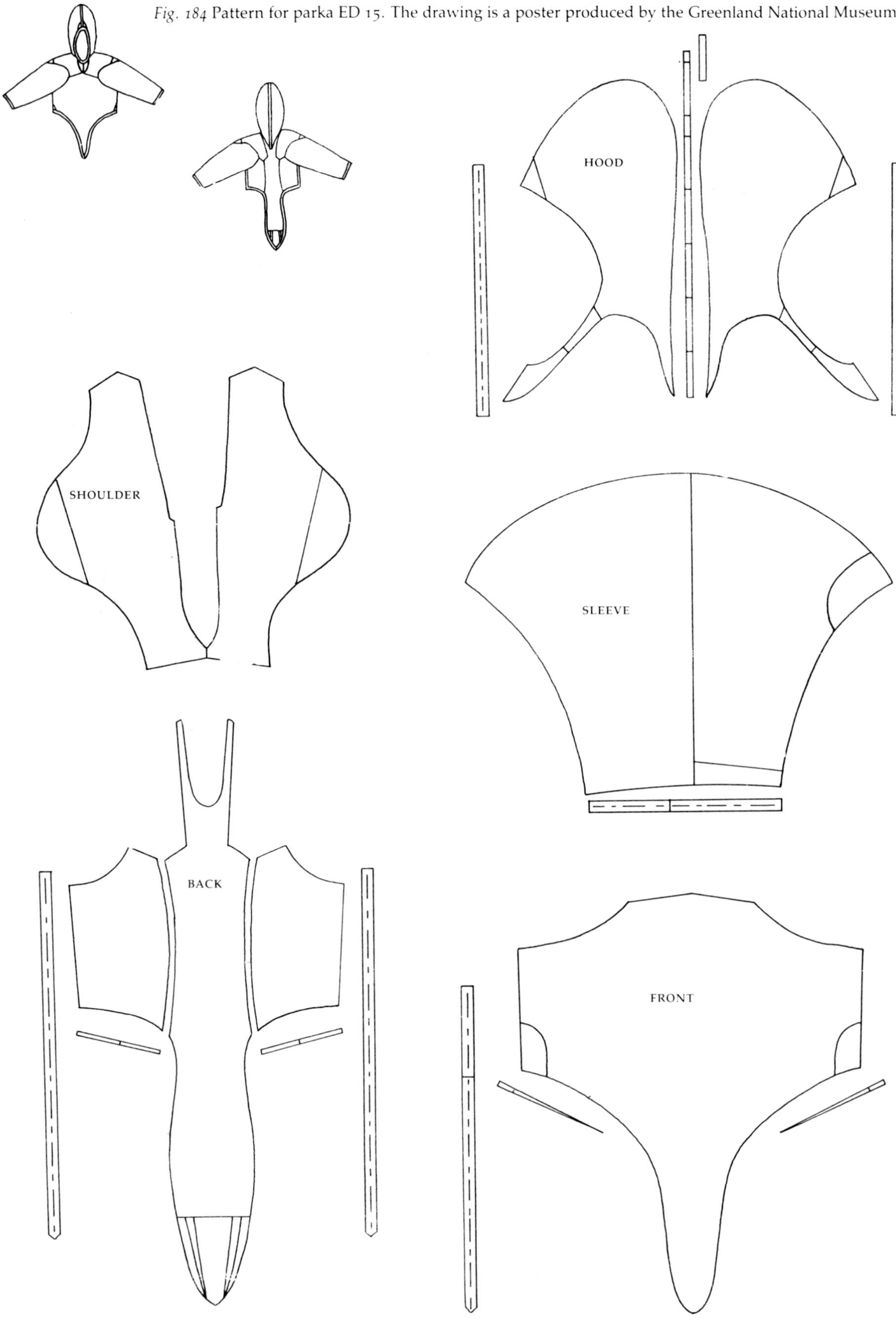

of bone. The back of the front flap bears traces of something having been sewn on about 20 cm from the point.

ED 29 is the largest of the parkas and the only one in which the dark and light skin pieces are not used decoratively. The side panels of the back are made of seal back, not belly; there are no light insertions by the sleeves, and the hood is made of dark skin from a seal back.

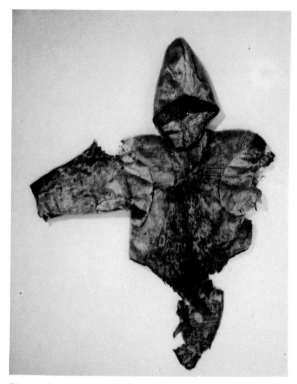

Fig. 185 Front view of parka ED 26.

ED 30 is very badly preserved, and large areas are missing in the front, on one sleeve and on the hood. The front is made of one sealskin whose back forms the centre. It ends at the bottom in a tail and at the top is cut off level with the chest. There are light shoulder sections which are joined with the front. In the middle of this seam a loop has been sewn on. The shoulder sections are connected by a light chin-piece. The back and the hood are made in one piece, from one sealskin. The parka is hip-length, and a back tail, most of which is missing, is sewn on. The shoulder sections, which are from 6 to 7 cm wide on the back, are joined to the back section at the shoulder blades. Over the shoulders they widen in a tongue shape towards the sleeves; each

measures about 20 cm. The hood, which is very difficult to describe because of its poor state of preservation, consists of chin-piece in the front with the addition of two gussets and is connected with the shoulders at the sides. The hood is edged with a dark, turned-in fur band. Along this band there are coarse stitches made with thick sinew-thread, probably the remains of a piece of skin which was first sewn on, then removed. The sleeves are set in on a curve and are very full.

This garment seems to have been made as an *amaat*, a parka designed so that a child can be carried on the back in an inside pouch. The child is prevented from sliding down by a strap which goes round its back and is fastened in front of the adult, perhaps passed through a loop.

ED 78 is badly preserved, and has lost much fur. This parka consists of a front, back, hood and sleeves. The front is made of one piece of sealskin whose back forms the centre. This piece goes to the shoulders, where it is joined to the back by a shoulder seam. The back is made of a skin which forms a wide, tongue-shaped tail towards the bottom, a tail unlike that of the other parkas. The bottom 10 cm consist of dark skin which was added on. The hood, which lacks its top, is edged with a dark, turned-in fur band. In the front it forms a light chin-piece which has been sewn into the front section, and which at the back is joined to the back in a slightly curving seam. The sleeves, which are set in from straight to slightly curved, have an extremely wide armhole and are very roomy at the shoulders. A piece of light skin, 21 cm wide, forms a cuff at the bottom front. The cut of this parka is totally unlike that of the others and must be regarded either as a transitional type, as a man's parka, or as a design influenced from elsewhere.

Inner parka ED 77 is a bird-skin parka which is very poorly preserved – the front, most of the back, one sleeve and part of the hood are missing. A hood and front and back flaps remain. This garment is edged with caribou skin along the hood, armhole and at the bottom along the flaps.

Trousers ED 12 are a pair of well-preserved, carefully-sewn, handsome short trousers of sealskin. They are made of two symmetrical halves with a centre seam. There is a casing at the top in which there is a strap to be tied at the back, and at the bottom is a turned-in fur band. Each of the two halves is composed of ten pieces of skin; at the back the light and dark skin has been used so as to form a most decorative pattern.

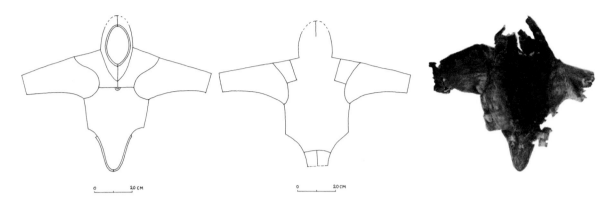

Above Fig. 186 The different sections of parka ED 30. *Far right* The back of the parka.
Below Fig. 187 The different sections of parka ED 78. *Far right* The front of the parka.

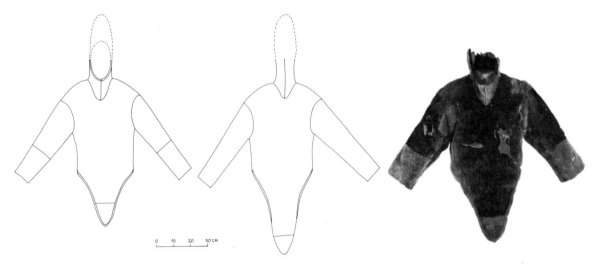

ED 13 are a pair of short, quite beautiful trousers of caribou skin. Their cut is similar to that of ED 12, and they also have a casing at the top in which there is a strap to tie at the back. The cut and an ornamental pattern are made by using at least twenty skin pieces and strips for each half. The larger pieces of skin are caribou, and on the front of the trousers two skins have been placed so that both a white dot and a light stripe in the skin are positioned symmetrically on either side of the centre line. The rest of the ornamentation is made by the insertion of white and dark strips of skin. In the back middle seam two small skin patches, which protrude intentionally have been sewn on. The trousers are worn, especially at the seat, where the fur has been worn away above the buttocks.

ED 24 are a pair of very short caribou skin trousers. The fur is worn in both the front and back, and the

Fig. 188 Trousers ED 13 of reindeer skin.

waistband is missing. Each half is composed of seven pieces of skin. On the seat a long piece of dark sealskin, measuring about 12 cm, has been sewn on. At the bottom of both trouser legs hang a number of pieces of thick sinew-thread which have been cut

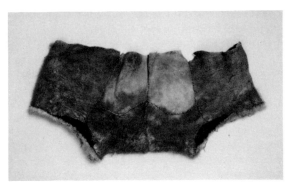

Fig. 189 Trousers ED 24 of reindeer skin.

regular backstitches in a single row, using sinew-thread. The leg is seamed in front.

ED 4 is a kamik of water skin with a stocking (ED 3). This well-preserved kamik shows signs of wear, with two patches on the bottom of the sole, at the heel and toe. The entire kamik is sewn with sinew-thread, in a single row of regular backstitching. There are eyes for a kamik strap.

ED 14 is an entire kamik of water skin. It shows signs of wear, as there are two patches sewn under the delapidated sole, at the heel and toe. Within the casing at the top of the 34-cm-long leg there is a strap to be laced at the back. The sole is gathered evenly. There are two eyes for a kamik strap. The kamik is sewn with braided or twined sinew-thread in a double row of backstitching both at the front and back of the leg.

ED 15 is a water skin kamik. A patch at the heel of the delapidated sole indicates that the boot was much worn. The leg, which is 36 cm long, is seamed

off. This indicates that the trousers may originally have had legs added on.

Boots ED 1 is a kamik with a stocking (ED 2). The kamik is called 'stumpy-cut' because the upper part of the leg has been cut off. The kamik is made of water skin and shows signs of having been used. It has two patches on the bottom of the sole, under the heel and toe. There are two eyes for a kamik strap. This well-preserved kamik was sewn with

Fig. 190 Kamik ED 4.

Fig. 191 Kamik ED 15.

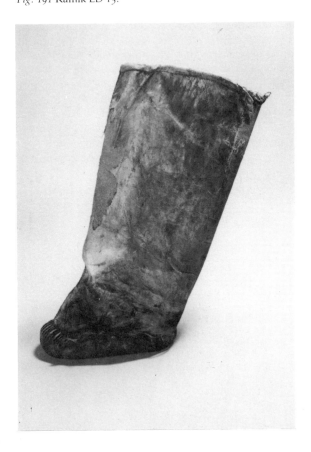

in the front. Large holes were later made in the front and back. There is a strap in the casing at the top to be laced at the back. There are two eyes for a kamik strap. The boot is sewn using twined or braided sinew-thread in a single row of backstitching except for at the instep, where it is double.

ED 17 is a water skin kamik with a stocking (ED 18). It is in a poor state of preservation, with a large hole on the sole and with parts missing from the top of the leg. The leg, which is 35 cm long, is sewn using braided sinew-thread in a single row of stitching in front. There are two eyes for a kamik strap.

Stockings ED 2 is a stocking made of ringed sealskin, and is the stocking from the kamik ED 1. The entire stocking is in a good state of preservation, with wear beneath the heel and toe. The leg has no edging band.

ED 3 is a ringed sealskin stocking from kamik ED 4. The entire stocking is in a good state of preservation, with wear at the toe and a hole at the heel. This stocking is seamed at the front and back of the leg with sinew-thread in overcast stitching.

ED 16 is a stocking made of ringed sealskin. It is relatively well-preserved, with holes at the lower side of the leg, which is seamed in the front with a single sinew-thread. At the top of the leg a casing has been sewn on, with a strap inside to be laced at the back. The sole is gathered to the leg at the toe, slightly less at the heel.

ED 18 is a stocking of ringed sealskin (from the kamik ED 17). It is poorly preserved, with large areas missing at the top and a big hole on the bottom of the sole. This stocking is sewn using quite thick sinew-thread in even overcast stitching. The leg, which is 35 cm long, is seamed in front.

ED 19 is a stocking made of ringed sealskin. There are holes at the top of the leg, at the toe and under the sole. The 35-cm-long leg is seamed in front. Two pieces are sewn at the top of the leg. This stocking is sewn, using sinew-thread, in even overcast stitching.

ED 20 is a stocking made of the skin of unborn or newborn seal. The leg, 34 cm in length, is intact, with several extra pieces. The edging band at the top is made of sealskin. This stocking was sewn with sinew thread in overcast stitching. The foot has rotted away.

ED 21 is a stocking made of ringed sealskin. The leg, which measures 33 cm, is in good condition, with a few holes. It is seamed using sinew-thread in even overcast stitching at the front and back, and with a piece added in front. Belly skin was used for one half and back skin for the other. A sealskin edging band has been sewn on at the top of the leg. The foot of the stocking is partially rotted away, and only small parts of the sole remain.

Half-sleeves ED 22 are half-sleeves of ringed seal skin. The sleeves, which are 23 cm long, are partially rotted away by the edging band. They are sewn with sinew-thread in an even overcast stitching and comprise three pieces of skin with a triangular piece at the top. Two loose sinew-threads with knots hang from the top edge, which may indicate that some garment had been attached here. There are a number of lice eggs and lice in the fur.

ED 23 is a half-sleeve made of ringed sealskin, 22 cm in length. It is composed of three pieces of skin and has a turned-in fur band at the wrist, where it is most narrow. The half-sleeve widens toward the top by about 7 cm.

Fig. 192 Greenlanders in their summer camp at Roeve, near Egedesminde, 1909.

Bibliography

Chapter 1

BIRKET-SMITH, KAJ. *The Eskimos*. Copenhagen 1971.
DAMAS, DAVID (ed.). *Arctic Handbook of North American Indians*, vol. 5. Washington DC 1984.
DUMOND, DON E. *The Eskimos and Aleuts*. London 1977.
GAD, FINN. *The History of Greenland*, vol. 1. London 1970.
KROGH, KNUD J. *Viking Greenland*. Copenhagen 1967.
MATHIASSEN, THERKEL. 'Inugsuk. A Mediaeval Eskimo Settlement in Upernavik District, West Greenland', in *Meddelelser om Grønland*, vol. 77. Copenhagen 1930.

Chapter 3

PETERSEN, ROBERT. 'The Greenland Tupilak', in *Folk*, vol. 6. Copenhagen 1964.
— 'Burial Forms and Death Cult Among the Eskimos', in *Folk*, vols 8–9. Copenhagen 1967.

Chapter 4

COCKBURN, A. and COCKBURN, E. (eds). *Mummies, Disease and Ancient Cultures*. London 1980.
BALSLEV JØRGENSEN, J. 'The Eskimo Skeleton', in *Meddelelser om Grønland*, vol. 146, no. 2. Copenhagen 1953
BODENHOFF, J., GEERTINGER, P. and PRAUSE, J. 'Isolation of Sporothrix fungorum from a 500-year-old mummy found in Greenland', in *Acta path. microbiol. scand.*, Sect. B 87: 201–3. 1979.
DAVID, A. R. (ed.). *The Manchester Museum Mummy Project*. Manchester 1979.
FOGED, N. 'Diatoms in Human Tissues', in *Greenland ab. 1460 AD – Funen 1981–2 AD* Nova Hedwigia 36: 345–79. 1982.
HANSEN, H. E. and GÜRTLER, H. 'HLA Types of Mummified Eskimo Bodies from the 15th Century', in *Amer. J. Phys. Anthropol*, 61: 447–53. 1983.
HARRIS, J. E. and WENTE, E. F. (eds). *An X-ray Atlas of the Royal Mummies*. Chicago 1980.
HENRIKSEN, K. L. 'A revised index of the insects of Greenland', in *Meddelelser om Grønland*, vol. 119, 1–111. 1939.
HØJGAARD NIELSEN, N., MIKKELSEN, F. and HART HANSEN, J. P. 'Nasopharyngeal Cancer in Greenland', in *Acta path. microbiol. scand*, Sect. A 85, 850. 1977.
KISSMEYER-NIELSEN, F. 'The HLA System. An Overview', *Triangle*, 20: 59–69, 1981.
PEDERSEN, P. O. 'The East Greenland Eskimo Dentition', in *Meddelelser om Grønland*, vol. 142, no. 3. Copenhagen 1949, 2nd edn 1965.
— 'Some Dental Aspects of Anthropology', in *Dent. Record* 72, 170–8. 1952.
STRYER, L. 'Connective tissue proteins: collagen, elastin and proteoglycans', in L. Stryer (2nd edn), *Biochemistry* 185–204. San Francisco 1981.
ZIMMERMANN, M. R. *et al*. 'The Paleopathology of an Aleutian Mummy', in *Arc. Pathol. Lab. Med.*, 105: 638–41. 1981.

Chapter 5

KJELLSTRØM, ROLF. 'Eskimåiska och ostsibiriska tatueringer', in *By og Bygd*. Norsk Folkemuseums Årbok 27. Oslo 1979.

SMITH, G. S. and ZIMMERMANN, M. R. 'Tattooing found on a 1600 year old, frozen, mummified body from St Lawrence Island, Alaska', in *American Antiquity*, 40: 434–7. 1975.

Chapter 6

BIRKET-SMITH, KAJ. 'Ethnography of the Egedesminde District', in *Meddelelser om Grønland*, vol. 66. Copenhagen 1924.
BROUQUI, M., CORNUET, R. and DE TASSIGNY, C. 'Traitement par rayonnements gamma, de la momie de Ramses II', in *Revue Generale Nucleaire*, 1: 10–14. 1978.
HATT, GUDMUND. 'Arctic Skin Clothing in Eurasia and America', in *Arctic Anthropology*, 5 (2): 1–132. 1969.
HOLTVED, ERIK. 'Contributions to Polar Eskimo Ethnography', in *Meddelelser om Grønland*, vol. 82, no. 2. Copenhagen 1967.
KAALUND, BODIL. *The Art of Greenland*. Berkeley 1983.
MATHIASSEN, THERKEL. 'The Eskimo Archaeology of Julianehaab District', in *Meddelelser om Grønland*, vol. 118. Copenhagen 1936.

Chapter 7

BRESCIANI, J., HAARLØV, N., NANSEN, P. and MØLLER, G. 'Head louse (*Pediculus humanus suscp. capitis deGeer*). From mummified corpses of Greenlanders, AD 1460 (+/−50)', in *Acta Entomologica Fennica*, 42: 24–7. 1983.
BÖCHER, TYGE W., HOLMEN, KJELD and JACOBSEN, KNUD *The flora of Greenland*. Copenhagen 1968.
DANSGAARD, W., JOHSEN, S. J., REEH, N., GUNDESTRUP, N., CLAUSEN, H. B. and HAMMER, C. V. 'Climatic Changes, Norsemen and Modern Man', in *Nature*, 255: 24–8. 1975.
ESCHER, A. and WATT, W. S. 'Geology of Greenland', in *Grønlands Geologiske Undersøgelse*. 1976.
FEILBERG, JON, FREDSKILD, BENT and HOLT, SUNE. *Flowers of Greenland*. Ringsted 1984.
FREDSKILD, BENT. 'The natural Environment of the Norse settlers in Greenland', in *Proceedings of the international symposium Early European Exploitation of the Northern Atlantic 800–1700*, 27–42, at the Arctic Centre, University of Groningen, Netherlands. 1981.
— 'Studies in the vegetational history of Greenland. Paleobotanical investigations of some Holocene lake and bog deposits', in *Meddelelser om Grønland*, vol. 198, no. 4. 1973.
— 'Paleobotanical investigations at Sermermiut, Jakobshavn, West Greenland', in *Meddelelser om Grønland*, vol. 178, no. 4. 1967.
— 'Paleobotanical investigations of some peat deposits of Norse age at Qagssiarssuk, South Greenland', in *Meddelelser om Grønland*, vol. 240, no. 5. 1978.
HANSEN, J. C. 'A Survey of Human Exposure to Mercury, Cadmium and Lead in Greenland', in *Meddelelser om Grønland, Man & Society 3*. 1981.
TAUBER, H. 'Carbon–13 evidence for dietary habits of prehistoric man in Denmark', in *Nature*, vol. 292: 332–3. London 1981.
TORIBARA, T. Y., MUHS, ANN and CLARKSON, T. W. 'Hair – A Keeper of History', in *Arctic Anthropology*, 21: 99–108. 1983.

Index